Patterns in child phonology

Wyn Johnson and Paula Reimers

Edinburgh University Press

Edinburgh University Press Ltd
22 George Square, Edinburgh

www.euppublishing.com

Reprinted 2011

Typeset in Adobe Sabon by
Servis Filmsetting Ltd, Stockport, Cheshire and
printed and bound in Great Britain by
CPI Antony Rowe, Chippenham and Eastbourne

A CIP record for this book is available from the British Library

ISBN 978 0 7486 3819 2 (hardback)
ISBN 978 0 7486 3820 8 (paperback)

PATTERNS IN CHILD PHONOLOGY

CONTENTS

PREFACE

Phonological acquisition and development in children has long been the object of research, considered from various theoretical and disciplinary perspectives. Child data have been called upon to lend weight to claims of naturalness being attributed to various linguistic theories, however, these various perspectives have not been brought together before.

Our aim in this book is to present an overview of patterns observed in the development of phonology. The intention is to give pointers to the issues that arise in the study of phonological acquisition. We have concentrated on normal acquisition and have avoided, as much as possible, delayed or disordered speech, although there are studies using data from children with delayed acquisition which parallel, at a later age, the paths followed by normally acquiring children and, therefore, present useful confirmation of some of the patterns we have discussed. We also believe that a knowledge of what is 'normal' is important to those studying deviant speech. It is not in any sense a monograph, nor does it present any new research. The data we present are taken, for the most part from published material, although there are a few unpublished data included where a certain point needs to be reinforced. Certain sources, in particular Smith (1973) have been heavily plundered because of their richness and we are grateful to those who have contributed so generously to the overall stock of data available. Others have provided fewer data but have, nevertheless, helped to enrich our examples. Because the main focus of studies is on Indo-European languages, in particular English, there is a heavy concentration on these languages to the exclusion of those languages that have been neglected or only very cursorily studied. Except in the first chapter, the children in question are named, some by their full name (or pseudonym) and others are identified just by initials. Nevertheless, in all cases it is possible to develop a familiarity with subjects. The reader is encouraged to return to original sources to confirm the information we have provided.

Although many of our chapters are concentrating on the patterns of the title and are, therefore, rich in data as well as possible explanations, both from general phonological theory and from particular theories that purport to explain the findings, we also look at the pre-production stage of acquisition since it is clear that the child has experienced many months of his or her native language before he or she attempts to produce language. In addition, we have discussed some studies that attempt to explain acquisition and processing of speech from outside mainstream linguistic theory. For the most part, we have employed the type of theoretical model that has been used to attempt to explain the phenomena observed. We have endeavoured to give the reader some idea of these theories and their particular efficacy in explaining the patterns. We do not necessarily espouse any particular theory and leave the reader to make up his or her mind as to their relative explanatory powers.

In the first chapter, we set the scene by introducing phenomena found in children's speech and relating these to similar phenomena occurring in the languages of the world. We hope that what this demonstrates is that variation is not infinite and that the processes observed in young language acquirers are also active in adult language. The second chapter is devoted to investigating some of these phenomena in more depth and considering the various strategies that are employed by learners to deal with patterns they are not yet ready to produce. We find that, although more than one strategy may be adopted, there are, in fact, patterns which seem not to occur and we hope that general phonological theory might have an explanation for this. In Chapter 3, we pick up the theme of universally observed patterns and consider the notion of Universal Grammar and markedness as a guiding principle. Universal Grammar is the device that underpins language acquisition and is claimed to be innate in the human species. However, these studies make the assumption that the grammar starts with production, so bearing in mind that the onset of production lags well behind that of perception, in Chapter 4, we try to trace the child's phonological grammar to its initial state in the pre-production phase to try to locate what is human-specific. Here we find that the story is somewhat less clear and, indeed, the evidence does not point clearly and unequivocally to speech perception being a human-specific attribute. We, therefore, in Chapter 5, investigate other explanations, outside the field of true linguistics, offered for the ability of children to acquire language. Chapter 5 also looks at other influences on acquisition, such as the nature of the input and physiological factors. In Chapter 6, we return to the theme of early phonological production and consider explanations of how the child might build up a phonological structure of segments, syllables and prosody. In Chapter 7, we look at the influence of the building process on the segmental output and return to the theme of the early chapters attempting to explain the same patterns. Some of the data from the first two chapters are revisited but more are introduced. Chapter 8 summarises the main discussion of the book and suggests further avenues to be pursued. The appendices provide sources for the data in Chapter 1 and some definitions of terms used in the text. There is a chart of IPA symbols for reference purposes after this Preface.

Wyn Johnson and Paula Reimers 2010

CONVENTIONS: In accordance with the conventions used in the majority of the child language literature, child surface forms appear in square brackets, adult or target forms in slanted lines, glosses in single quotes, and target words written orthographically are italicised. The ages of the children are presented as years;months.days, so '4;8.2' reads 'four years, eight months and two days'.

THE INTERNATIONAL PHONETIC ALPHABET (revised to 2005)

CONSONANTS (PULMONIC)

	Bilabial	Labiodental	Dental	Alveolar	Post alveolar	Retroflex	Palatal	Velar	Uvular	Pharyngeal	Glottal
Plosive	p b			t d		ʈ ɖ	c ɟ	k ɡ	q ɢ		ʔ
Nasal	m	ɱ		n		ɳ	ɲ	ŋ	ɴ		
Trill	ʙ			r					ʀ		
Tap or Flap		ⱱ		ɾ		ɽ					
Fricative	ɸ β	f v	θ ð	s z	ʃ ʒ	ʂ ʐ	ç ʝ	x ɣ	χ ʁ	ħ ʕ	h ɦ
Lateral fricative				ɬ ɮ							
Approximant		ʋ		ɹ		ɻ	j	ɰ			
Lateral approximant				l		ɭ	ʎ	ʟ			

Where symbols appear in pairs, the one to the right represents a voiced consonant. Shaded areas denote articulations judged impossible.

CONSONANTS (NON-PULMONIC)

Clicks		Voiced implosives		Ejectives	
ʘ	Bilabial	ɓ	Bilabial	ʼ	Examples:
ǀ	Dental	ɗ	Dental/alveolar	pʼ	Bilabial
ǃ	(Post)alveolar	ʄ	Palatal	tʼ	Dental/alveolar
ǂ	Palatoalveolar	ɠ	Velar	kʼ	Velar
ǁ	Alveolar lateral	ʛ	Uvular	sʼ	Alveolar fricative

VOWELS

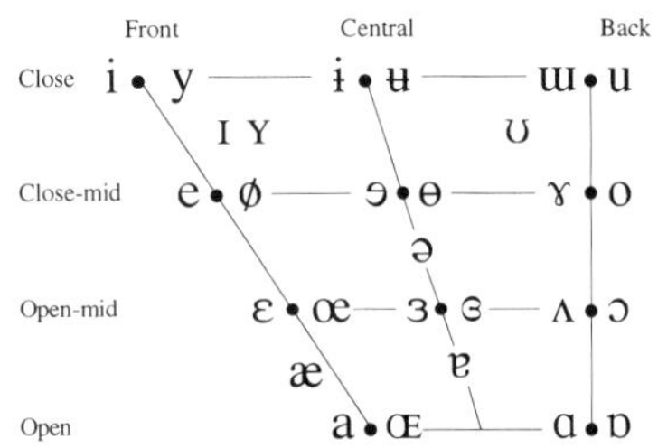

Where symbols appear in pairs, the one to the right represents a rounded vowel.

OTHER SYMBOLS

ʍ Voiceless labial-velar fricative

w Voiced labial-velar approximant

ɥ Voiced labial-palatal approximant

ʜ Voiceless epiglottal fricative

ʢ Voiced epiglottal fricative

ʡ Epiglottal plosive

ɕ ʑ Alveolo-palatal fricatives

ɺ Voiced alveolar lateral flap

ɧ Simultaneous ʃ and x

Affricates and double articulations can be represented by two symbols joined by a tie bar if necessary. k͡p t͡s

SUPRASEGMENTALS

ˈ	Primary stress
ˌ	Secondary stress ˌfoʊnəˈtɪʃən
ː	Long eː
ˑ	Half-long eˑ
̆	Extra-short ĕ
|	Minor (foot) group
‖	Major (intonation) group
.	Syllable break ɹi.ækt
‿	Linking (absence of a break)

DIACRITICS Diacritics may be placed above a symbol with a descender, e.g. ŋ̊

◌̥	Voiceless	n̥ d̥	◌̤	Breathy voiced	b̤ a̤	◌̪	Dental	t̪ d̪
◌̬	Voiced	s̬ t̬	◌̰	Creaky voiced	b̰ a̰	◌̺	Apical	t̺ d̺
ʰ	Aspirated	tʰ dʰ	◌̼	Linguolabial	t̼ d̼	◌̻	Laminal	t̻ d̻
◌̹	More rounded	ɔ̹	ʷ	Labialized	tʷ dʷ	◌̃	Nasalized	ẽ
◌̜	Less rounded	ɔ̜	ʲ	Palatalized	tʲ dʲ	ⁿ	Nasal release	dⁿ
◌̟	Advanced	u̟	ˠ	Velarized	tˠ dˠ	ˡ	Lateral release	dˡ
◌̠	Retracted	e̠	ˤ	Pharyngealized	tˤ dˤ	◌̚	No audible release	d̚
◌̈	Centralized	ë	◌̴	Velarized or pharyngealized ɫ				
◌̽	Mid-centralized	e̽	◌̝	Raised	e̝ (ɹ̝ = voiced alveolar fricative)			
◌̩	Syllabic	n̩	◌̞	Lowered	e̞ (β̞ = voiced bilabial approximant)			
◌̯	Non-syllabic	e̯	◌̘	Advanced Tongue Root	e̘			
˞	Rhoticity	ɚ a˞	◌̙	Retracted Tongue Root	e̙			

TONES AND WORD ACCENTS

LEVEL			CONTOUR		
e̋ or	˥	Extra high	ě or	˩˥	Rising
é	˦	High	ê	˥˩	Falling
ē	˧	Mid	e᷄	˦˥	High rising
è	˨	Low	e᷅	˩˨	Low rising
ȅ	˩	Extra low	e᷈	˧˦˧	Rising-falling
ꜜ		Downstep	↗		Global rise
ꜛ		Upstep	↘		Global fall

1

UNIVERSAL PATTERNS

Our aim in this book is to investigate the acquisition and development of the child's phonological system. It has long been assumed that, unique among animal species, humans are pre-programmed to acquire language and, if this is the case, then, the assumption goes, the newborn infant must come equipped with a template for language that is common to all human languages. As we know, the phonological systems of languages can vary greatly but, to some extent, there is a remarkable similarity between the patterns produced by young children regardless of the language they are acquiring. Our first task will be to introduce such patterns and observe their universal status. This will be done in an unconventional way, since data presentation is followed by explanation, rather than the other way around. Depending on the background of the reader, this method of introducing child patterns will either train or test the analytical skills necessary in working with child language.

In this chapter, we will concentrate on analysing the different patterns that emerge as the child progresses towards the mastery of the adult phonological system. Since most accounts are based on the assumption that the child's target is the adult form, the data we present show examples of the typical deviations from the adult target that occur in child phonology. We will not discuss the implications of these data in this chapter; we merely invite the reader to consider them and attempt to identify the patterns in them.

Most of the data shown in this chapter are from well-known published sources, although not all of them. Similar data from adult language systems appear from time to time in order to observe to what extent child patterns are universal. The reader is encouraged to analyse any child data phonologically, as one would with any adult language, rather than treating child data as child language. Since the focus of this chapter is to get familiarised with common child phonology processes through active analyses of illustrative data sets, some of the data sets have been mixed and grouped together in order to highlight particular phenomena. Thus, their sources are intentionally omitted from their presentation. However, they can be found in the Appendix 1, which is listed in alphabetical order of the target (adult) words for English and glosses for non-English data. Also, most of the data sets will reappear, properly labelled with their sources, when we return to them with a full discussion in subsequent chapters.

1.1 The first step

Let us now take a plunge into our first data, which is from French child language. We ask the reader to bear in mind to perform an objective analysis when attempting to identify what is going between the target forms, that is the adult output forms, and the child output forms.

(1.1)	Child output	Target		
	[pɔpɔ]	/po/	*pot*	'pot'
	[nene]	/ne/	*nez*	'nose'
	[dodo]	/dɔrmir/	*dormir*	'sleep'
	[pipi]	/pise/	*pisser*	'urinate'

What is most noticeable with the child form in (1.1) is that whether the target word is a monosyllable or a disyllable, the child output always takes the form of a disyllable in which the syllable-initial or onset consonants and the vowels are identical. When we consider the relationship between the target words and their child production forms, in the case of the first two words, [po] and [ne], the target word consisting of a single CV (consonant + vowel) syllable is repeated twice in the child form. As for the repetition in the other two words, it is the first CV syllable of the target form that is repeated twice. The repetitive process going on in (1.1) is called **reduplication** and it is thought to be the first and most fundamental step in the linguistic development of children, since it occurs in all children in varying degrees. During the earliest stage, reduplication coincides with the transition from playful babbling to first signs of communication and can persist well into the second year. Now consider the following French data.

(1.2)	Child output	Target		
	[meme]	/grãmɛr/	*grandmère*	'grandmother'
	[fãfã]	/ãfã/	*enfant*	'child'
	[tutu]	/ʒu/	*joue*	'play'

[toto]	/gato/	*gâteau*	'cake'
[gogo]	/kokot/	*cocotte*	'hen'
[bobo]	/ʃapo/	*chapeau*	'hat'
[lala]	/vwala/	*voila*	'here'
[mimi]	/minu/	*minou*	'pussycat'
[papa]	/lapɛ̃/	*lapin*	'rabbit'
[nene]	/done/	*donné*	'to give'
[toto]	/oto/	*auto*	'car'

As is apparent in (1.2), the phenomenon of reduplication is not restricted to monosyllabic and disyllabic targets or the first syllable being reduplicated, and children can also reduplicate a syllable after changing the onset consonant. What happens when children are confronted with target forms that they are not able to reproduce accurately is that they have a choice of not producing anything at all or changing the forms into those that they can manage in production. In other words, target words are simplified in order to match the production capacity. We saw above that reduplication is clearly a productive strategy and the diversity of the data in (1.3) should convince the reader that this strategy is used universally by all children, regardless of whether or not reduplication is present in the target language of the children.

(1.3) Reduplication in Jordanian ARABIC child language

Child output	Target	
[mama]	/mayy/	'water'
[bobo]	/boːt/	'shoes'
[baba]	/baab/	'door'

Reduplication in Mandarin CHINESE child language

Child output	Target	
[t^{h}aŋ t^{h}aŋ]	/t^{h}aŋ k^{w}oʊ/	'sweet/candy'
[jiji]	/jiːfuː/	'clothes'
[maʊ maʊ]	/maʊ tsɪ/	'hat'

Reduplication in ENGLISH child language

Child output	Target	
[gɒ́gɒ]	/dɒg/	'dog'
[bebe]	/beɪbɪ/	'baby'
[baba]	/blænkət/	'blanket'
[dada]	/dædɪ/	'daddy'
[mama]	/mʌmɪ/	'mummy'
[kaka]	/kɪtɪ/	'kitty'
[gaga]	/kwæk kwæk/	'quack-quack'

Reduplication in GERMAN child language

Child output	Target	
[nana]	/naːzə/	'nose'
[bebe]	/bɛr/	'bear'
[baʊbaʊ]	/baʊχ/	'belly'

Reduplication in JAPANESE child language

Child output	Target	
[ʤuʤu]	/ʤuːsu/	'juice'
[tenten]	/tentɔːmuʃi/	'lady bird'
[meːmeː]	/ɒsembeɪ/	'rice cracker'
[ʤunʤun]	/gitaː/	'guitar'
[manman]	/anpanman/	'Anpanman' (Japanese cartoon character)

Reduplication in MALTESE child language

Child output	Target	
[baba]	/banana/	'banana'
[nana]	/banana/	'banana'
[gaga]	/gazaza/	'dummy/pacifier'

Reduplication in RUSSIAN child language

Child output	Target	
[kɔl-kɔl]	/u'kɔl/	'sting/injection'
[tuk-'tuk]	/stu'ʧu/	'hammer' (1.Sg.Pr.)
[gɔm-gɔm]	/bʲi'gɔm/	'running'
[kap-kap]	/'kapətʲ/	'drip' (Inf.)
[pɨk-pɨk]	/prɨg/	'jump'

Reduplication in SWEDISH child language

Child output	Target	
[gaːgaː]	/tak/	'thank you'
[dada]	/tak/	'thank you'
[dædːæ]	/tɪtʊt/	'peek-a-boo'

Reduplication in ZUNI (native American) child language

Child output	Target	
[tata]	/tatʧu/	'father'
[mama]	/ʦitta/	'mother'
[titi]	/ʃiwe/	'meat'
[wewe]	/waʧita/	'dog'

It is not the case that children's reduplicated production is as simple as shown in (1.1–1.3), and it may not consist of identical syllables. Take a look at the data in (1.4). The data in (1.4a) come from the same French child who also produced identical syllables in

(1.1); (1.4b) is from a Catalan-acquiring child, and (1.4c) is from English:

(1.4)		Child output	Target	
	a.	[dadap]	/dam/	'lady'
		[tutup]	/sup/	'soup'
		[babab]	/bal/	'ball'
	b.	[βεβέzə]	/sərβέzə/	'beer'
		[papátəs]	/səβátəs/	'shoes'
		[ʒɔʒɔ́nta]	/tərɔ́nʒə/	'orange'
	c.	[dagda]	/dɒg/	'dog'
		[ladla]	/slaɪd/	'slide'
		[dεbdε]	/teɪp/	'tape'

It should be apparent by now that reduplication can be total or partial. At the same time, what is copied in the process of reduplication can vary from a single consonant to a whole syllable. The reduplication of monosyllabic targets has been reported to be less common than target words consisting of two or more syllables. This is based on the view that since reduplication is a strategy used by children to simplify both the structure and the articulation of the word, a disyllabic production of monosyllabic target is a complication, rather than simplification. We will return to the issue of why some children should choose to reduplicate monosyllabic targets later, but for now we will focus on the universality and the function of reduplication.

Reduplication is not restricted to child language. For example, when we consider *Djemba-Djemba* and *Lualua*, the surnames of two African-born footballers currently playing in English football clubs, *Chipolopolo* and *Bafana Bafana*, which are the national football teams of Zambia and South Africa, respectively, and a conservation area in Tanzania called *Ngorongoro*, it is not hard to see that reduplication is commonly found in Bantu languages, usually to form a frequentive verb or for emphasis. As for other examples, which are not proper nouns, the Swahili phrase, *ana-sumbua* (ana = 'to be'; sumbua = 'annoying'), meaning 'X is annoying', is reduplicated to *ana-sumbua-sumbua*, meaning 'X is very annoying'. Likewise, the phrase *mtoto-analia-lia* (mtoto = 'child'; ana = to be'; lia = 'crying'), which means 'the child is crying a lot', is derived from *mtoto-analia*.(Data source for African languages: Bagamba Bukpa Araali, personal communication.)

Although reduplication may seem rare or even exotic to those of us whose language repertoire is restricted to Indo-European languages, it is more widespread in the languages of the world than one might think. In fact, besides the Bantu languages spoken in many parts of Africa, this process is common in languages of Austronesia, Australia, South Asia, and also occurs in those spoken in the Caucasus and Amazonia. Take a look at the examples of total reduplication in Nukuoro, an Austronesian language, in (1.5).

(1.5) Total reduplication in Nukuoro (Rubino 2005)

gada	'smile'	→	*gadagada*	'laugh'
vai	'water'	→	*vaivai*	'watery'
hano	'go'	→	*hanohano*	'diarrhoea'
ivi	'bone'	→	*iviivi*	'skinny'

Furthermore, it is interesting to note how reduplication frequently penetrates into pidgins and creoles that have developed from Western European languages, in which reduplication is not found. See (1.6) data for demonstration.

(1.6) Reduplication in Nigerian Pidgin English (Rubino 2005)

dem	'them'	→	*demdem*	'themselves'
mek	'make'	→	*mekmek*	'scheme/plot'
kop	'cup'	→	*kopkop*	'by the cup'

Reduplication in Seychelles Creole French (Rubino 2005)

ver	'green'	→	*ê rob ver-ver*	'a greenish dress'
roz	'ripe'	→	*roz-roz-roz*	'as ripe as can be'

Reduplication in Berbice Dutch Creole (Rubino 2005)

inga	'thorn'	→	*inga-inga*	'many thorns'
mangi	'run'	→	*mangi-mangi*	'keep running'

However, apart from child-directed speech, total reduplication in adult language seems to be less common. Although there are languages with only total reduplication, but no language with only partial reduplication, which means that languages with partial reduplication also allow total reduplication, the overall picture is there are more languages with both types than with only total reduplication and a more sophisticated reduplication is employed for grammatical reasons. Take a look at the examples of morphological alternations below from Ilokano, a language spoken in the Philippines, and the Bantu language, Feʔ Feʔ Bamileke, spoken in Cameroon in (1.7).

(1.7) Reduplication in Ilokano (Rubino 2005)

[pusa]	'cat'	→	[puspusa]	'cats'
[kaldiŋ]	'goat'	→	[kalkaldiŋ]	'goats'
[dakkel]	'big'	→	[dakdakkel]	'bigger'

Reduplication in Fe? Fe? Bamileke (Rubino 2005)

[si-sii]	'to spoil'	[pi-pii]	'to get'
[su-su]	'to vomit'	[ku-kuu]	'to carve'
[ji-jee]	'to see'	[ti-tee]	'to remove'
[ci-cen]	'to moan'	[ti-ten]	'to stand'
[ci-cæ?]	'to trample'	[ti-tæ?]	'to bargain'

What we see in (1.7) is prefixation, the more common form of reduplication in adult languages. In the case of Ilokano, the plural form is formed by reduplicating a whole syllable, including the initial consonant from the following syllable to form a syllable-final consonant or coda, and in Fe? Fe? Bamileke, the prefixation consists of reduplicating the onset of the monosyllabic stem, but possibly with coda exclusion and a vowel change.

The fundamental difference between reduplication in adults and children is that in adult languages reduplication is a morphological process with a clear grammatical function, that is the meaning of a word changes after a full or a partial reduplication, while children do not reduplicate to change the meaning of a word. In this sense, reduplication in child language is extra-grammatical, since it does not have a morphological function, but is merely a strategy used to alter the target word in accordance with the developing production capacity. In terms of phonology, on the other hand, it clearly seems to be the first step in speech production, since children reduplicate even when reduplication is absent from the target language and it is a systematic operation of decomposing and/or composing target words, which is even considered by some researchers as children creating the grammatical link to the phonetic component. We will return to this topic in Chapter 3, where we will be examining the link between babbling and first words.

1.2 Avoidances

Just as there are no two people who are identical in every respect (not even twins), we cannot expect all children to use the same strategies in the same ways in order to cope with speech production. From this point of view, it is only natural to expect differences among children acquiring different languages. However, not only do we see differences among children acquiring the same language, but also different strategies are found within each child, as we shall see later on. Nevertheless, simplification strategies in child language must be universal, since their cross-linguistic occurrence is adequately widespread to be labelled child language patterns.

While some child language processes are optional and some more common than others, some processes are simply unavoidable by children, as we saw in the case of reduplication. Let us now take a look at another common, probably unavoidable, process in children. What are the English-acquiring children doing in (1.8)?

(1.8)	[u]	/ʃu/	*shoe*
	[baɪ]	/baɪk/	*bike*
	[bʊ]	/bʊk/	*book*
	[ʧi]	/ʧiz/	*cheese*
	[bebɪ]	/beɪbɪ/	*baby*
	[bɛd]	/brɛd/	*bread*

It will, we hope, be clear that the target words are being shortened or truncated by only one sound in (1.8). Although the phenomenon of **segmental deletion** is seen in all word positions, word-final segmental deletion is said to occur more frequently than any other positions and consonant deletion is more frequent than vowel deletion. We will address the question of why this should be in the next chapter. For now, let us focus on another type of deletion in child language. Considering the obvious fact that the younger the child is, the more the need to simplify and therefore delete; deletions can naturally involve more than a single segment, for example *bounce* → [bʌ], and even whole syllables. Take a look at the English data in (1.9). What is the **syllable deletion** pattern there?

(1.9)	Child output	Target
	[weɪ]	*away*
	[nɑnə]	*banana*
	[ækʊs]	*abacus*
	[æːsʌn]	*Allison*
	[sɪmɛn]	*cinnamon*

All words in (1.9) are polysyllabic and the target words are truncated to make them more manageable. After looking at the first two words, one could gather that children like to omit the first syllable when their target contains more than one syllable. However, when the focus is shifted from ‘what is deleted’ to ‘what is retained’ and the rest of the data are considered, we see that the deletion in (1.9) is not related to position of the word, but to stress placement – the weakest syllable is deleted in each word. This type of truncation is, of course, reminiscent of one form of truncation used in adult English to form diminutives of names (1.10).

(1.10)	[rɒni]	*Veronica*	[trɪʃə]	*Patricia*
	[ʤɜɪni]	*Virginia*	[lɪz]	*Elizabeth*
	[gʌs]	*Augustus*	[mænɪ]	*Emanuel*

Weak syllable deletion or strong syllable retention is not specific to English. Children acquiring other languages have been reported to use exactly the same strategy as English-acquiring children we just saw. For example, the Jordanian Arabic word [ba'tata] for 'potato' has been reported to be produced as [tata] and the examples in (1.11) come from Portuguese child language.

(1.11)	['patu]	*sapato*	/sa'patu/	'shoe'
	['munu]	*menino*	/mə'ninu/	'boy'

As for examples of a weak syllable deletion process in adult lan guages, it also occurs in Hawaiian, and Latvian has vowel deletion in final unstressed syllables. As we can make an analogy to how weaker colours are easily absorbed by stronger colours, the simple phonetic fact is that there is a difference in the articulation of the vowels between those in stressed syllables and unstressed syllables. Hence, it should be easy to understand that weak syllable deletion or strong syllable retention is not at all rare in adult languages of the world. Moreover, deletion is not restricted to segments and syllables. For example, tone sandhi processes in many Chinese dialects involve spreading of the tone of the stressed syllable, preceded obviously by deletion of the unstressed syllable tone.

Deletion patterns in child language vary and there are many more patterns than the straightforward ones exhibited in the examples above. The English data in (1.12) should give some flavour of deletion patterns that occur in different children.

(1.12)	[bɑnə]	*banana*
	[ziː]	*chimpanzee*
	[bʌfo]	*buffalo*
	[fɛvɪt]	*favourite*
	[bɒŋ]	*belong*
	[tɛfo]	*telephone*
	[baki]	*broccoli*

The first word in (1.12) shows stressed syllable deletion, the opposite of what we saw earlier. As for the second word, *chimpanzee*, without looking at other patterns of the child producing its token [ziː], it is not entirely clear whether it is a case of weak syllable deletion, strong syllable retention, or final syllable retention. Although the deletions in *buffalo*, *favourite*, and *belong* result in these words becoming one syllable shorter, these are not cases of syllable deletion, but that of segments, as with the last two words. Note that deletions do not always involve segments adjacent to each other. Furthermore, when we consider the word *behind* being produced as [aɪnd] by a child, we can see that deletions can involve a combination of a syllable and a segment.

We now invite you to observe the data in (1.13).

(1.13)	a.	[bæʧʌ]	*spatula*
		[geɪp]	*escape*
		[beɪdu]	*potato*
		[mɑdu]	*tomato*
		[ɛʔvɛn]	*elephant*
	b.	[twaɪkl]	*tricycle*
		[waf]	*giraffe*
		[wuː]	*kangaroo*

It should now be obvious that what is going on in (1.13a) and (1.13b) is weak syllable deletion. However, at the same time as the weak syllables being deleted, there is a change in voicing in (1.13a) and in (1.13b) /r/ is substituted with [w], which is called **gliding**. Gliding is said to be a very common in children cross-linguistically and affects two other segments; the light [l] as in *light* /laɪt/ → [jaɪt] and its dark counterpart, [ɫ] as in *milk* /mɪɫk/ → [mɪwk].

1.3 From nothing to something

Now take a look at (1.14) and see what is going on at the word-initial position. The first two words come from English-acquiring children, the third from a French-acquiring child, and the last from a Japanese-acquiring child.

(1.14)	[hɛgɜdə]	/ælɪgeɪtə/	'alligator'	(English)
	[hæmstədæm]	/æmstədæm/	'Amsterdam'	(English)
	[hailo]	/alo/	'hello'	(French)
	[hebi]	/ebi/	'shrimp'	(Japanese)

Although the data in (1.14) come from children acquiring different languages, the same process is going on. Straightforwardly, all input words begin with a vowel and all child forms begin with [h]. While there are no syllables being deleted, the words in (1.14) are a clear case of **epenthesis**, [h]-insertion to be exact. It is worth noting that /h/ is not found in the phonemic inventory of the target language for the French child. Although epenthesis is generally not as common as deletion, we will show later that it is quite natural and expected under certain circumstances. Still focusing on the word-initial position, take a look at the next data set from two English-acquiring children.

(1.15)	a.	[fi-giɾo]	*mosquito*
		[fi-bejə]	*umbrella*
		[fi-dinə]	*Christina*
		[fi-vajzə]	*adviser*
		[fi-geɾi]	*spaghetti*
		[fi-tenə]	*container*
		[fi-bɛkə]	*Rebecca*
		[fi-wajn]	*rewind*
	b.	[ridʌktə]	*conductor*
		[ristɜb]	*disturb*
		[riskeɪp]	*escape*
		[rirɔst]	*exhaust*

Quite obviously, all the child forms in (1.15a) begin with [fi] and (1.15b) with [ri]. Notice that the children in (1.15) are being faithful to the number of syllables in the input words, that is, the number of syllables in the input and the output is the same, and that the initial syllable in all target words is unstressed. Since these children are deleting the initial unstressed syllable and replacing it with another, we can see here that epenthesis is not restricted to segments. The epenthesis in (1.15) is one of a 'dummy syllable', since the epenthesised syllable is a uniform syllable which does not bear any real resemblance to the one it is apparently replacing, and it is not a very common process in children. However, what occurs more frequently is the process demonstrated in the Portuguese and Dutch child data in (1.16). Try to find out what phonological process the children in (1.16) are using.

(1.16)	[ɑmɑˈmɑ̃]	/mɑˈmɑ̃/	'mummy'	(Portuguese)
	[ɑˈbiˈbi]	/ˈbɑ̃bi/	'Bambi' '	(Portuguese)
	[ɑˈpɑ]	/ˈpɑ̃w̃/	'bread'	(Portuguese)
	[ˈjoeRək]	/jyrk/	'dress'	(Dutch)
	[ˈmɛlək]	/mɛlk/	'milk'	(Dutch)
	[ˈbálə]	/bɑl/	'ball'	(Dutch)

We hope that, without much effort, the process in (1.16) can be identified as vowel insertion. Again, this process is widespread in both adult and child languages of the world. To name a few, vowel insertion is applied in morphological operations in Berber languages and in Spanish, which disallows /s/-initial consonant clusters, /e/ is inserted before /s/, as in *España*, *escudo*, *esperanza*, and so on. Perhaps the most recognisable examples for the reader are from English, in which vowel epenthesis occurs in pluralisation, for example *dogs* [dɒgz], but *matches* [mæʧɪz], and in past tense formation, for example *walked* [wɔkt], but *hated* [heɪtɪ̠d]. Furthermore, the strategy of vowel insertion is most vividly demonstrated in Japanese loanword phonology. Look at the Japanese words in (1.17), borrowed from English, and see whether you can figure out the reason behind the vowel insertion in Japanese loanwords.

(1.17)	[kurisumasu]	'Christmas'
	[tekisuto]	'text'
	[sutoraiku]	'strike'
	[aisukuriːmu]	'ice-cream'
	[puraido]	'pride'

If the English words are transcribed into IPA first and then compared with the Japanese loanwords with the inserted vowels highlighted, it is quite easy to see the purpose of this vowel insertion: it is to break up consonant clusters, which Japanese phonology does not allow. We will be expanding on how children deal with consonant clusters in the next chapter, but for now it suffices to underscore that child phonology is no different from any adult phonology in the view that different strategies are used in order to deal with disfavoured structures.

1.4 Modifications

When a child is confronted with a structure that his or her phonology disallows, there is another way to overcome the problem in production besides reduplicating, deleting and inserting. Observe the English data in (1.18).

(1.18)	a.	*pig*	[bɪg]
		pear	[bɛə]
		car	[ga]
		cup	[gɐp]
		two	[du]

b. *big* [bɪk]
bead [bit]
bad [bæt]
flag [flæk]
Bob [bɒp]
c. *peg* [bɛk]

Apparently, there are no syllable structure changes or segments being deleted or inserted in (1.18), but a segment in each target word is changed to another in the output form. Since we can stipulate that all the words (in the input as well as the output) are monosyllabic, we can refer to segments in the context of syllable positions. We can ignore the vowels, as they are produced accurately, and observations can be made as to what is in the onset and the coda positions: The onset of the target words in (1.18a) are all voiceless obstruents, and the target codas in (1.18b) are all voiced obstruents. What is the difference between these target onsets and codas and the obstruents in the onsets and the codas of the child forms in (1.18)? The manner and the place of articulation of the obstruents are the same and the only difference is in the voicing. The voiceless onset obstruents in (1.18a), [p], [t], and [k], gain voice in child production and surface as [b], [d], and [g]. What is happening in (1.18b) is the reverse; the voiced coda obstruents of the targets in (1.18b) lose their voice and appear as their voiceless counterparts in child production. It should now be clear that the word in (1.18c) demonstrates a clear case of these two processes going on at the same time, namely onset obstruent voicing and coda obstruent devoicing. These processes both classify as position-specific processes and are, indeed, quite common child languages of the world. In adult languages, while onset obstruent voicing seems to be non-existent, coda obstruent devoicing is fairly common, with the most cited examples being German, Dutch, Polish, Russian, Catalan and Turkish.

In addition to **voicing changes**, there are two more basic ways in which segments can change. Consider how segments can be grouped in other ways than in terms of voicing and examine the next data set from English child language in (1.19). Any changes in the voicing should be ignored.

(1.19) [deɪn] *Jane*
[dʌmp] *jump*
[du] *zoo*

[daɪ]	*shy*
[do]	*show*
[di]	*see*
[tɔk]	*sock*

It is very obvious that the onset consonant is changing in all the words in (1.19). The consonants of the target words that are being changed are affricates and fricatives, and they all change into a stop, either [d] or [t], in the child output. This change is in the manner of articulation and the process that is shown in (1.19) is a very common phenomenon in child language known as **stopping**. Stopping is not restricted to any specific word position, for example *house* → [haʊt], and it can even occur at both ends of a monosyllabic word, for example *this* → [dɪt].

Stopping is not the only type of **manner change**. In fact, we have already seen another common type of manner change earlier, which is gliding. Furthermore, the first two words in (1.19) can be specified as **deaffrication**, which can also occur without stopping, for example *chip* → [ʃɪp]. Thus, we have identified three different types of manner change in child language: stopping, gliding and deaffrication, which are all cross-linguistic child phenomena. While manner changes are cross-linguistically extremely frequent in adult languages, they do not occur in the same forms as in child language, but as a result of assimilation, that is changes triggered by another segment.

Consider the word *fish* being produced by an English-acquiring child as [tɪs]. We now know that this child is stopping the onset fricative, [f] → [t]. But the change that is going on in the coda, [ʃ] → [s], is not stopping and not even a change in the manner or voicing, since both segments are voiceless fricatives. This exact change can also occur in the onset, for example *ship* → [sɪp], and this process can take other forms, for example *sun* → [θʌn] and *soap* → [θoʊp], voiceless fricatives again. The next data set from Japanese child language, (1.20), may be helpful in identifying this substitution pattern. Although the first four words may seem to point in the direction of stopping, the last word should provide the best hint.

(1.20)	Target		Child output
	/sakana/	‘fish’	[takana]
	/semi/	‘cicada’	[temi]
	/rappa/	‘bugle’	[dappa]
	/saru/	‘monkey’	[sadu]
	/neko/	‘cat’	[neto]

The change that is taking place in the last word in (1.20) is from the dorsal stop, [k], to its alveolar counterpart, [t]. When we consider the place of articulation, we can see that the Japanese child in (1.20) is articulating the consonants in question more or less towards the front than their respective targets. This is also the case for the English data where the palatal [ʃ] fronts to the alveolar [s] and the alveolar [s] to the dental [θ]. For obvious reasons, this **place change** is known as **fronting**. The fronting that occurs in the last word in (1.20) is specifically known as velar fronting, which is a phenomenon not found in adult languages, but cross-linguistically common in child languages, for example *kiss* → [tɪs] and *cat* → [tæt] by English-acquiring children. Changes in the place of articulation can go in the opposite direction, namely towards the back, for example *bat* → [dæt]. Since we will be returning to this later, we will leave it as place changes being cross-linguistically very common in child language.

As is the case of changes in voicing and manner, place changes are commonly seen across adult languages, but take the form of assimilation. We need to look no further than English to demonstrate a familiar case of voice assimilation. Take a look at (1.21), which shows examples of English regular plural nouns.

(1.21)	*book*[s]	*leg*[z]	*lip*[s]	*robe*[z]	*cat*[s]	*bed*[z]
	wedge[z]	*creche*[z]	*bee*[z]	*axe*[z]	*carton*[z]	*wall*[z]

By looking only at the first line of (1.21), it is immediately noticeable that the voicing of the word-final consonant and the plural morpheme is the same. With the knowledge of English spelling system that regular plural nouns are formed by adding the letter '*s*' to the right edge of the noun, a quick analysis of (1.21) might be that the plural morpheme /s/ is voiced to [z] when words end in voiced consonants. However, the second line contradicts this analysis, since *creches* and *axes* end in [z] in spite of the fact that their singular forms end in voiceless sibilants. It is not necessary to consider whether this has to do with the insertion of the vowel [ɪ] in front of the plural morpheme when words end in sibilants, because the plural form of *bee* provides us with the plural morpheme in neutral context by ending in a vowel. Thus, the correct analysis is that the plural morpheme /z/ assimilates to [s] after voiceless obstruents.

Still staying with English and to get a taste of place assimilation in adult language, take a look at the data in (1.22), which are transformations that take place in fluent adult speech (second column).

(1.22)

some books	so[m] books
some pens	so[m] pens
some cars	so[m] cars
ten books	te[m] books
ten cars	te[ŋ] cars
top table	to[p] table
top door	to[p] door
that book	tha[p]book
that pen	tha[p]pen
that car	tha[k]car
red book	re[b]book
red pen	re[b]pen
red car	re[g] car

Obviously, there is no assimilation going on in the first five words. However, when the first word ends in a coronal stop and the second word begins with a non-coronal obstruent, place assimilation generally takes place between these two adjacent obstruents in fluent speech.

To see adult place assimilation in a morphological context and also to see that assimilation is not restricted to obstruents, try analysing the data set in (1.23), which is reduplication in Selayarese, an Austronesian language spoken in Indonesia.

(1.23) Selayarese reduplication (Mithun & Basri 1986)

Non-reduplicated form		Reduplicated form	
/pekaŋ/	'hook'	[pekampekaŋ]	'hook-like object'
/tunruŋ/	'hit'	[tunruntunruŋ]	'hit lightly'
/keloŋ/	'sing'	[keloŋkeloŋ]	'sort of sing'
/maŋŋaŋ/	'tired'	[maŋŋammaŋŋaŋ]	'sort of tired'
/gitaŋ/	'chilli'	[gitaŋgitaŋ]	'chilli-like object'
/roŋgaŋ/	'loose'	[roŋganroŋgaŋ]	'rather loose'
/dodoŋ/	'sick'	[dodondodoŋ]	'sort of sick'
/bambaŋ/	'hot'	[bambambambaŋ]	'sort of hot'
/soroŋ/	'push'	[soronsoroŋ]	'push lightly'

All the words in the first column end in the velar nasal [ŋ], which is clearly the target place assimilation in (1.23), obviously occurring as a result of the morphological process of reduplication. When the velar nasal is followed by a labial consonant, for example [p], [m], and [b], it transforms into a labial nasal, namely [m]. If the place of the following consonant is the same as the velar nasal, that is dorsal, [ŋ] is allowed to remain unchanged. However, with coronal consonants following, for example [t], [d], [r], and [s], the velar nasal assimilates and changes into its coronal counterpart, [n].

1.5 Harmony

While changes in voicing, manner, and place in child language we have seen so far were not products of assimilation or dissimilation, it is not the case that substitutions in child language are never triggered by another segment within the word. In (1.24) we present a set of English child data, which should be considered at the word level, rather than the syllable, since the process involves both monosyllabic and disyllabic words.

(1.24)	a.	[gɔg]	*dog*
		[gɪg]	*big*
		[gʌk]	*duck*
		[gʊk]	*book*
		[kako]	*taco*
		[kek]	*take*
	b.	[bʌb]	*tub*
		[bɒp]	*top*
		[wæwæ]	*flower*
		[dæt]	*bat*
		[nɛt]	*neck*
		[gɪk]	*kiss*
	c.	[pɛm]	*pen*
		[bum]	*spoon*
		[non]	*stone*
		[minz]	*beans*
		[lɒli]	*lorry*
		[lɛlo]	*yellow*

First of all, we can note that all the target words contain at least two different consonants while all the child output forms contain exactly two consonants that are either identical or similar. This phenomenon of consonant assimilation is specific to child language and the broader term for it is **consonant harmony**. What we see in (1.24) is the different types of consonant harmony found in child language. In (1.24a), as the change that is taking place is on the first consonant (C1) of the target and not the second consonant (C2), we know immediately that the direction of the influence is from C2 to C1. Since both C1 and C2 are obstruents and the voicing of both consonants remain unchanged in the child output forms, we can arrive at the observation that it is the dorsal (phonetically velar) place of C2, namely [g, k], that is spreading to C1, whose place is originally coronal or labial. This is known as **dorsal harmony**.

Bearing in mind that in phonological analyses articulation is categorised into three places: labial, coronal and dorsal, one could speculate that there must be at least two more types of consonant harmony: **labial harmony and coronal harmony**. A practical overview of consonant harmony can be facilitated by writing down the relevant places at the same time as taking note of the direction. It might be helpful to take a look at the chart in (1.25), which is a visual overview of the process in (1.24a), and apply it for (1.24b).

(1.25) Consonant harmony overview for (1.24a)

Child output	Target	C1 place	Direction	C2 place
[gɔg]	*dog*	Coronal	⇦	Dorsal
[gɪg]	*big*	Labial	⇦	Dorsal
[gʌk]	*duck*	Coronal	⇦	Dorsal
[gʊk]	*book*	Labial	⇦	Dorsal
[kako]	*taco*	Coronal	⇦	Dorsal
[kek]	*take*	Coronal	⇦	Dorsal

Once an overview of the consonant harmonies in (1.24b) is achieved, with or without the help of the chart in (1.25), it should be easy to make out that the first three child forms in (1.24b) display labial harmony, while the fourth and fifth ones, *bat* and *neck*, are cases of coronal harmony. In the first two words, besides C1 taking the labial place from C2, the voice of C1 is also changed. In the case of *flower*, C2 is simply copied to replace the word-initial consonant cluster. Furthermore, we can also see in this child's reduplicated form that there is vowel harmony, since the vowels are identical. As for coronal harmony, while the child's C1 simply takes the coronal place of C2 in *bat* without voice change, the direction of the harmony in *neck* is the other way around, going from C1 to C2, known as progressive harmony, whereas the earlier examples display regressive harmony. This direction of harmony is also exhibited in the child form of *kiss*, a case of dorsal harmony in (1.24b), in which there is a voicing change in C1, but not in C2.

Having identified three types of consonant harmony, which can go in either direction, it is immediately noticeable in (1.24c) that the first two examples are cases of labial harmony, in which the coronal nasal in the coda changes to its labial counterpart. It should also be fairly straightforward to note that there is no spreading of place features in the last four child tokens of (1.24c). In the child forms of *stone* and *beans*, it is the nasality of C2 that spreads to C1, understandably termed nasal harmony: After the initial /s/-deletion in *stone* the alveolar stop [t] is nasalised to [n] and in *beans* C1 (labial stop) changes into the labial nasal [m]. Finally, the cases of *lorry* and *yellow* demonstrate lateral harmony in two different directions.

As can be guessed by now, consonant harmony is not specific to English-acquiring children, which is exactly what the Dutch, Greek, and Spanish data in (1.26) exhibit.

(1.26) Consonant harmony in DUTCH child language

Target	Gloss	Child form	C1	Direction	C2
paard	'horse'	[paːp]	Labial	⇨	Coronal
slof	'slipper'	[pɔf]	Coronal	⇦	Labial
boot	'boot'	[tɔt]	Labial	⇦	Coronal
tram	'tram'	[ten]	Coronal	⇨	Labial
blokken	'blocks'	[kɔkoː]	Labial	⇦	Dorsal

Consonant harmony in GREEK child language

Target	Gloss	Child form	C1	Direction	C2
petái	'fly' (3.Sg.Pr.)	[pepái]	Labial	⇨	Coronal
típos	'type'	[pípo]	Coronal	⇦	Labial
káto	'down'	[káko]	Dorsal	⇨	Coronal
síko	'get up'(imp.)	[kíko]	Coronal	⇦	Dorsal
kápa	'Kappa' (surname)	[pápa]	Dorsal	⇦	Labial

Consonant harmony in SPANISH child language

Target	Gloss	Child form	C1	Direction	C2
peine	'comb'	[popa]	Labial	⇨	Coronal
sopa	'soup'	[popa]	Coronal	⇦	Labial
casa	'house'	[kaka]	Dorsal	⇨	Coronal
troca	'truck'	[koka]	Coronal	⇦	Dorsal

Whether consonant harmony also occurs in adult languages is a very good question. In fact, there are different types of consonant harmony in adult languages, too. However, the fundamental difference between consonant harmony in children and adults is that child consonant harmony is a long-distance primary place harmony involving agreement in the primary place of articulation, which is claimed to be unattested in adult languages of the world. We will be discussing the different patterns of child consonant harmony and their distribution in detail in the next chapter.

2

STRATEGIES

In the previous chapter, we presented data showing processes very commonly found in child phonology. In this chapter, we shall show some of the strategies employed by children in pursuit of a similar target and to offer some explanation for those strategies and data. In Chapter 3, we shall see how theoreticians have attempted to account for the data.

2.1 Cluster simplification

2.1.1 Canonical clusters

First, consider the examples in (2.1) of what we have hitherto been considering as deletion of consonants. The data sets we are discussing are provided by two children, Amahl (Smith 1973) and Gitanjali (Gnanadesikan 2004), at roughly the same age, around two and a half. Both children are acquiring English and the pattern exhibited is typical of children of that age.

(2.1)	Amahl (Smith 1973)		Gitanjali (Gnanadesikan 2004)	
	[b̥eɪ]	*play*	[kin]	*clean*
	[b̥u]	*blue*	[piz]	*please*
	[g̊in]	*clean*	[fen]	*friend*
	[g̊aɪ]	*sky*	[dɔ]	*straw*
	[b̥ɔt]	*sport*	[gɪn]	*skin*
	[b̥un]	*spoon*	[bun]	*spoon*

You will have noticed that neither child can pronounce consonant clusters. Here we are concentrating on word-initial clusters, although there is one example in the data of the reduction of a word-final cluster. These, however, will be discussed later. Most of the target adult clusters would have contained two consonants, although there is one example in the data set in (2.1) of a three consonant one.

The question we want to address here is: What is the pattern apparent in the forms produced of both children? The question must be: What is retained? – rather than – What is deleted? Before we continue, see if you can work out what the pattern is.

The key to these simplifications lies in the idea of 'preferred onset' and in **sonority**. The term 'sonority' refers to the loudness, all other factors (stress, pitch, velocity, muscular tension, and so on) being equal, of a sound. Relative sonority can be correlated with the amount of air resonating in the vocal tract. Thus a low vowel such as [ɑ] where the area of the resonating chamber is fairly large will be louder, or more sonorous, than a high vowel and considerably louder than an obstruent such as [p]. The scale of relative sonority is as follows:

Non-high vowels (ɑ, æ, etc.) > high vowels and glides (i, u, j, w) > liquids (l, r) > nasals (m, n, ŋ) > fricatives (s, f, etc.) > stops (p, b, t, k, etc.).

This is, of course, a very crude scale and there may be refinements that could be made within it (see, for example, Selkirk 1984 for an expanded version of this scale). It will serve our present purposes very well, however.

You will, no doubt, have noticed that both the children retain the less, or least, sonorous of the segments in the adult cluster. Therefore, if the choice is between stop [p] and liquid [l] (*play, please*) they opt for the [p]. Notice that this is not because this is the word initial sound since if the initial is a fricative [s] and the second sound is a stop it is the stop that is retained and the fricative is not pronounced. The two patterns combine in Gitanjali's rendering of *straw* [dɔ] where both the target /s/ and the target /ɹ/ fail to materialise. Nor is the reason that the children cannot pronounce a liquid – both children exhibit word initial [l] when there is no other consonant (2.2).

(2.2)	Amahl		Gitanjali	
	[lɒli]	*lorry*	[læb]	*lab*

Substitution of target /ɹ/ does occur in both children, but this will be discussed in a later chapter.

An explanation for the retention of the less sonorous of the consonants is provided by general theory of the syllable and the sonority dispersion principle. This can be stated in very simple terms as the requirement that the preferred onset of a syllable is of minimal sonority and the preferred nucleus is of maximal sonority – thus permitting a maximum dispersion of sonority that is a maximum sonority contrast between adjacent segments. In a nutshell, the 'ideal syllable' has a low sonority onset preceding a vowel, preserving maximal contrast (Clements 1990).

So far it has appeared that what we shall call the sonority pattern holds good for both the children, as indeed it does for other children (2.3).

(2.3) Julia: English (Pater & Barlow 2001, 2002, 2003)

[bæki]	*blanket*		
[kaʊn]	*clown*		
[fut]	*flute*		
[pet]	*plate*		
Annalena: German (Goad & Rose 2004)			
[bɯmə]	/bl/*ume*	'flower'	
[kɑin]	/kl/*ein*	'small'	
[fɪkə]	/fl/*iege*	'fly'	
[gɪf]	/gr/*iff*	'grip'	
Clara: French (Rose 2000)			
[βœj]	/flœʁ/	*fleur*	'flower'
[kejɔ]	/kχɛjɔ̃/	*crayon*	'pencil'
Theo: French (Rose 2000)			
[ke]	/kle/	*clé*	'key'
[pize]	/bʁize/	*brisé*	'broken'

It can be seen, also, that cluster reduction occurs in European Portuguese (João Freitas 2003), as we show in the (2.4).

(2.4) Inês

[kɛ]	/kɾɛmɨ/	*creme*	'cream'
[abi]	/abɾɨ/	*abre*	'open' (imperative)
[pajɐ]	/pɾajɐ/	*praia*	'beach'
[tikiko]	/tɾisiklu/	*triciclo*	'bicycle'

As well as this common strategy for overcoming the problems posed by clusters, examples from European Portuguese also show the strategy of vowel epenthesis to break up the clusters (2.5).

(2.5) Luis

[kɨɾɐ̃dɨ]	/gɾɐ̃dɨ/	*grande*	'big'
[mõʃtɨɾu]	/mõʃtɾu/	*monstro*	'monster'
[pɛdɨɾɐ]	/pɛdɾɐ/	*pedra*	'rock'
[fɨɾawdɐ]	/fɾaɫdɐ/	*fralda*	'nappy'
[fɨlojʃ]	/floɾɨʃ/	*flores*	'flowers'

Vowel epenthesis can also be found in Jordanian Arabic (2.6).

(2.6)	Ameera	[bawaat]	/bwaat/	'boots'
	Khaleel	[kitaab]	/ktaab/	'book'
		[kalaab]	/klaab/	'dogs'
	Maya	[tileen]	/treen/	'train'
		[muʔallem]	/mʔallem/	'teacher' (masc.)

However, as we commented in the previous chapter, sometimes the preferred pattern breaks down for a number of reasons. In (2.7) we show examples of the different strategies employed by Amahl and Gitanjali when it comes to certain /s/-clusters.

2.1.2 /s/-Clusters

(2.7)	Amahl		Gitanjali	
	[no]	*snow*	[so]	*snow*
	[mɔ]	*small*	[sʊki]	*snookie*
	[laɪt]	*slide*	[sip]	*sleep*
	[wip]	*sleep*	[fok]	*smoke*
	[ŋeɪk]	*snake*	[fɛrə]	*sweater*
	[mɛu]	*smell*	[fɛw]	*smell*

You will notice that the two children have totally different strategies for dealing with target /s/ plus sonorant clusters. The most obvious difference is that Gitanjali sticks to the sonority pattern exhibited above in (2.1), while Amahl diverges from it. Let us deal with the two patterns separately.

For Gitanjali, an onset with a fricative is preferable to one with a nasal or a liquid. On the other hand, Amahl appears to have a problem with the articulation of fricatives. Let us look at how he deals with singleton target fricatives (2.8).

(2.8)	Amahl				
	a.	[d̥ʌt]	*shut*	[d̥aɪ]	*shy*
		[g̊ɪŋɪŋ]	*singing*	[d̥id̥in]	*sitting*
		[d̥ɪdə]	*scissors*	[d̥i]	*see*
		[g̊ɛgu]	*thank you*	[d̥id]	*these*
		[wɑpt]	*laughed*	[maɪp]	*knife*
	b.	[wɪt]	*fish*	[wæː]	*fire*
		[wæwæ]	*flower*	[wʊt]	*foot*
	c.	[it]	*seat*	[ɑp]	*sharp*
		[up]	*soap*	[aʊt]	*house*
		[nu]	*nose*	[b̥i]	*please*

As you can see, fricatives are avoided in a number of different ways. The most usual way, following from what we showed in (1.19) in the previous chapter, is to produce the nearest stop consonant in terms of place of articulation, which, in most of the examples shown, is coronal. This strategy is shown in (2.8a). We will return to the apparent exceptions to replacement by stops with the closest place of articulation in 2.2, later. The second strategy appears to apply only to target /f/. While in the words *laughed* and *knife* the stopping strategy is employed in syllable codas, in data set (2.8b) /f/ is replaced by a more vowel-like glide [w], with which, of course, it shares a labial place of articulation. The third strategy, shown in data set (2.8c) is to omit the fricative altogether. While we might want to suggest that the replacement of a fricative by a less sonorous stop was in order to increase sonority dispersion, this cannot be the explanation, since stopping is not the only fricative avoidance strategy used. In (2.8b) the replacement onset segment is of higher sonority than the target. Clearly, the strategies in (2.8b and 2.8c) indicate conclusively that Amahl cannot articulate fricatives.

2.1.3 Coalescence

All the data from Gitanjali in (2.7) indicate that she can, indeed, produce fricatives and that the sonority pattern holds strongly for her. We have very few examples of target fricatives in isolation, rather than the result of reduced clusters, from Gitanjali, although we can compare her production of *please* [piz] with that of Amahl [bi]. Gitanjali is also the child whose dummy syllables [fi] we saw in (1.15) of Chapter 1. However, in spite of this, there are unexpected forms in her data. As we might expect of a child who is faithful to this pattern, target *snow* becomes [so] and target *sleep* is [sip] – both merely losing the more sonorous element from the onset. However, when we turn to words such as *smoke* and *sweater* we are given a taste of this unexpected aspect. These are produced as [fok] and [fɛɾə]. Here, again the sonority pattern is respected but neither segment from the target form results. Gitanjali does indeed produce a fricative but a labial one rather than the target coronal. Notice, however, that in both these cases the missing sonorant is labial. Gitanjali retains the labial place of the sonorant and combines it with the fricative manner of the /s/. This is a process known as 'coalescence', a combination of features of two sounds. Coalescence of this type is widespread among young children, as we can see in examples from Lucy from about 2;5 and Amahl at a later stage in his development, from around 2;9. (See 'Conventions' in the preliminary pages of the book).

(2.9)

Lucy (unpublished data)		Amahl	
[fɪmɪn]	*swimming*	[fɪmɪn]	*swimming*
[fɒn]	*swan*	[fɪŋ]	*swing*
[ɬaɪd]	*slide*	[ɬip]	*sleep*
[ɬipɪn]	*sleeping*	[ɬʌg]	*slug*

The examples in (2.9) differ from Gitanjali's, in that neither child is producing /s/-approximant clusters but is combining the fricative manner with the place and, regardless of the place. This means that both produce a coronal lateral fricative [ɬ] which incorporates the laterality of /l/. Notice that it is only with a target approximant that either of these children resorts to coalescence. /s/-nasal targets are correctly pronounced by Lucy, while Amahl steadfastly maintains his avoidance of /s/ although nasals are devoiced, indicating an effect from the missing /s/ ([m̥ɛl] *smell* [n̥eɪl] *snail*).

2.1.4 Favourite sounds

Gitanjali's coalescence appears to serve a different purpose. She seems to have a great liking for labial sounds and these will be retained in some form or other at all costs. As we can see from the data in (2.10), Gitanjali's labial preference extends to her cluster reduction of stop+labial clusters. It should be borne in mind that she appears to have reanalysed [ɹ] as a labial. The relationship between [ɹ] and [w] will be discussed in Chapter 5.

(2.10)

Gitanjali	
[pi]	*tree*
[paɪ]	*cry*
[paɪt]	*quite*
[bɪk]	*drink*
[bep]	*grape*
[pɪkəw]	*twinkle*

Julia also exhibits a preference for the retention of the labial. Her strategy is different from Gitanjali's, however, as we can see from the data in (2.12), Julia's normal cluster reduction strategy is similar to Gitanjali's, in other words the sonority pattern, as we show in (2.11):

(2.11) Julia

[bʌʃ]	*brush*
[pet]	*plate*
[piz]	*please*
[pɪdɪ]	*pretty*
[pun]	*spoon*
[sip]	*sleep*
[saɪt]	*slide*

Now, however, consider the data in (2.12).

(2.12) Julia

[wɪk]	*drink*
[waɪv]	*drive*
[wæmə]	*grandma*
[wɪŋ]	*swing*

Again, you will notice, that [ɹ] appears to have been reanalysed as a labial. In (2.8) we can see that labial obstruents are retained, as expected. The target in the data of (2.9) is a non-labial obstruent followed by a labial sonorant. In such cases, the labial alone is retained, causing a violation of the sonority pattern. Pater and Barlow (2001) show more than one pattern in the reduction of non-labial obstruent+labial sonorant clusters in Julia's data. However, the pattern shown in (2.12) appears to be the most common.

Spencer (1986) in his reanalysis of the Amahl data, draws our attention to an interesting twist in the labial preference story. There is no overt preference shown, as we have demonstrated in the examples shown so far, however, the labial place is apparently present in an unexpected way. Consider the data in (2.13).

(2.13) Amahl

a.	[kɪp]	*quick*
	[kim]	*queen*
	[kib]	*squeeze*
	[kaɪp]	*quite*
	[daɪp]	*twice*
b.	[wɪn]	*win*
	[wit]	*sweet*
	[pun]	*spun*

Amahl does exhibit consonant harmony, as we can see from some of the examples in (2.2) and (2.7) above, as well as two of the unidentified data in (1.24) of Chapter 1. However, in (2.13a) there is no overt reason why the word-final consonants should be labial, since the target consonants are coronal and the initial consonants are not labial. Indeed, we can see that where the initial consonant is overtly labial as in (2.13b), no harmony is evidenced. The common thread running through the data in (2.13a) is that sonority-based cluster reduction has, as expected, left the stop consonant (either dorsal or coronal) but has caused the loss of the labial approximant [w]. It is this labiality that has combined with the manner of articulation of the final consonant to produce a labial. In other words the labial feature has lingered but, instead of attaching itself to the initial sound it has attached itself to the final.

2.2 Coda cluster simplification

So far, we have been looking at word initial cluster simplification and its consequences. There was, as we commented, one example of a simplified final cluster in Gitanjali's data. Let us look at the patterns in Amahl's word-final cluster simplification.

(2.14) Amahl

a.	[ɛt]	*ant*	[ɛn]	*hand*
	[bʌp]	*bump*	[bɛn]	*band*
	[dʌp]	*jump*	[mɛn]	*mend*
	[mɛt]	*meant*	[daʊn]	*round*
	[dæp]	*stamp*	[wɛn]	*friend*
b.	[gud]	*cold*	[ɛp]	*help*
	[mɪk]	*milk*	[wɛp]	*self*
	[dɒt]	*salt*	[ud]	*hold*
	[bot]	*bolt*	[wɛp]	*shelf*

In (2.14) we show a reasonably representative selection of the patterns to be found in Amahl's speech during the period around two years of age (Amahl's stages are generally of only a few days' duration). If we study the data, we can see that there is a clear pattern emerging in data set (2.14a) and a somewhat different one in data set (2.14b). Smith (1973) comments that Amahl's [final] nasal cluster simplification varies as to the voicing setting of the obstruent. You will have noticed that if the obstruent is voiceless, it is retained and the nasal deleted. If, on the other hand, it is voiced, then the obstruent is deleted and the nasal retained. If the target cluster contains a lateral /l/ (2.14b), the voicing setting of the following obstruent is irrelevant; if cluster simplification is to take place, the lateral is never retained.

We might want to suggest some possible explanations for these findings. We could start by considering sonority dispersion as one of the possible causes. You will, however, immediately notice that there appear to be strange anomalies here. As presented so far, the impression of sonority dispersion is that of the preservation of a maximal contrast. The deletion of the nasal before a voiceless stop and the liquid everywhere would, therefore, seem to be in conformity with this principle and present a mirror image to the case of the sonority pattern in onsets. The problem here would be: Why do voiced obstruents delete in preference to nasals?

Another observation by Clements (1990) indicates that syllable codas are not, in fact, mirror images of onsets. In terms of what he calls the 'sonority cycle principle', Clements makes the claim that codas are preferably of relatively high sonority. This tendency is more apparent word-medially, but, according to Clements, the overall tendency is towards a profile that 'rises maximally towards the peak and falls minimally towards the coda'. Thus, by this principle, the cluster simplification leaving the nasal in preference to the voiced obstruent would seem to be better. Notice also, that the only post-nasal word-final voiced stop permitted in English is /d/. There are no words ending in [mb] or [ŋg], although there are, of course, dialects of English where this second cluster is permitted word-finally. However, examples of this would not show up in the data, since Amahl was acquiring standard Southern-British English. Furthermore, by also deleting the /d/ Amahl would seem to be ironing out an anomaly.

It appears, then, that we now have to return to the question of why the nasal is lost in favour of voiceless obstruents and why the liquid is lost in general, regardless of the voicing of the following obstruent.

In conflict with the sonority cycle principle, the applicability of which appears to be primarily limited to word-medial syllable contact, is the observation that voiceless obstruents are less marked than voiced ones, in particular in coda position. Indeed, as we observed in Chapter 1, in many languages, voiced obstruents are not permitted in the coda and any voicing contrast is neutralised in this position. This particular tendency is very noticeable in Amahl's early utterances (2.15), up to around 2;0.4.

(2.15) Amahl

[bɛt]	*bed*
[bɪk]	*big*

[gup] *cube*
[dɛt] *dead*
[ɛk] *egg*
[bɛk] *peg*
[laɪt] *slide*

This same tendency is also manifested by Joan (2.16), who also preferred to replace other vowels with [u] (Velten 1943).

(2.16) Joan
[nap] *knob*
[mat] *mud*
[but] *bread*
[but] *bed*
[ut] *egg*
[hus] *hose*

As we shall see in Chapter 3, Stampe (1972, 1979) suggests that there are certain 'natural processes' in language that will surface in early language acquisition but may be suppressed by speakers of some languages in the interests of introducing contrast. One such process, according to Stampe, ensures that all obstruents, in particular those in final position, will be voiceless. Some languages, such as German, Dutch, Catalan and Turkish, never suppress this process and thus always devoice these final obstruents. Others, such as English or French have introduced this contrast. Thus, in English, the words *bed* and *bet* contrast in the voicing of the final sound, whereas in German, *Rad* 'wheel' and *Rat* 'advice' are both pronounced as [ʁat], although the voicing contrast is maintained in intervocalic position when suffixation occurs.

It appears that the sonority dispersion principle is winning out over the sonority cycle principle in the case of the nasal plus voiceless stop. Now, if we turn to the examples in (2.14b) the situation here is even stronger endorsement of the sonority dispersion principle. Although Amahl is able to pronounce clear /l/ in onset position, as we saw in (2.2) above, but since dark /l/ is more vowel-like, he, like most other children and many English speaking adults, replaces dark /l/ in a rhyme with a vowel. We shall discuss the vocalisation of /l/ and other related matters in Chapter 3. Examples of vocalisation of /l/ in various children can be seen in (2.17).

(2.17)	Amahl		Gitanjali	
	[bebu]	*table*	[biw]	*spill*

[gɪgu]	*tickle*	[fɛw]	*fell*
[æbu]	*apple*	[fɛw]	*smell*
[æməu]	*Amahl*		
Daniel (Menn 1971)		Trevor (Pater 1997)	
[kʌdu]	*cuddle*	[ʃɛu]	*Michelle*
[bʌbu]	*table*	[gɪgu]	*tickle*
		[kɪku]	*pickle*
Joan			
[waw]	*well*		
[baw]	*bell*		

When target /l/ is in a cluster, Amahl invariably deletes it, although this is not the case with Joan. English contains a number of forms which demonstrate the historic deletion of dark /l/ from clusters, in particular containing labial or dorsal consonants, as we can see exemplified in (2.18).

(2.18)

[kɑm]	*calm*
[fok]	*folk*
[wɔk]	*walk*
[tɔk]	*talk*
[pɑm]	*palm*
[jok]	*yolk*

In general, then, the preferred syllable shape appears to conform to the sonority dispersion model, yet we still have the somewhat anomalous situation with the target nasal+voiced stop. Could this be an attempt at disambiguation, even although very few of the forms would cause a problem? Remember that Amahl generally devoices all final consonants. Amahl also adopts the same deletion model intervocalically, even although the consonants in question would be heterosyllabic (for example [ɛŋi] *angry* [wɪnu] *window cf.* [gɛgu] *thank you* [gɪgɪn] *thinking*).

It is, however, interesting that there are exceptions to these final cluster simplifications.

(2.19) Amahl

[waɪnd]	*find*
[wɪnd]	*wind*
[aɪnd]	*behind*
[bɛnd]	*bend*
[gaɪnd]	*kind*
[dænd]	*stand*

All the examples of nasal+stop which are not subject to simplification are nasal+voiced stop. Notice that, here, no devoicing occurs (2.19). It could be suggested that these clusters are being treated as complex segments, like the prenasalised stops that are commonly found in the African language Fula. This must remain a matter for speculation, however.

Aspects of word final consonant clusters and of codas in general will be discussed further in Chapter 7.

2.3 Consonant harmony

In Chapter 1, we give many examples of reduplication which appears to be very prevalent in children in the early stages of development and which we might want to view as an extension of babbling. These disyllabic CVCV utterances may well give way to CVC where the initial and final C share a place or manner of articulation, although harmonised forms may also be disyllabic, for example Lucy's [gɒgɒ] *dog* later gave way to [gɒg] or to [gɒgi].

2.3.1 Harmony targeting the coronal

We have seen in the examples in this chapter, in particular from Amahl, but also in some of the data from Daniel and Trevor, of such harmony. Unlike simple reduplication, consonant harmony involves the mere sharing of features as we can see from the following examples.

(2.20)

Amahl		Daniel	
[ŋeɪk]	*snake*	[gʌk]	*duck*
[gʌk]	*stuck*	[gɔg]	*dog*
[gɑk]	*dark*	[gɪk]	*stick*
[gɪk]	*drink*	[gʌg]	*Doug*

The examples in (2.20) share common features. In the first place, harmony is regressive, that is to say that the site of the harmonised consonant is to the left of the triggering consonant, in these cases the word initial coronal is anticipating the place of the word final dorsal. This form of harmony is very widespread among children as we can see from the selection in (2.21).

(2.21)

Julia (Pater & Barlow 2001)		Richard (O'Neal 1998)	
[gʌk]	*duck*	[gɑk]	*dark*

[kak]	*sock*	[gɒg]	*dog*
[kɪgəs]	*tickles*		
Trevor (Pater & Werle 2001)		Jennika (Ingram 1974)	
[gɔg]	*dog*	[kɔk]	*talk*
[gɪgu]	*tickle*	[gɔk]	*dog*
[krʌk]	*truck*	[kek]	*take*
[kiŋk]	*sink*	[gɪk]	*dig*
[gækit]	*jacket*	[gɪk]	*Dick*
		[gək]	*duck*
		[kako]	*taco*

In the examples shown, the place of articulation of the triggering segment is dorsal but we can find examples in many children of labial harmony as well (2.22).

(2.22)

Amahl		Daniel	
[wip]	*sleep*	[bʌb]	*tub*
[bɒp]	*stop*	[bap]	*top*
[bebu]	*table*	[bɛp]	*step*
[maɪp]	*knife*	[bap]	*stop*
[waɪbɪn]	*driving*	[bip]	*jeep*

Again the targeted sound is a coronal and harmony is regressive. Regressive harmony does seem to be more prevalent in the data in general although we find examples, although to a less significant extent of progressive harmony, in the output of both Amahl and Trevor (2.23).

(2.23)

Amahl		Trevor	
[gɪk]	*kiss*	[kog]	*cold*
[gɒk]	*cloth*	[gɛːg]	*good*
[gɑgi]	*glasses*	[kɪk]	*kiss*
[gʊg]	*good*	[kaʊg]	*cloud*
		[kɪkar]	*guitar*

As with assimilation cross-linguistically, regressive, or anticipatory, harmony is more common than progressive, or perseverative. This sort of anticipation could be the result of forward planning in speech. This is certainly the case with assimilation.

The relative weakness of the coronal is also exemplified in data from Spanish and Greek, which we showed in Chapter 1. In both these languages, we find that coronal is targeted by both dorsal and labial, as it is in English. In the Spanish data in (2.24) and the Greek in (2.25) we can find both regressive and progressive harmony.

(2.24) Si (Macken & Ferguson 1983)

[kaka]	/kasa/	‘house’
[koka]	/troka/	‘truck’
[popa]	/peine/	‘comb’
[popa]	/sopa/	‘soup’

(2.25) Sofia (Kappa 2001)

[kiko]	/siko/	‘get up’ (imp.)
[kika]	/siɣa/	‘slowly’
[kako]	/kato/	‘down’
[kika]	/kita/	‘look’ (2. imp.)
[poma]	/stoma/	‘mouth’
[pipo]	/tipos/	‘type’
[pe(pai)]	/petai/	‘fly’

It is not only coronals that are targeted in English, however, as we show in the data in the next section.

2.3.2 Targeting labials

Amahl and Julia appear only to target coronals in instances of place of articulation harmony but this is not necessarily always the case. Both Daniel and Trevor also exhibit harmony involving labial and dorsal:

(2.26)

Daniel		Trevor (Rose 2000, from Pater 1996)	
[gʌg]	*bug*	[gæk]	*back*
[gaɪk]	*bike*	[gɪg]	*big*
[gɪg]	*pig*	[gægi]	*blanket*
[gɪg]	*big*	[kɪku]	*pickle*
[gʊk]	*book*		

All the data in (2.26) show regressive harmony and, indeed, the only examples of harmony exhibited by Daniel appear to be regressive. Trevor does, to a lesser extent, exhibit progressive labial-dorsal harmony, although, according to Rose (2000) only in a mere 15 per cent of potential targets.

Overall, then, it looks as though the pattern from English favours regressive harmony and that the coronal is the preferred, although not exclusive, target. The tendency of the dorsal to trigger harmonisation is greater than that of the labial or coronal, indeed from what we have seen so far, from published data, the coronal never acts as trigger and the labial does not target the dorsal, although of course, the reverse is true.

Rose (2000) suggests that the findings for Amahl and Trevor indicate a strength hierarchy for place of articulation as shown in (2.27):

(2.27) dorsal > labial > coronal

which we can see applies to the other English acquiring children sampled above.

2.3.3 Other harmony patterns

Clara acquiring Canadian French also displays consonant harmony but her pattern is somewhat different. Consider the following examples.

(2.28) Clara (Rose 2000)

a.	[bɑbuː]	/dəbu/	*debout*	'standing'
	[vævæl]	/ʃəval/	*cheval*	'horse'
	[fədɔː]	/savɔ̃/	*savon*	'soap'
b.	[pæpæː]	/gaspaʁ/	*Gaspard*	'Gaspard'
	[papæb]	/kapab/	*capable*	'capable'
	[pəfɛ]	/kafe/	*café*	'coffee'
c.	[tɔlo]	/gʁəlo/	*grelot*	'little bell'
	[tæto]	/gɑto/	*gâteau*	'cake'
	[tajæ]	/kaju/	*Caillou*	'Caillou'

What you will observe in the data in (2.28) is that labial can target coronal (2.28a), labial can target dorsal (2.28b) and coronal can target labial (2.28c). The instances of labial targeting coronal and dorsal occur in 93 per cent of possible targets, whereas the instances of coronal targeting dorsal occur in only 61 per cent of possible tokens. The picture resulting from this particular little girl is that dorsal is the most likely target and labial the most likely trigger – a very different strength hierarchy (2.29) from that exhibited by the English children.

(2.29) labial > coronal > dorsal

All Clara's harmonic patterns are regressive, there is no evidence of progressive harmony at all in the data presented. There is, however, evidence of progressive harmony in another child (2.30) who exhibits the same strength hierarchy as Clara, but who is acquiring Spanish.

(2.30) José (Lléo 1996)

a.	[pɛjba]	/mesa/	*mesa*	'table'
	[bɐbɛ]	/plato/	*plato*	'dish'
	[ʔubobo]	/unloβo/	*un lobo*	'a wolf'
b.	[pɐpa]	/boka/	*boca*	'mouth'
	[pɔpa]	/foka/	*foca*	'sea-lion'
	[babajɔ]	/kaβaʎo/	*caballo*	'horse'
c.	[totɐ]	/toka/	*toca*	'(he) plays'
	[ʔutato]	/uŋgato/	*un gato*	'a cat'
	[diːtada]	/gitara/	*gitarra*	'guitar'

A similar picture emerges from Robin acquiring Dutch (Levelt 1994; Fikkert, Levelt & van de Weijer, submitted to *First Language*). As with Clara's data, Robin appears to indicate the strength of the labial relative to coronal and dorsal, as we can see from the examples in (2.31) and (2.32).

(2.31) Robin

[fup]	/stup/	'pavement'
[pap]	/tʀɑp/	'stairs'
[fɔp]	/sɔp/	'suds'
[mef]	/nef/	'cousin'
[mimat]	/nimɑnt/	'nobody'

(2.32) Robin

[vomə]	/sχɔmələ/	'swing'
[pɪmə]	/klɪmə/	'climb'
[pofi]	/kɔfi/	'coffee'
[bamɑɹ]	/kaməɹ/	'room'
[popə]	/kopə/	'buy'
[mɔpjə]	/knɔpjə/	'button' (dim)

Robin does produce some examples where we could argue that coronal is targeting dorsal, although these data may also represent examples of 'velar fronting', which we shall discuss later.

Like Robin, Melanie (2.33) acquiring German (Berg 1992, cited in Buckley 2003) exhibits regressive harmony with the labial targeting both dorsal and coronal.

(2.33) Melanie (2;7–2;11)

[poːmas]	/toːmas/	'Thomas'
[biːbən]	/ʃiːbən/	'to push'
[meːmən]	/neːmən/	'to take'

[bɛlp]	/gɛlp/	'yellow'
[pɔmt]	/kɔmt/	'comes'
[boːm]	/doːm/	'cathedral'

The languages we have looked at so far have been European but consonant harmony can be found in non-European languages as we can see from the data from Jordanian Arabic (2.34).

(2.34) Farah (Daana 2009)

[bubun]	/sufun/	'ships'
[bab]	/kalb/	'dog'
[bub]	/dub/	'bear'
[baab]	/ktaab/	'book'
[butub]	/kutub/	'books'
[baab]	/klaab/	'dogs'
[babbaaχ]	/Tabbaaχ/	'cook'

Notice that Farah seems to prefer the labial and to target either the coronal or dorsal. It appears, then, that Dutch, German and Jordanian Arabic have the hierarchy in (2.35).

(2.35) labial > coronal, dorsal

One overall observation we can make about these various patterns of place of articulation harmony is that the coronal is never the strongest in the hierarchy. We shall return to this matter in Chapter 6.

2.3.4 Nasal and lateral harmony

So far, we have only investigated examples of consonant harmony involving the spreading or anticipation of a place of articulation. However, we also find examples of other features spreading. Consider the following forms from Daniel (2.36) (Menn 1971), which develop over the period of 22½ months and 25½ months:

(2.36) Daniel

[mum]	*broom*
[nun/mum]	*prune*
[non]	*stone*
[mum]	*spoon*
[non]	*stone*
[mʌm]	*plum*
[næn]	*stand*
[næʊn]	*down*

Amy (unpublished data) was producing similar processes at the age of 2;0, some of which persisted for several months (2.37).

(2.37) Amy

[mʌmi]	*tummy* (also *Mummy*)
[nɪnə]	*dinner*
[mɒməs]	*Thomas*
[mɪŋgə]	*finger*
[mɪnɪʃ]	*finish*

Notice that Daniel's forms show place harmony as well as nasal. This is not entirely true of Amy's, where only initial coronals seem to harmonise, while initial labials retain their place and it is these forms that persist longer. Interestingly, like Gitanjali and Julia above, Amy appears to have a great predilection for labial-initial words and even, unlike any of the other English acquiring children in our discussion, harmonises both dorsal and coronal to the labial place (2.38).

(2.38) Amy

[bʌv]	*glove*
[bæmmɑ]	*grandma/grandpa*
[bæbɪt]	*rabbit*

As we know, Amahl demonstrates place of articulation harmony very strongly, in particular that which targets the coronal, and we have suggested that this place is the weakest in his (and Trevor's) hierarchy. Not only do we find coronal obstruents and nasals targeted in this way, but we can also find instances of approximants thus targeted both by labials and dorsals (2.39).

(2.39) Amahl

[wip]	*sleep*
[wʌb]	*love*
[wæp]	*lamp*
[gɪk]	*lick*
[gaɪk]	*like*
[gɛgo]	*Lego*
[wæbɪt]	*rabbit*
[wæm]	*ram*
[wum]	*room*
[g̊ɪŋ]	*ring*
[g̊ʌk]	*rug*
[g̊ɒk]	*rock*

[g̊ok] *yolk*
[g̊æk] *yak*
[g̊ʌŋ] *young*

However, as Goad (1996) points out, the coronal place can also effect a substitution of /l ɹ j/, but never /w/, as we can see from (2.40).

(2.40) Amahl
[d̥ʌt] *lunch*
[d̥aɪt] *light*
[d̥edə] *later*
[dɛdə] *letter*
[d̥eɪdi] *lady/lazy*
[d̥ɛt] *red*
[d̥ʌn] *run*
[d̥æt] *rat*
[d̥ud] *used*
[d̥ɛt] *yet*

When there are two approximants other than /w/ in the word, on the other hand, it appears that the lateral is stronger and so we find examples such as those in (2.41).

(2.41) Amahl
[lɒli] *lorry*
[liu/lil] *real*
[lili] *really*
[lolin] *rolling*
[luli] *usually*
[lɛlo] *yellow*
[lɛlɪn] *yelling*
[læli] *Larry*

Interestingly, we also find examples of lateral harmony where the target is not an approximant, demonstrating the relative strength of the lateral (2.42).

(2.42) Amahl
[lilin] *ceiling*
[wɪdo lɪl] *window sill*
[lɒli] *trolley*
[lɪlɪŋ] *shilling*
[lælo] *shallow*

With the exception of the /tr/ in *trolley*, the targeted segments are all coronal fricatives and it should be remembered, as we saw in the data in (2.5) above showing his various substitution patterns, that Amahl was late acquiring fricatives, in particular coronal fricatives. We could speculate that the reason *trolley* falls into the lateral substitution set is that the sequence /tɹ/ could well be perceived as /ʧɹ/, in other words containing a coronal affricate. The target form *troddler* is also subjected to the same treatment.

The findings of the latter part of this section seem to confirm the place hierarchy suggested for English in (2.27). The strength of the labial /w/ gives it precedence over the others which are all coronal. There are no dorsal approximants, although it could be argued that /w/ contains a dorsal element but we note that, for all the children discussed, it appears to behave as a labial.

2.4 Consonant–vowel interaction

Thus far, we have been considering the effects that consonant features have on other consonants in the same domain and have been suggesting that it is the anticipation or preservation of such features that accounts for the processes we have been studying. In the data that follow, we shall look at examples of child forms where consonant substitutions cannot be explained by the nature of other consonants in the domain (usually at this stage the word). In many of these examples, no other consonant is present in the word.

The observation was made by Fudge (1969), regarding his (unnamed) son at the age of 1;4, actually in the context of the child's syllables at that stage, that labial consonants occurred only with rounded vowels and front vowels tended to co-occur with coronal consonants (2.43).

(2.43) Fudge's son (Fudge 1969)

[bo]	*book* or *ball*
[bɔm]	'beating drum' or 'playing piano'
[ti]	*drink*
[den]	*again*

What we can witness here is the affinity between the articulators, that is to say that both rounded vowels and labial consonants use the lips and front vowels and coronal consonants use the front part of the tongue. Braine (1974) discusses the development of his son Jonathon who, at the stage between twenty and twenty-three months has developed a contrast between labial and coronal sounds but never produces labial consonants before high front vowels (2.44).

(2.44) Jonathan (Braine 1974)

[di]	*pee, penis, B*
[diʔ]	*big*
[nɪʔ]	*milk*
[didi]	*baby*

Braine remarks that when he tried to persuade Jonathan to produce /b/ before such a vowel he repeated [bʌbʌbʌbi] as [bʌbʌbʌdi].

The relationship between front vowels and coronal consonants is also apparent in the sample from Levelt's data (2.45) from Dutch (1994, 1996).

(2.45) Eva 1;4.12 (Levelt 1996)

[dɛt]	/bɛt/	*bed*	'bed'
[dɛ]	/bɛɹ/	*beer*	'bear'
[tɛit]	/kɛik/	*kijk*	'watch'
[tɪt]	/prɪk/	*prik*	'injection'
Noortje 2;1.7 (Levelt 1996)			
[teə]	/bɛɹ/	*beer*	'bear'
[ti]	/di/	*die*	'that one'
[tis]	/fits/	*fiets*	'bike'
[te]	/tʋe/	*twee*	'three'

There are examples from these children that might indicate that the affinity between labial vowels and labial consonants is active; there is less clear evidence in the data of this.

Although this type of phenomenon does not persist very long in children acquiring language normally, it is significant that it does persist in children with delayed acquisition (see Bates et al. 2002), indicating that the cause may be biological rather than phonological.

2.5 Velar fronting

We have seen that coronals tend to be the targets of harmony processes but that they can be the product of their affinity with front vowels. Joshua at three years (unpublished data) was given a toy train and a toy crane for his birthday, both of them were pronounced as [ʧɹeɪn]. Now the fact that the dorsal place in the latter was fronted to a coronal could be construed as the result of its adjacency to coronals, which we have shown to be the case in one datum from Eva and one from Fudge's son above, there is widespread evidence in the literature for a phenomenon known as 'velar fronting'. In (2.46) we show examples that cannot all be attributed to the place of the following vowel.

(2.46) Subject LP 2;0 (Stoel-Gammon 1996)

[dɪt]	*Kit*
[tʰi]	*key*
[tʊdi]	*cookie*
[taː]	*car*
[dus]	*goose*
[doz]	*grows*
[dan]	*gone*
[dʌt]	*duck*
[dadi]	*doggy*
[pɪdi]	*piggy*
[bʊt]	*book*
[bʌd]	*bug*

Clearly subject LP produces all dorsals as coronals, regardless of word position but, as we can see in the following data, also from Stoel-Gammon (1996), this is not always the case and position may play a part in the determination of whether the dorsal is produced correctly or not.

(2.47) Subject MK 1;6–2;0

[tʌp]	*cup*
[tʌtɪt]	*cut it*
[twaɪm]	*climb*
[dɪdʌp]	*get up*
[tʊk]	*cook*
[teɪk]	*take*
[fɔk]	*fork*
[bæk]	*back*

Subject ML 2;6

[tʌp]	*cup*
[tɪd]	*kid*
[dʊd]	*good*
[deɪm]	*game*
[daʊf]	*golf*

[tʊk]	*cook*
[teɪk]	*take*
[tɪk]	*kick*

Kylie 2;0 (Stoel-Gammon 1996, from Bleile 1991)

[tiz]	*keys*
[tæni]	*candy*
[do]	*go*
[dʊ]	*girl*
[teɪk]	*cake*
[mʌk]	*Mark*
[sak]	*sock*
[fɔg]	*frog*
[bʌg]	*bug*

What is clear from all the data in (2.47) is that word initial dorsals are produced as coronals but that final ones are produced faithfully. These words, of course, are short and do not give us an opportunity to find out what can happen to word-medial dorsals. The data in (2.48), from Inkelas and Rose (2007), give some indication of the other influences that might affect the fronting of dorsals.

(2.48) E. 1;9–2;0

[tʌp]	*cup*
[doː]	*go*
[tuwɔ]	*cool*
[tɪs]	*kiss*
[ədɪn]	*again*
[dʊdʊ]	*Gügü*
[tadɛɾə]	*together*
[hɛwtɔptɛə]	*helicopter*
[æwədɛɾə̃]	*alligator*
[hɛksədɔn]	*hexagon*
[tʌndʌktə]	*conductor*
[maŋki]	*monkey*
[bejgu]	*bagel*
[bʌkɪt]	*bucket*

[ækʧwi]	*actually*
[ɑktəpʊs]	*octopus*
[ɑktəgʊn]	*octagon*
[bɪg]	*big*
[bʊk]	*book*
[pædjɔk]	*padlock*
[bæk]	*back*

The overall pattern shown in (2.47) seems to be repeated here up to a point, that is to say that dorsals are produced as coronals word-initially and final dorsals are produced faithfully. The interest here lies in the picture word-medially. Syllable codas, whether final or medial remain faithful but the reverse is not always true of onsets. Notice that in words such as *again, together, helicopter,* etc., syllable initial dorsals are also produced as coronal but in such words as *monkey, bagel* and *bucket* they remain faithful to the dorsal place. The difference, of course, is that in the first set, the syllable following the segment in question bears some degree of stress, either primary as in *together* or secondary as in *helicopter*, whereas in *monkey, bagel* and *bucket* the following vowel is unstressed. A similar distinction can also be found in further data from Stoel-Gammon (1996), as we can see in (2.49).

(2.49) ML 2;6 and KG 2;0 (Stoel-Gammon 1996)

[tɪko]	*tickle*
[twækʊ]	*cracker*
[pʌŋfo]	*finger*
[ʊgə]	*sugar*
[bitʌz]	*because*
[ot^{h}eɪ]	*OK*
[wətun]	*racoon*
[ədɛn]	*again*

2.6 Positional variation

A similar observation to velar fronting can be made about the articulation of fricatives. We saw in (2.8) above that Amahl had difficulty with the articulation of fricatives in the earlier stages of the data set we have available and, indeed, for some time. The result of this difficulty with fricatives resulted in their omission or replacement with stops and even with laterals (see (2.42) above). Other children, on the other hand, appear to dislike fricatives in a strong position but be perfectly capable of producing them in other, weaker, positions. Consider the examples in (2.50) taken from Edwards (1996).

(2.50) Kevin 1;6 and 1;8
[dʊɪs] *shoes*
[tɪs] *fish*
[dɪʒə] *feather*
[daʃ] *giraffe*
[taʒa] *zebra*
[dʊʃ] *shoes*
Linda 2;3
[kwʌm] *thumb*
[mæʊf] *mouth*
[bæ:tɪn] *valentine*
[gwʌf] *glove*

A more extreme case of this can be seen in Daniel between 1;10.5 and 2;0 (Menn 1971). Daniel (2.51) can produce fricatives and affricates in weak position but, instead of strengthening them in strong position, he omits them entirely in the same way as Amahl shown in (2.8c) above.

(2.51) Daniel 1;10.5 and 2;0
[it] *seat*
[dos] *toast*
[iz/is] *cheese*
[æʃ] *watch*
[ɨʃ] *ish*
[ejndʒ] *change*
[uz] *shoes*
[ufs] *juice*

Similarly, we can find a positional difference with fricatives in data from German. Initial fricatives are either deleted or realised as stops, as we show in data from Naomi and Annalena (2.52) in the period between 1;1 and 1;7 (Grijzenhout & Joppen 1998).

(2.52)	[abɐ]	/zaʊbɐ/	*sauber*	'clean'	(Naomi)
	[at^{h}]	/zat/	*satt*	'satisfied'	(Annalena)
	[dat^{h}]	/zat/	*satt*	'satisfied'	(Annalena)
	[aka]	/ʋa:gn̩/	*Wagen*	'car'	(Annalena)
	[gaga]	/ʋa:gə/	*Waage*	'scale'	(Annalena)

In final position, however, fricatives are realised (2.53).

(2.53)	[af]	/ʔaʊf/	*auf*	'on'	(Naomi)
	[ax]	/ʔaʊx/	*auch*	'also'	(Annalena)
	[buχ]	/buːx/	*Buch*	'book'	(Naomi)
	[miç]	/mɪlç/	*Milch*	'milk'	(Naomi)

2.7 Conclusion

The main object of this chapter has been to consider in more detail some of the prevalent phenomena found in children's attempts to produce target forms and to consider the diverse strategies that children employ to achieve the same ends. Although we have presented different strategies employed by the same child at various points, we have perhaps glossed over the fact that many of these strategies overlap in individual children. However, the fact remains that strong patterns emerge. Now we need to start considering explanations for our observations. Before we do this in the next few chapters, however, it is worth taking note of certain points.

First, children's earliest word forms are more or less similar across languages, but they differ from their target (adult) word forms in ways which can be regarded as systematic and predictable. Second, in all normally developing children, acquisition is quick and effortless, irrespective of the target language. In other words, any normally developing child is capable of mastering any one of the thousands of languages of the world equally well, within a relatively short period of time, without any instruction. Finally, in spite of the incredibly speedy advance of computer technology, where there are many examples of computer performance surpassing that of humans, not only does computer-generated speech still sound unnatural and non-human, but also computers are not able to acquire language in the way that children do.

We will not attempt to provide any explanation for the last observation, but we can examine the reasons behind the first two observations fairly systematically by referring to theories of acquisition.

Models attempting to account for cross-linguistic generalisations fall mainly into two groups, depending on the assumption made about what it is that the child brings to the task of language learning. This can be described as the 'nature or nurture' debate. On the one hand, we have linguistic models assuming that the child is naturally or genetically pre-programmed to acquire language. Such models suppose that the recurrent properties of adult and child languages are the result of a cognitive concept of Markedness embodied in Universal Grammar (UG), that is these simplification strategies are innately given by UG to guide the child in acquisition, and predictions are made regarding what are possible and impossible patterns in child language. By proposing an explicit theory of how cross-linguistic patterns emerge in language, UG-based models focus on similarities among children acquiring different languages, as well as among child and adult languages.

Alternative models do not view cross-linguistic patterns that emerge in child phonology as products of UG or of the 'language gene', but rather they account for the recurring patterns as effects of the environment (nurture) in addition to other cognitive mechanisms. Such models obviously assume that the human infant is not equipped with an innate knowledge that is specific to language and that the innate state of the human is basically the same as that of any other species.

In the next few chapters, we will see how these two different views provide explanations for child language patterns. Interestingly, however, in spite of the nature-or-nurture debate, all researchers studying child language agree that simplification or *unmarkedness* characterises early phonological production. Since both linguistic and non-linguistic accounts commonly refer to the term markedness when explaining frequent development phenomena, although the definition of markedness is unclear and diverse due to its wide usage, we will start with a search for what exactly is meant by the term at the beginning of the next chapter. Once we disentangle the different definitions associated with the term, we shall investigate various linguistically-based markedness accounts of child patterns and see how they fare in coming to terms with observations from acquisition, before moving on to explanations outside linguistic theory.

3

LINGUISTIC MODELS

3.1 Markedness and its definitions

Since Trubetzkoy (1939) first introduced it in the late 1930s in the phonological study of adult language typology, the term markedness has been extended to other fields and areas, with the result that its meaning has not remained constant. Unfortunately, the inconsistent usage of the term in different domains makes it difficult to reach a consensus about the exact meaning of markedness, even in purely linguistic terms.

Sometimes markedness claims are based on adult language typology; that which occurs most frequently in the languages of the world is unmarked. At other times they are based on child language; that which children do first is unmarked. And sometimes they are based on both; that which is found frequently in adult languages is argued to be unmarked if evidence for its early appearance in child language can be provided, and vice versa. Although the notion of markedness continues to occupy a position of substantial importance in phonology, evidenced by the fact that markedness is commonly relied upon, its definition has remained unclear and its usage tends to exploit any one or several criteria which seem most suitable for the purpose (for an overview of different markedness criteria, see Rice 2007: 80).

The term is generally used in explanations of universals and naturalness. It appears in numerous domains, but mainly in phonetics, descriptions of specific languages, typological studies, first language acquisition and language change. It is commonly used to indicate simplicity or commonness as opposed to complexity or rarity. It has been claimed that an unmarked phenomenon is simple, common, normal, basic, natural, ordinary, of high frequency within a language and/or across languages, the implied in an implicational relationship, acquired early by children, lost late in aphasia, and targeted in language change.

A good number of scholars have defined markedness as naturalness and equated it directly or indirectly with cross-linguistic tendencies, both inside and outside the field of phonology. However, if markedness is naturalness, which is equal to cross-linguistic occurrence frequencies of, for example, phonological processes and forms, why do we need the term, markedness, in the first place? Or if markedness is naturalness in terms of phonetics, 'phonetic difficulty' would be a better label for it.

A major problem in identifying markedness is the diversity in the usage of the term. Whether it is based on observations of cross-linguistic data, child language, or phonetics, it seems that markedness is used as an umbrella term for properties of 'naturalness' which happen to appear in more than two domains. Such usage makes the origin of markedness unclear and creates circularity: is X frequent because it is unmarked or is X unmarked because it is frequent?

Since the linguistic approaches to child language rely on markedness to account for what the child brings to the task of language learning and any such account is easily refuted without a consistent definition of markedness, we need to evaluate whether the various ways of approaching markedness mentioned above converge on a consistent definition, before we can proceed with our investigation of linguistic theories of child patterns. A good starting point is to formulate a set of markedness 'definitions'. As is clear in the set of statements in (3.1a–f), the notion of markedness is comparative and used for expressing a relation between at least two elements.

(3.1) a. X is marked with respect to Y if and only if X is phonetically more difficult than is Y.
b. X is marked with respect to Y if and only if X occurs after Y in acquisition.
c. X is marked with respect to Y if and only if X is less frequent in a particular language than is Y.
d. X is marked with respect to Y if and only if X is less frequent in the languages of the world than is Y.
e. X is marked with respect to Y if and only if the presence of X implies the presence of Y.
f. X is marked with respect to Y if and only if X is avoided in language change more than is Y.

It may be worth mentioning two points with regard to the data in (3.1). The first is that a markedness definition based on language loss or aphasia is not included. If aphasia is the reverse of language acquisition, as proposed by Jakobson (1941/1968), we might suppose that an investigation of sound loss is not trivial. However, there is very little that can be said about the loss of sounds in aphasia, since recent research in aphasiology has found that language does not break down along traditional linguistic lines. The second point is that (3.1e) is distinct from (3.1d), since the entailment relationship between (3.1e) and (3.1d) only goes in one direction, from (3.1e) to (3.1d): from the fact that the presence of X implies the presence of Y in a particular language, it follows that the unmarked Y must at least be cross-linguistically as frequent as is the marked X. However, nothing follows regarding the implicational relationship between X and Y from the distributional fact that X occurs in fewer languages than does Y.

What is crucial to note here, is that a truly consistent definition of markedness requires a sound correlation between ALL the concepts identified by the statements in (3.1). An ideal correlation would be if Y is phonetically simpler than X, (3.1a); children acquire it before X, (3.1b); it is not only the more frequent than X in a particular language, (3.1c), but also across languages of the world, (3.1d); its presence is implied by the presence of X, that is, if a language allows X, then it also has Y, but the reverse is not true, (3.1e); diachronic changes always go in the direction of Y, that is Y never disappears in language change, (3.1f).

One example that appears to fit all of the criteria in (3.1) is that of /l/-vocalisation (Johnson & Britain 2007). This phenomenon was alluded to in Chapter 2, where the dark /l/ loses alveolar contact and is produced as a vowel-like sound. The phonetic explanation that can be suggested for this has to do with the gestures involved in the production of /l/. Where a language or dialect exhibits positional /l/ allophony, the clear and more consonantal /l/ will occur in prevocalic position, in syllable onsets, and the more vocalic dark /l/ will occur in non-prevocalic position in syllable rhymes. Both clear and dark /l/ involve consonantal coronal and vocalic dorsal gestures but it is the timing of these gestures that varies. In the case of the clear /l/ the coronal (alveolar) gesture precedes the dorsal tongue retraction making the latter somewhat weaker, whereas in the case of the dark /l/ the timing of the gestures is reversed (Sproat & Fujimura 1993). This makes the margin for error in the coronal gesture greater, resulting in a greater potential for the coronal target being missed. The loss of the coronal gesture makes the segment phonetically simpler, thus satisfying criterion (3.1a). As we commented in Chapter 2, children acquiring English overwhelmingly appear to vocalise their dark /l/s as we show in the examples below (3.2), repeated from (2.17) in that chapter, thereby satisfying criterion (3.1b).

(3.2)	Amahl (Smith 1973)		Gitanjali (Gnanadesikan 1996)	
	[bebu]	*table*	[biw]	*spill*
	[gɪgu]	*tickle*	[fɛw]	*fell*
	[æbu]	*apple*	[fɛw]	*smell*
	[æməu]	*Amahl*		
	Daniel (Menn 1971)		Trevor (Pater 1997)	
	[kʌdu]	*cuddle*	[ʃɛu]	*Michelle*
	[bʌbu]	*table*	[gɪgu]	*tickle*
			[kɪku]	*pickle*
	Joan (Velten 1943)			
	[waw]	*well*		
	[baw]	*bell*		

Interestingly, children acquiring languages with no such /l/ allophony do not vocalise as we can see in the data in (3.3) from Clara, who is acquiring Canadian French.

(3.3)	Clara (Rose 2000)		
	[liɸ]	/liv/	*book*
	[pɔl]	/bɔl/	*bowl*
	[pwæl]	/pwal/	*hair*

Criteria (3.1d) and (3.1f) are satisfied by numerous cross-linguistic examples of alternations and change. We pointed out that historic /l/ disappeared from pre-labial and pre-dorsal position in English (see data in (2.18) of Chapter 2). The process of this deletion was caused by the vocalisation of the /l/ yielding [kaʊm] for *calm* and then the subsequent monophthongisation of the diphthong resulting in [kɑːm]. Examples of similar changes can be found in Old French (Gess 1998, 2001), in Serbo-Croatian (Kenstowicz 1994) and Polish, Belear Catalan and Mehri which all exhibit [l]~vowel alternations (Walsh Dickey 1997). In addition, vocalisation of dark /l/ has occurred in many dialects of Romance (Recasens 1996), and for the last 100 years a new wave of vocalisation has been spreading through numerous dialects of English although this is by no means yet complete. We list in (3.4) some examples from the above languages and refer the reader to Johnson and Britain (2007) for further details of the changes occurring in English.

(3.4)	Old French	[albə] → [aubə]	'dawn'
	Catalan	[alba] → [auba]	'dawn'
	Mehri from the root /ɬlθ/ 'third'		
		[ɬoːləθ]	'third' (masc.)

[ɬəwθeːt]	'third' (fem.)
Serbo-Croatian from the stem /debél/ 'fat'	
[debéo]	'fat' (masc.)
[debelá]	'fat' (fem.)
Old Provençal → Modern Provençal	
[falsu] → [faus]	'false'
[dulse] → [douts]	'sweet'

Indeed, in the majority of the examples listed in (3.4), criterion (3.1c) is also satisfied since the unmarked vowel has replaced the marked dark /l/. Finally, the fact that there are no languages with the dark /l/ as the only lateral substantiates the link between the implicational criterion (3.1e) and the others and it can be said that the correlation between the statements in (3.1) is absolute for the case of /l/-vocalisation.

However, it is extremely rare to find such cases as the one we have just shown. In fact, /l/-vocalisation is probably the only reported case, and when the correlation between the markedness criteria in (3.1) has been put to the test, the general picture is that, although there is a clear link between many of them, it is not absolute. Some counter-examples are:

1. Despite the general trend for phonetically simpler segments to occur more frequently than those that are not and for epenthesis to involve segments that are relatively phonetically simple within the language, the French epenthetic vowel is the rounded mid-front [œ] (Féry 2003), which is phonetically more complex than its unrounded counterpart [ɛ] and also highly frequent within the language.
2. While there is an implicational universal statement claiming that the presence of the labial nasal consonant /m/ implies the presence of its coronal counterpart, /n/, not only do we find a clear preference for /m/ in child language, but it is also more often the only nasal consonant, rather than /n/, in early words (Vihman 1996).
3. Based on phonetics and cross-linguistic occurrence frequency, while we would not expect obstruents to change into sonorants in language changes, Biggs (1965) reported Fijian, a Polynesian language, to have undergone a change from the obstruent /d/ to the sonorant /r/.
4. Although it has been claimed that children commonly substitute [t] for /k/ (for example, Stemberger & Stoel-Gammon 1991), thus validating the claim for the acquisition of /t/ occurring before /k/

and the unmarked place of articulation being coronal, Japanese-acquiring children seem to acquire /k/ before /t/ (Beckman et al. 2003).

The above examples are merely exceptions, which are few in number by definition. Observations show that the norm is that marked or unmarked phenomena usually satisfy at least two criteria listed in (3.1). The extent to which the counter-examples are exceptions can only be seen through a systematic investigation of a very large number of pair-wise comparisons between markedness diagnostics in different domains. We do not propose to undertake such an exhaustive comparison (see Reimers 2006 for more examples and detailed discussions). Our point here is that (a) since the definitions in (3.1) cannot be equated with each other, (3.1a–f) can only be diagnostics, and not definitions, of markedness and (b) we cannot ignore the fact that the recurrent patterns generally go across adult and child languages in different domains, that is, there seems to be enough correspondence between the different manifestations of markedness for us to be persuaded that there must be some unifying concept underlying them. Consequently, we need to refer to markedness as a cognitive concept and examine claims of markedness originating in linguistic analysis itself.

3.2 Universal order of acquisition

Following Trubetzkoy, Roman Jakobson took up the notion of markedness and attempted to form a unified theory. His hypothesis in his well-known book *Kindersprache, Aphasie und allgemeine Lautgesetze* first published in 1941 and translated into English as *Child Language, Aphasia and Phonological Universals* (1968) was that there was a relationship between these three definitions of markedness. Concentrating on acoustic properties and on ease of articulation, he hypothesised that those contrasts that are learned early in child language will be present in all the world's languages and will, furthermore, be the last to be lost in cases of aphasia. One such contrast he discussed is that between the openness of the low vowel [a] and the total closeness of the labial consonant [p]. This contrast, he claimed, would be the first to be acquired by the child and would also occur in all the languages of the world. He also suggested that the more marked a certain contrast, the more likely it was that it would be avoided in language change.

Although Jakobson studied some published accounts of child language, he based his predictions of the order of acquisition largely on what he perceived to be marked and unmarked contrasts cross-linguistically. First, we need to include a caveat. When we are talking about acquisition, it is not at all clear whether the predictions made by Jakobson necessarily have any true validity. Let us look at the predictions made and consider them in the light of the child data in the literature (3.5).

(3.5)
a. Vowels are acquired before consonants; /a/ is the first vowel
b. Single consonants are acquired before multiple consonants (clusters); generally the first consonant is labial ('front' consonants are acquired before 'back' consonants – this means that dorsal must be assumed to be the last)
c. Consonant–vowel contrast is the first to be acquired
d. The distinction between nasal and oral; generally [m] vs [p]
e. The distinction between grave (labial) and acute (dental) sounds; generally [p, m] vs [t, n]
f. The first vocalic opposition is low vs high; [a] vs [i]
g. The expansion of the vocalic system into three vowels by splitting the high vowel into front and back to form the fundamental vowel triangle /a, i, u/ or adding a more central degree of opening to form the linear vowel system /a,e,i/
h. The pair /o~u/ cannot precede the pair /e~i/
i. Secondary vowels are acquired later than primary vowels (in other words, front rounded after both front spread and back rounded and so on)
j. The acquisition of stops; velar stops are acquired shortly after dentals
k. The acquisition of fricatives (since no language has fricatives without stops); if the child has only one fricative is it /s/
l. Acquisition of affricates
m. Acquisition of liquids and glides
n. Acquisition of obstruent liquids
o. Nasal vowels are acquired after the remaining vowels
p. The distinction between nasal and oral vowels
q. The distinction between pulmonic and non-pulmonic airstream mechanisms

Studies on developmental phonology since Jakobson have some found evidence to support the idea that the above order is a typical order in acquisition cross-linguistically. However, at the same time, studies have also shown again and again that there are problems with Jakobson's claims.

The first and greatest difficulty with Jakobson's markedness theory is that the prediction made for universal segmental acquisition is *strictly ordered*, while there is no single order of acquisition. It is commonly observed that vowels appear before consonants and that single consonants appear before clusters in all children. Although it is found that in very early production, where the ratio of vowels to consonants is in the order of 4.5:1 and the consonants produced tend to be glottal [ʔ] and [h], in most, though not all, children, the first consonant in babbling is indeed a labial. However, it is difficult to know whether this is due to an open mouth producing a vowel and a closed one producing a labial consonant or whether the child is conforming to the principle of maximal contrast, since not all children start with vowels and the first consonant isn't always labial.

Menn's (1976) Jacob acquired his first contrast between dental and velar stops before producing any labial consonants. Studies on the acquisition of vowels tend to show that the early acquired vowels are not, as Jakobson predicts, /i e a o u/ but instead /ɪ, ʊ, a, o, ʌ/ (Kent & Miolo 1995), although vowels are acquired first as predicted by Jakobson. Joan (Velten 1943) replaced other vowels with [u]. /f/ and /v/ emerged as the earliest fricatives in Amahl's productions, indeed the first appearance of /s/, which, according to the above predictions should be the first fricative, was more than two months later.

Ferguson and Farwell (1975) analysed the productions of three children during the development of the first 50 words. By and large their development went along the same course and to some extent tallied with Jakobson's predictions, in spite of the fact that the children's phone trees showed lexical rather than phonemic contrasts. One striking similarity among the three children that was not predicted by Jakobson was that all of them developed voiced labial and coronal first, but their velars were voiceless.

Furthermore, although it has been suggested that rhotics are the unmarked liquid, based on a typological observation by Maddieson (1984: 83) that if a language has only one liquid, then it would be the rhotic, it is not the case that the rhotic liquid is always acquired before the lateral counterpart in languages with a rhotic/lateral opposition. In fact, Rice (2005) proposes that the relationship between

Table 3.1 Examples of rhotic substitution

Language	Adult word	Gloss	Child SR	Age	Source
Czech	/dira/	'hole'	[di ːja]	1;3	Pačesová 1968
			[diːla]	1;4	
	/ruka/	'hand'	[luʧiʧki]	1;5	
English	/reɪn/	'rain'	[lein]	2;4	Smith 1973
			[rein]	2;5	
Japanese	/remɒn/	'lemon'	[liːmaʔ]	1;11	Kobayashi 1980
	/harɔː/	'hello'	[ᵘloʊweː]	2;11	Vihman (unpubl)

rhotics and liquids is language-specific. While Jakobson would predict [l] to be one of the last consonants to be acquired, it has been observed that French children do not seem to have problems producing the lateral onset of the French definite article [l] and it is not uncommon for French children at around 12–15 months of age to be able to produce laterals, but not rhotics (data in Vihman 1993; Vihman & Boysson-Bardies 1994). Furthermore, in a developmental study of a Czech boy, Pačesová (1968) documents rhotics substituted by laterals. The same substitution was observed by Smith (1973) for English. Moreover, this substitution has been reported in infants acquiring Japanese, a language with only the rhotic liquid, by Kobayashi (1980) and Vihman (1996). Some examples are listed in Table 3.1.

A further problem is the connection between babbling and speech. Jakobson considered canonical babbling to be articulatory exercises during the pre-linguistic period and nothing to do with speech. Subsequent studies have shown that sounds and syllable structure in babbling and early language are closely connected. The following examples are to be found in Stoel-Gammon and Cooper (1984). They undertook a longitudinal study of three children from babbling through to the acquisition of the first fifty words. During this period babbling continued alongside the production of words and the phonemes present in both babbling and words provide evidence of the fact that babbling in the later period tends to become more ambient language-specific. The three children, Daniel, Sarah and Will, were all acquiring English, and, as we can see from the Table 3.2, to some extent showed a degree of similarity in both the frequency of certain phones in babbling and in those used in their early word forms.

Table 3.2 Relative frequency of consonantal phones accounting for 1 per cent or more of the total consonants in the babbling samples

Subjects	Age	No. of consonants	30–40%	10–29%	1–9%
Daniel	11;2–12;2	405	d	b n w j	m s x ð ř
Sarah	10;0–11;0	453	d	b g m	n β h j ř l
Will	11;2–12;2	512	d	b t s z	m ʃ h w j

Table 3.3 Comparison of consonants occurring with a frequency of 1 per cent or more in babbling (B) and in at least two of the first fifty words (W)

Subject	B and W	B only	W only
Daniel	b d m n s w	ð x ř j	p t k g ʔ z ʒ
Sarah	b d m n l h	g β ř j	t k s w
Will	b d t m s z h w	ʃ j	g ʔ tθ pw fw

(Stoel-Gammon & Cooper 1984: 252, Tables 1 and 2.)

As Stoel-Gammon and Cooper point out, to a certain extent, the data in Table 3.2 support the claim that the sounds used in early babbling are the same as those used in early words. Some of the phones used in babbling are not phonemes of English and are, therefore, unlikely to occur in meaningful speech. Notice also that Sarah was the only one to use /l/ in babbling and also used it in early speech, while Will was the only one not to use /n/ in either.

Third, the behaviour of phonemes in different positions (allophones) poses a serious problem for the Jakobsonian system. If a bunch of features that make up a segment is based on articulation and acoustics, and phonemes may surface differently depending on the position, then surely a theory on the order of acquisition must at least include syllable shapes and syllabic positions. Furthermore, the question of what might constitute an acceptable allophone of a consonant phoneme is not mentioned at all in Jakobson's work.

To summarise, although Jakobson's rough outlines have been confirmed over the years, his proposed order of acquisition does not always hold and his markedness theory cannot always account for the variations in early speech, since it was derived from the principle of maximal contrast based on the phonetic nature of the phonemes in terms of acoustics, rather than articulation. Furthermore, although Jakobson's theory assumes adult surface forms to serve as the child's underlying forms, there is no formal mechanism for mapping child underlying representations to adult surface representations. Thus, we can conclude that Jakobson's markedness theory should not be considered as a theory of acquisition. His implicational statements which are based on distributional properties of languages and which define what the child brings to phonological acquisition have difficulties in accounting for the variability observed in children cross-linguistically, within each language, and within each child.

3.3 NATURAL PHONOLOGY

The concept of markedness, by another name, plays a significant role in Natural phonology. David Stampe (1972/9) makes the claim that language is governed by a set of what he terms 'natural processes', which might be equated to unmarkedness. These are based on phonetic criteria. His view that children are endowed with these natural processes and that language acquisition is the suppression of these processes. These natural processes can be equated to ease of articulation and their suppression to the introduction of contrast.

The markedness theory of Natural phonology is formulated by linking together children's substitutions in their inaccurate reproduction of adult speech, adult substitutions in casual or fast speech (as opposed to careful, attentive, or slow speech), foreign accents and historical language change. If we take a concrete example, based on typological observation, Stampe claims that it is more natural for obstruents to be voiceless. Accordingly, this natural process is inherent in child language and Hawaiian lacks voiced obstruents, but totally suppressed in Italian and partially suppressed in English and German.

By incorporating articulatory ease, Stampe's theory of markedness is more flexible than that of Jakobson. With only certain orders being fixed and natural processes which may or may not combine, variability is accounted for. For example, the transition between the nasal and the fricative in word such as *dance* [dɑns], requiring the release of an oral closure to coincide with the closure of the velum, can be resolved in two possible ways.

1. If the velum closes before the release of the stop, then we find an interim oral stop, sharing the place of articulation with the nasal (thus [dɑnts] or for *hamster* [hæmpstə]).

Table 3.4 Delateralisation

Child (name)	Target word	Surface form	Source
Daniel	*lamb*	[jæ̃]	Stampe 1972/9
Mackie	*balloon*	[bəjun]	Albright & Albright 1956
Amahl	*light*	[jait]	Smith 1973
Hildegaard	*lie*	[jai]	Leopold 1947
	lutscht (German)	[ju]	
Charles	*la* (French)	[ja]	Grégoire 1937
Edmond	*clef* (French)	[kje]	

2. If the two gestures are reversed, then the vowel will tend to become nasalised ([dɑ̃s]).

The difference between the two surface forms is down to which of the two solutions is preferred by the speaker(s).

The substitutions found in child language according to Stampe are by no means unpredictable. A series of natural processes explain the types of substitution found for /l/ in children. These substitutions are listed as 'delateralisation', which give us [j] for /l/ – as we earlier described as 'gliding'; 'spirantisation' which is a form of **fortition**, then turns the /j/ into [ʒ]. This form of fortition aids audibility, particularly in prominent positions, and is frequently found, for example, in adult Spanish, where *yerno* 'son-in-law' [jerno] may be produced as [ʒerno] or even strengthened further to [ʤerno]. The last stage is termed 'depalatalisation' leading to the palato-alveolar [ʒ] being produced as alveolar [z]. As can be seen in the Table 3.4, delateralisation seems to be more common in child language.

The existence of these three processes, for Stampe, explained the variability among children in their substitutions for /l/. Joan (Velten 1943) consistently substitutes [z] for /l/ ([zab] *lamb* [zuf] *leaf* etc.) thus, apparently availing herself of all three processes. Daniel (Stampe 1972/9) has all initial [j] for /l/ ([jæ̃] *lamb*, [ji:v] *leave*) using only one of the processes. Stampe does not give any examples of [ʒ] but Tess (unpublished data) produced [ʒæp] for *lap*. It is not clear, however, why spirantisation should be considered to be natural, since the motor control required to produce a fricative is greater than that of a glide (or indeed of a stop). We saw that Amahl could not produce fricatives at the earlier stages of his production and this is true of many children. It could be said that the suppression of a process would yield such a form in the quest for increased audibility.

Although, the combinatorial mechanism seems to have the advantage not only of accounting for the variability observed across children and within each child, but also of providing a natural explanation for how the variability decreases within each child and across children with their development, the main critique of Natural phonology is that it cannot explain any phonological phenomena lacking phonetic motivation, which links to several consequences.

First of all, while the starting point in every child must be a set of unsuppressed natural processes, variability across children seems to exist from the onset of speech production. For example, Eleni (Edwards 1970) first produced [uk] for *look* progressing subsequently to [juk]. The claim that the first CV syllable will be non-nasal followed by [a] is contradicted by Daniel (Stoel-Gammon & Dunn 1985) whose first word was [nænæ] *banana*.

Second, there are a number of phenomena that are found in child language that are not found in language change, which seem to indicate that what is natural in child language is not natural in historical change. These include the rounding of front vowels [i] → [y] and [e] → [ø] which is a change in the direction of the marked and is not attested in diachronic change. The tendency we have seen for children to change fricatives into stops is rare in language change where the tendency is to spirantise.

Problematic also for the theory as an explanation of language acquisition, are cases where child language appears to be more marked than adult language, such as the common child language phenomena of stopping and initial syllable deletions, which are very rare in adult languages. A case in point is consonant harmony which, as we saw in Chapter 2, is very common in children but rarely, if ever, attested in adult language. Since the only difference between children and adults is that adults have to suppress more processes than children, it is problematic for any phenomenon in child phonology to be relatively more marked or unattested in adult languages.

To recapitulate, compared with Jakobson's phonemic model of markedness, the advantages of Natural phonology lie in its capacity to incorporate the two forces (ease of perception and ease of articulation) in phonology and to provide an account for the variability observed in child data. Ironically, however, it is the theoretical aspect of basing phonology on phonetic capacities that questions its status as a theory of acquisition (or even of phonology), since it cannot account for phonological phenomena lacking phonetic motivation, for example non-phonetic factors influencing developmental phonological behaviour, or acknowledge the fundamental difference between child and adult grammars.

3.4 Optimality theory

Markedness has been revived as a vital constituent of Optimality Theory (OT). While the approach to phonology before OT (Prince & Smolensky 2004) was to apply sequential rules or processes to underlying representations in order to derive their grammatical surface representations and the focus was on the process of transformation, there are no rules in OT, but non-sequential interaction of constraints. OT is an output-oriented approach focussing on the hierarchy of ranked constraints, which varies according to language. Within OT, markedness constraints provide the structure of 'language'. For example, the basic syllable is reckoned to be CV, this is the syllable type that would occur if neither of the two constraints Onset (syllables must have onsets) and NoCoda (syllables must not have codas) were to be violated. However, if one or both of these constraints is violated, we build a richer syllable structure. An Onset violation gives us V and a NoCoda violation allows for CVC and a violation of both gives VC. In other words relative degrees of markedness can be calculated in terms of the constraint violations involved.

OT views language as being controlled by a (minimally) violable set of constraints that determine for any given input which of any number of possible output candidates is the most harmonic. Markedness constraints, of the type listed, vie with faithfulness constraints. 'Faithfulness' means faithfulness to a contrast in languages. Clearly, if markedness constraints were consistently to dominate any other constraints, then all languages would be roughly the same and homophones would abound. Languages have, therefore, introduced phonemic contrast to widen their scope. You will notice that, up to this point, the similarity to Stampe's Natural phonology is very striking. The markedness constraints, favouring the unmarked in fact, can be compared to the natural processes and their gradual demotion below the faithfulness constraints has remarkable similarities to the suppression of those natural processes

Although the focus of investigation is on the theory itself, rather than phonological development, Gnanadesikan (2004) is the earliest work to analyse child data using a constraint based model which finds strong support for the OT approach in child phonology. The advantage of such a model is that it is no longer necessary to postulate the application of more rules or representation levels to adult forms in order to derive child forms. The universal constraints alone are adequate to account for child phonology, since the grammar is assumed to be the same for children and for adults; that is the hierarchy of universal constraints and their interactions. What differs is the ranking of these constraints. Developmental phonology can now be explained in terms of the child re-ranking its hierarchy from some initial state of the grammar into that of its target language. The data and analysis she presents are based on the development of her daughter Gitanjali between the ages of 2;2 and 2;9, although it is claimed that her /s/-cluster reduction persisted longer.

Gnanadesikan's hypothesis is that the initial state of a grammar is the unmarked state. That is to say that, at this stage, all markedness constraints dominate all faithfulness constraints. Cross-linguistic studies have, to a great extent, shown that the earlier words produced by children show amazing similarities. At this stage, then, faithfulness constraints are violated. A further claim that Gnanadesikan makes is that Gitanjali's input is the same as the adult output.

The focus of the study is onset clusters. We shall outline, briefly, the analysis of Gitanjali's productions and refer also to other children's patterns. As we have seen, all children at this stage simplify clusters, in particular in onsets, so there is a vast literature on the subject. The explanation for this is that a constraint *Complex (no complex onsets) dominates all others in the child's grammar. If we look at the following two simple tableaux, we can see the difference between the child's and the adult's ranking with regard to this markedness constraint and faithfulness to contrast.

Before showing a tableau depicting the information we have just mentioned, it might be useful to any uninitiated reader to show the 'interpretation of a tableau'. The fundamental principle of OT, as we have said above is that there are constraints on the production of language. The architecture of the tableau in which we display constraint interaction requires that constraints be ranked horizontally from left to right in order of their severity. Possible candidates are listed vertically.

We can see in Tableau 3.1 that the ranking of the constraints is crucial. Constraints are ranked in such a way that a violation of the higher ranked constraint will rule out the candidate that violates it. The optimal, or favoured, candidate is the one which has the fewest serious violations. Each violation is indicated with an *asterisk* (*). An exclamation mark (!) after the asterisk indicates that the violation in question is fatal to the candidate incurring it and means that any consideration of lower ranked constraints is unnecessary.

Tableau 3.1 Gitanjali's production of *grow*

/gro/	*COMPLEX	FAITH
gro	*!	
☞go		*

Tableau 3.2 Adult production of *grow*

/gro/	FAITH	*COMPLEX
☞gro		*
go	*!	

In the case of the adult, whose grammar ranks faithfulness higher than markedness, the output violates *COMPLEX in order to remain faithful to the input. However, when a grammar ranking markedness above faithfulness confronts a marked input, as is the case of Gitanjali, the output would have to violate a faithfulness constraint in order to satisfy the higher ranked markedness constraint. When there is only one consonant in the input, Gitanjali uses it, regardless of markedness (it is not too clear from the data how many apparently marked onsets she uses). However, when her input contains more than one consonant, *COMPLEX forces onset cluster simplification which can be achieved either by coalescing two or more segments, violating the faithfulness constraint NO-COAL or by deleting one or other of the segments in order to achieve a singleton, thus violating MAX (=maximality, for every input X there is a corresponding output X, that is, no deletion).

When the solution is deletion, as in /gro/ above, the phonology has to choose which of the pair of consonants is to be deleted: [go] or [ro]? Evidence from Gitanjali's s-consonant clusters indicates that the decision as to which segment of the cluster is to be retained is determined by the relative sonority of the segments in contention, based on the universal sonority hierarchy. As we explained in Chapter 2, in the context of Clements' theory of sonority dispersion, universally, preferred onsets are the least sonorous possible based on the (3.6) slightly condensed scale (Selkirk 1984).

(3.6) 1. voiceless stops
2. voiced stops
3. voiceless fricatives
4. voiced fricatives
5. nasals
6. liquids
7. glides
8. vowels

Thus, the segment to be deleted in /gro/ will be the more sonorous /r/. Although we know from the Smith data that not all children employ the same strategy in cluster simplification, Gitanjali's data provide an excellent instantiation of 'the Emergence of the Unmarked' (McCarthy & Prince 1994) – that is to say that the segment selected for deletion is more marked as an onset than that retained.

*ONSET/V >> *ONSET/APP >> *ONSET/NAS >> *ONSET/VFRIC >> *ONSET/–VFRIC >> *ONSET/VSTOP >> *ONSET/–VSTOP

Both these hierarchies achieve the same ends in the case of the data we are presented with (although they could have other consequences in other circumstances). The ranking of *ONSET/APP above *ONSET/STOP ensures that the correct output prevails.

The ranking which works for Gitanjali also produces the correct results for some other children as we can verify from some of the Julia data presented in Chapter 2 (2.11), as well as for Subject 25 (3.7), a child with delayed acquisition, in Pater and Barlow (2002), from Barlow (1997).

(3.7) Subject 25 (age 4;10)

[din]	*queen*	[do]	*grow*	[beɪ]	*play*
[sowɪŋ]	*snowing*	[sip]	*sleep*	[sip]	*sweep*
[bun]	*spoon*	[daɪ]	*sky*	[dov]	*stove*

On the other hand this ranking would not produce the correct output for Amahl nor for Subject LP65 (3.8) (Pater & Barlow 2002), neither of whom produces any fricatives at all.

(3.8) Subject LP65 (Pater & Barlow 2002)

[wend]	*friend*	[wʊːt]	*fruit*
[jip]	*sleep*	[jɛd]	*sled*
[niːd]	*sneeze*	[noʊmæn]	*snowman*
[wɪnːt]	*drink*	[wɛːd]	*shred*
[wɪːn]	*swing*	[wɪəm]	*swim*

[mɛʊ]	*smell*	[maɪjʊ]	*smile*
[wi]	*three*	[woʊ]	*throw*

As we saw above, the effect of *COMPLEX is to rule out the faithful candidate, so let us now consider other candidates to see how they fare.

Tableau 3.3 Gitanjali's sonority based grammar

/gro/	ONSET	*ONSET/APP	*ONSET/STOP
o	*		
go			*
☞ro		*	

For children like Amahl, this would also work, both for obstruent-approximant clusters and for /s/-stop ones. However, when it comes to s-sonorant clusters, the two patterns diverge. Gitanjali retains the /s/ in words like *snow* → [so] or *sleep* → [sip]. Amahl, on the other hand reduces /s/-sonorant clusters to the sonorant: *snow* → [no] and *sleep* → [wip], which also show a very prevalent labial harmony. For Gitanjali the universal (unmarked) ranking *ONSET/SON >> *ONSET/FRIC will ensure that the s-initial form prevails. However, this creates problems in cases such as Amahl. Since the ranking of the sonority constraints must be fixed, re-ranking *ONSET/FRIC cannot be the solution, particularly in view of the fact that sonority plays an important part in Amahl's grammar generally. The solution (see for example Pater & Barlow 2002) is to propose that Amahl has a constraint *FRICATIVES which reflects the fact that he simply has not acquired them (this late acquisition is predicted by Jakobson's implicational universals). Thus, although [no] incurs a violation of *ONSET/SON instead of the lower ranked *ONSET/FRIC the ranking of the constraint against fricatives ensures that this form prevails.

Tableau 3.4 Amahl's grammar

/sno/	*FRIC	*ONSET/SON	*ONSET/FRIC
so	*		*
☞no		*	

At this point, we might turn again to Julia's data, repeated from Chapter 2 (2.12). In the case of most of her cluster simplifications, she follows the same pattern as Gitanjali, however, in one little batch (3.9).

(3.9) Julia

[wɪk]	*drink*
[waɪv]	*drive*
[wap˺tət]	*dropped it*
[wæmə]	*grandma*
[wips]	*grapes*
[wʌni]	*Grundy*
[wækə]	*cracker*
[wɪŋ]	*swing*

Julia consistently retains the labial in any cluster (bearing in mind that labial includes adult /r/). In a word like *pretty* [pɪdi] or *froggie* [fɔgi], the labial is also contained in the less sonorous member of the cluster, so the constraint ranking already predicted will ensure that the stop/fricative surfaces. In the words above, however, the labial feature attaches to the approximant. Thus, we have to find another constraint to outrank those suggested for Gitanjali. In this case, it has to be a constraint which requires faithfulness to the input labial: FAITH$_{[lab]}$ >> *ONSET/SON >> *ONSET/OBS.

Tableau 3.5 Julia's grammar

/dwaɪv/	FAITH$_{[lab]}$	*ONSET/SON	*ONSET/OBS
daɪv	*		*
☞waɪv		*	

Gnanadesikan makes claims for segmental accuracy for the child's inputs, through Gitanjali's use of a dummy syllable in words containing more than two syllables. A word-initial unstressed syllable in Gitanjali's phonology is replaced by a dummy syllable [fi-], as shown in (3.10) (the transcriptions are taken from Gnanadesikan (2004) who uses the upper case 'D' for the sound generally notated with /ɾ/):

(3.10) Gitanjali

a.	[fi-giDo]	*mosquito*	b.	[fi-kala]	*koala*
	[fi-gɛDi]	*spaghetti*		[fi-pis]	*police*
	[fi-tenə]	*container*		[fi-bo]	*below*
	[fi-bɛkə]	*Rebecca*		[fi-bɛt]	*barrette*

Although Gitanjali's words may seem to display segmental inaccuracy in the output, the difference between the words in the two columns above show that there is more to her dummy syllable replacement than merely deleting a word-initial unstressed syllable and replacing it with [fi]. Following the pattern of dummy syllable replacement in (a) it would be natural to predict that the words in (b) would be produced as in (3.11).

(3.11) Gitanjali

koala	*[fi-ala] or *[fi-wala]
police	*[fi-lis] or *[fi-jis]
below	*[fi-lo] or *[fi-wo]
barrette	*[fi-rɛt] or *[fi-wɛt]

However, since this is not the case, the output forms in (3.10b) show that the unstressed syllables are not deleted and replaced, but that the segments (at least the onset) of the replaced syllable are retained and used as the onset of the stressed syllable when required by the sonority constraints on the onset of the stressed syllable.

When the onset of the stressed syllable is zero, a /j/ or a liquid, the highest ranked constraint ONSET demands the presence of an onset be less sonorous than a glide or liquid. This is achieved at the cost of violating the faithfulness constraint and I-CONTIG (input contiguity) which requires that corresponding segments in the input and the output form a contiguous string (McCarthy & Prince 1995). There is one exception in the data, which is *rewind* → [fi-waɪn]. We can explain this exception by the fact that there is no obstruent available in the input to be appropriated. We illustrate the rankings in Tableau 3.6 for *mosquito, police* and *koala*.

Gitanjali's use of dummy syllables demonstrates the segmental accuracy of her inputs by showing that the onset of the deleted syllable is somehow retained and used when required by the sonority constraints.

The earlier tableau made the assumption that the constraint that Gitanjali violates in order to satisfy *COMPLEX is MAX (meaning maximality = input segments must have correspondents in the output, in other words no deletion). However, we found that she also produces some output forms which do not apparently contain either of the input segments. In cases like *grow* she merely deletes the more sonorous of the two onset consonants, but in a case like *tree* → [pi] (and the other examples in the list), the only explanation can be that she is coalescing the [-son -cont -voice] features (voiceless stop)

Tableau 3.6

	ONSET	*ONS/glide	I-CONTIG	*ONS/m,n	*ONS/v,z	*ONS/b,d
mosquito						
☞fi-giDo						*
fi-jiDo		*!				
police						
fi-jis		*!				
☞fi-pis			*			
koala						
fi-ala	*					
fi-wala		*!				
☞fi-kala			*			

with the labiality of the following sonorant (input [twi] → output [pi]). Gnanadesikan mentions the possibility of misperception (see Macken 1980, with reference to Amahl), that perhaps Gitanjali hears adjacent syllables of the onset as one labial consonant, but rejects this explanation based on the evidence of some of Gitanjali's *fi-* words, where the coalesced segments are not contiguous:

(3.12) Gitanjali
gorilla (go-wijə) → [fi-bijə]
giraffe (ʤɪ-wæf) → [fi-bæf]
direction (dɪ-wɛkʃn) → [fi-bɛkʃn]

Instead of replacing the onset glide of the stressed syllable by the onset of the unstressed syllable (as she does in *koala*, etc.) so *gorilla* would be *[fi-gijə], the onset of the first syllable coalesces with the stressed syllable /w/. Long distance coalescence shows that Gitanjali's labialisation is not the result of misperception.

What we have shown represents snapshots of the constraint rankings which attempt to explain child forms at a certain point in their development. We said, however, that the progress towards the adult form is claimed to be the gradual demotion of the highly ranked markedness constraints so that the child's output becomes more similar to the adult form, eventually reaching the point of identity to the adult form. Let us discuss the rationale behind this claim.

As acquisition progresses and constraints are re-ranked towards the ranking of the target grammar, it is tempting to term re-ranking as 'the child learning to promote certain constraints'. However, the most accurate and practical way to handle the movement of constraints is through demotion, and not through promotion. The reason is based on logic and becomes apparent when we take a hypothetical example: A child who has been producing [ta] for the input /iːt/ *eat* has learned to say [iːt] and must therefore re-rank the constraints accordingly. In this scenario, the competing structures are a loser/winner pair, [iːt] and [ta]. Tableau 3.7 shows the child's grammar before re-ranking takes place, where the winner, [iːt], violates the markedness constraints NoCoda and Onset, [ta] violates the faithfulness constraints Max-IO (no deletion) and Dep-IO (no insertion).

Tableau 3.7

/iːt/	NoCoda	Max-IO	Dep-IO	Onset
→[iːt]	*			*
[ta]		*	*	

There are two ways for re-ranking: The winner's marks (NoCoda and Onset) can be dominated by the loser's marks through demotion or the loser's marks (Max-IO and Dep-IO) can dominate the winner's marks through promotion. At first, this may seem like giving the same result either way. However, there is a difference since *both* of the winner marks (NoCoda and Onset) must be dominated by *at least* one of the loser's marks (Max-IO or Dep-IO), formalised as:

(3.13) (Max-IO **or** Dep-IO) >> (NoCoda **and** Onset)
(*loser marks*) (*winner marks*)

The constraints corresponding to the winner marks are contained in a conjunction, since neither of them can be ranked above the loser marks. With respect to the two constraints corresponding to the loser marks, it is not at all clear which of the loser's violations (one or both) should be promoted, which is why they are in a disjunction (or). In demotion, the winner's marks are moved, so that the highest-ranked loser mark must dominate all of the winner marks. Thus, all constraints with winner marks, which are not already dominated by the highest-ranked loser mark, are demoted *as far as necessary*, which results in the following 'new' hierarchy, a re-ranking of (3.14).

(3.14) Max-IO >> NoCoda >> Dep-IO >> Onset

Promotion, on the other hand, moves both of the loser's marks up in the hierarchy, thus resulting in the following two possible hierarchies due to the problem caused by the disjunction:

(3.15) Max-IO >> Dep-IO >> NoCoda >> Onset
or
Dep-IO >> Max-IO >> NoCoda >> Onset

As is known in other fields, such as semantics and computational theories, disjunctions are problematic. By demoting the winner violation to be dominated by the highest-ranked loser violation, any winner violations already under such domination is left untouched, thereby avoiding any involvement in the problematic choice formulated by the disjunction. On the more practical or intuitive side, constraint demotion seems more natural, since it implies that what is involved in the re-ranking, whenever the child is 'converting' to adult structures, is the initially highly ranked markedness constraint(s) being forced down the hierarchy.

3.5 Conclusion

A conclusion that can be drawn regarding linguistic theories of markedness is that there are some difficulties surrounding the compatibility between linguistically-based markedness accounts and observations from acquisition. While the Jakobsonean markedness theory had difficulties with variability in child language and the Stampean markedness theory had problems in accounting for child language phenomena which have no phonetic basis, OT appears to offer more than just a remedy to the difficulties that the previous theories faced through the flexibility provided by its architecture: since evaluation of the structure (markedness) is separated from repair (constraint ranking), which varies according to the child, variability in child language is explained as individuality. Whether it is across developmental stages, across children or across languages, markedness constraints are satisfied in different ways. Furthermore, OT establishes a clear connection between acquisition and typology through markedness constraints. Ironically, however, there are a number of problems created by this explanatory efficiency of the theory and the extreme difficulty in distinguishing grammatical and extra-grammatical factors in the data.

First of all, we have to admit that some advances in the child's pronunciation occur due to increased command over coordination in the vocal tract. A linguistic markedness theory is too powerful, if such physiological development in child production is attributed to grammar. Second, while the current linguistic markedness theory assumes the child's underlying representations to be fully specified, there is good reason to believe that the child's underlying representation at the initial state may not contain the full set of phonological features to which markedness refers.

While modifications to the theory may enable it to overcome the first two points, the root of the third problem is the fact that perception precedes production in phonological acquisition. As most Universal Grammar (UG) models of first language phonological acquisition are production-based and therefore tend to equate the onset of speech production with the initial state of the grammar, this basic assumption leads to a far more serious predicament for the theory. Concretely, the standard assumption of the initial state of the grammar, which is MARKEDNESS >> FAITHFULNESS, and the concept of Markedness are incompatible, since the initial state ranking can simply not be valid for the stage at which first words appear in children.

While most researchers recognise now that the initial state of the grammar is much earlier than the onset of production, the assumption of an earlier initial state than the onset of production implies that the child's phonological grammar has already taken a turn towards language specificity at the onset of production. Consequently, it is reasonable to consider that child data are contaminated primarily by the influence of the linguistic input, which increases with the amount of exposure. Hence, if we are to investigate what the child brings to the task of language learning, ideally, we should be looking at a stage where there is no ambient language influence at all. However, since such a stage could be before the development of the auditory capacity in the foetus, making such a task infeasible, we can only take the initial state of the grammar as far back as possible. Thus, we turn to perceptual studies where we might find some clues regarding the child's underlying representation and the role of UG in phonological acquisition.

4

THE EARLIEST STAGES

The tradition in phonological analyses of acquisition has been to focus on children's production using adult language theories, with the consequence of equating the onset of production with the initial state of the grammar. By relating phonological theory to child language development, the application of child data was not only imperative in the validation of phonological theory, but also in revising or extending the theories. From the very first word, the child's underlying representation was assumed to be more or less the same as those of the adult (Smith 1973). Hence, the only consideration for the child's perceptual capacity was to justify the assumption of the child's adult-like underlying representation. However, in our investigation of how patterns emerge in child phonology, it is important to ascertain the time, or more specifically, the nature of the initial state of the grammar, since any theory is based on an assumption of what the child brings to the task of language learning.

4.1 The passive learner

There is evidence that children's speech output cannot be considered to exhibit the initial state of markedness domination. Whalen et al. (1991) studied the fundamental frequency (F_0) contours in the two- and three-syllable reduplicative babbling of five infants from monolingual American-English households and five from monolingual French households, in order to examine whether there were any differences in their pre-linguistic intonation patterns, which might reflect the influence of the ambient language. The ages of the children at the first stage of recording ranged from 5–9 months and at the last stage from seven months to 1;1. Recordings were made with a parent present at times when the child was 'least likely to be fussy' (Whalen et al. 1991: 512). On the two measures tested, the categorisation of intonation patterns into RISING, FALLING, RISE-FALL, FALL-RISE and LEVEL, and the F_0 of the early middle and late portions of each syllable, significant differences were found between the two language groups. While French children exhibited an equal proportion of rising and falling intonation, the English children exhibited 75 per cent falling intonation. Overall, the authors claim the contours found in the child intonation broadly reflects that found in the relative adult languages, based on Delattre (1961).

At the segmental level, similarities between the phonetic characteristics of babbling and the ambient language have also been found. When de Boysson-Bardies and her colleagues (1989) performed spectral analyses of vowels produced by preverbal infants acquiring English, French, Swedish, and Japanese using formant measurements, they found they matched the vowel patterns each of their own ambient language. A similar study was carried out for consonants, based on phonetic transcriptions this time (de Boysson-Bardies & Vihman 1991). Consonants were examined for their distribution of place and manner in infants of the same four language groups, from the babbling stage until the point at which they produced twenty-five words. Although all the infants produced more labials, dentals and stops than any other types of consonants, language-specific patterns could be observed in the babbling of the infants.

We should not take studies such as these as resolving the ongoing issue of continuity from babbling to first words (whether there is a connection between the phonetic characteristics of babbling and first words), since the babbling stage is not a prerequisite for language acquisition in the sense that every single normally developing infant goes through it and also, de Boysson-Bardies and Vihman (1991) found that the distribution of consonants in first words is more similar across the language groups than in babbling. Nevertheless, the vast majority of infants do go through the babbling stage and many acquisitionists consider babbling to be the first major milestone in infant vocal development (see Oller 2000 for detailed discussions). While Engstrand et al. (2003) found that Swedish and American adults could not distinguish their own native language prosodic patterns in the babblings of 12- and 18-month-old infants acquiring Swedish and English, analyses of infant babbling by child language experts have shown that babbling patterns is not entirely free from the linguistic environment influence. Hence, we can take studies of babbling patterns as an indication that the child learner has already moved in the direction of the target language at the onset of production through exposure to the input. More importantly, however, this means that we cannot assume the infant's first words to mark the initial state of the grammar.

Furthermore, when we take into consideration that it only takes about a couple of months from the babbling stage for infants to have acquired whatever information is necessary to produce their first words, we can confidently assume that passive learning is taking place long before he or she can produce any utterances. Consequently, if we are to get closer to what the infant brings to the task of language learning (in our investigation of the applicability of current phonological theory in explaining child patterns), we will need to look at pre-production stages before there is any influence from the linguistic environment. From the fact that hearing is a prerequisite for sound perception, which is intact in all (hearing) babies at birth and that prenatal maternal speech influences have been observed in newborn babies (newborns recognise mother's voice (DeCasper & Fifer 1980), stories and songs (DeCasper & Spence 1986), and native language (Mehler et al. 1988)), it is not at all implausible to speculate on linguistic development already commencing before birth. However, since we cannot take our investigation further back than birth due to obvious infeasibility involved in testing the prenatal state of mind, we can only go as far back as possible. Hence, our investigation will now steer us away from production data and take us to infant perceptual studies where we can hope to find a window to the initial state.

4.2 The perceptual capacity of the human infant

Compared with speech production, the study of speech perception is relatively new. It started with experiment-based behavioural studies of adult perception in the 1950s. The main focus then was to identify the basic unit of speech perception by investigating how acoustic signals are transformed into phonetic segments in perception. When Delattre et al. (1955) investigated acoustic invariants for speech sounds, they found that all acoustic signals were influenced by preceding and/or following signal(s). This is because the successive acoustic patterns in speech are not produced as discrete acoustic events. There is a certain overlap between adjacent sounds, known as coarticulation. Although a segment can be described in terms of a set of acoustic features, the feature specification of a particular segment varies according to the preceding and/or following segment. For example, Liberman et al. (1967) found that the second formant of [d] increased from about 2,200 to 2,600 Hz before [i], but fell from about 1,200 to 700 Hz before [u]. This led Liberman and his colleagues to investigate the relationship between acoustic patterns and phonemes by testing adults using phonemic discrimination tasks with computerised or synthetic speech stimuli. Since the subjects could not hear small acoustic changes within one phonemic category, it was concluded that human speech perception is categorical, ignoring all noises in acoustic signals that do not contribute to word meaning. Consequently, the earliest studies on infant perception in the early 1970s focused on whether infant perception is also categorical and investigated the ability of infants to perceive the presence (or the absence) of phonetic features which make up the segments.

The first study was on the discrimination of voicing contrast of stop consonants in 1- and 4-month-old American infants by Eimas and colleagues in 1971, using high-amplitude-sucking (HAS) procedure. This procedure involves infants sucking on an electronic dummy which measures the intensity and speed of the sucking gesture. First, the infant being tested is repeatedly presented with one of the two contrasting syllables. It is assumed that when the infant becomes adequately familiarised with a specific utterance through repeated exposure, the sucking rate decreases through boredom. That is when the other contrasting syllable is presented to the infant. If there is no change in the sucking rate, the infant is assumed to be incapable of perceiving the new utterance, and if the sucking rate increases, it is assumed that the infant is capable of discriminating the two contrasts. (For more details on this testing procedure as well as alternative methodology used in testing infant perception, see the Appendix in Jusczyk 1997.) The conclusion that Eimas and his colleagues reached was that since both 1- and 4-month-old infants could discriminate voicing contrasts of different phonemic categories, such as [ba] vs [pa], but not if the contrasts were within the same phonemic category, such as two different tokens of either [ba] or [pa], infants perceive these contrasts categorically in more or less the same way as adults.

The amount of research undertaken on the perceptual capacity of infants grew very quickly and subsequent studies showed that young infants (less than about six months of age) are also capable of perceiving phonetic contrasts other than voicing of onset stop consonants. The study of the infant's ability to discriminate different places of articulation of stop consonants was started by Moffit in 1971 who found that 5-month-old infants could discriminate place of articulation contrasts of onset stop consonants, for example [ba] / [ga] contrast. This was replicated and found to be valid for 2-month-old infants, by Morse (1972), who also found that infants could discriminate between speech and non-speech, which was consistent with the findings for adults by Mattingly and colleagues (1971). Furthermore, Eimas' (1974) investigation of place of articulation of onset stop consonants demonstrated that these contrasts are also perceived by infants in a categorical manner, like in adults. While most studies on place of articulation were of stop consonants in the onset position, experiments conducted on 2-month-old infants regarding this contrast in syllable-final positions by Jusczyk in 1977 and in medial positions by Jusczyk and Thompson in 1978, confirmed earlier findings. During the rest of the 1970s and the beginning of 1980s, numerous experiments were carried out which showed that, in addition to different places as well as manner of articulation, infants could also distinguish voicing of onset fricatives as well as sounds within the same category, such as different glides, liquids, nasals, and vowels.

The most remarkable milestone in infant perceptual study was perhaps made by Bertoncini and Mehler (1981) who found that newborns with no linguistic exposure were capable of discriminating different places of articulation of onset consonants. This finding led to the general consensus at the time that, since infants show categorical perception from birth, they are born with the capacity to perceive speech in terms of phonemes. The picture of research on infant perception is not so clear-cut that we could compile a list of speech sounds that infants can and cannot perceive. Some studies have been criticised on methodological grounds and in some cases studies were repeated using other methods, thus achieving different results. However, we have listed some representative studies in Table 4.1 for an overview (see Eimas & Miller 1981 for more details on earlier studies).

What is most interesting in the list in Table 4.1 is that some of the contrasts that infants less than six months of age can perceive are those acquired late in speech production. For example, the substitution of the voiceless onset fricative, [fa], for its inter-dental counterpart, [θa], often persists into later stages of speech production (for example Hodson & Paden 1981), and while at approximately two months of age, infants are capable of distinguishing onset liquids (Eimas 1975a) as well as glides (Jusczyk et al. 1978), the liquid contrast tends to not only be acquired late in speech production (Strange & Broen 1981; Templin 1957), but also substituted by glides (for example Prather et al. 1975). Furthermore, while Japanese learners of English are notorious for not being able to distinguish /r/ and /l/

Table 4.1 Perceptual discrimination (English-acquiring learners)

	Example	Age	Source/reference
Voicing			
Onset stops	[ba] – [pa]	1;0–4;0	Eimas et al. (1971)
Place of articulation			
Onset stops	[ba] – [ga]	5;0	Moffit (1971)
		2;0	Morse (1972)
	[bæ] – [dæ]	2;0–3;0	Eimas (1974)
		newborn	Bertoncini & Mehler (1981)
Syllable-final stops	[bag] – [bad] [ad] – [ag]	2;0	Jusczyk (1977)
Medial stops	[daba] – [daga]	2;0	Jusczyk & Thompson (1978)
Voiceless onset fricatives	[fa] – [θa]	6;0	Holmberg et al. (1977)
Voiced and voiceless onset fricatives	[fa] – [θa] [va] – [ða]	2;0	Levitt et al. (1988)
Manner of articulation			
Onset stop vs glide	[ba] – [wa]	6;0–8;0	Hillenbrand et al. (1979)
		2;0	Eimas & Miller (1980a, 1981)
Oral vs nasal onset consonants	[ba] – [ma]	2;0–4;0	Eimas & Miller (1980b)
Within-category			
Low vs high vowels	[a] – [i] [i] – [u]	1;0–4;0	Trehub (1976)
	[i] – [u] [a] – [i]	6;0	Kuhl (1979a,b)
Glides in initial and medial positions	[wa] – [ja]	2;0	Jusczyk et al. (1978)
Liquids in the onset	[ra] – [la]	2;0–3;0	Eimas (1975a)
Nasals in the onset	[ma] – [na]	2;0–3;0	Eimas & Miller (1980b)
Lax vs tense vowels	[i] – [ɪ]	2;0	Swoboda et al. (1976)
Non-high vowels	[a] – [ɔ]	6;0	Kuhl (1983)
Within-syllable			
Simple vs complex coda (stops)	[k] – [t] [ks] – [ts]	6;0–18;0	Fais et al. (2009)

Table 4.2 Perceptual discrimination: non-native contrasts

Non-native contrasts	Example	Age	Source/reference
English voicing contrast by Kikuyu infants	[pa] – [ba]	1;0–4;0	Streeter (1976)
English voicing contrasts by Spanish-acquiring infants	[pa] – [ba]	4;5–6;0	Lasky et al. (1975)
Thai prevoiced/voiced stop consonants by English-acquiring infants	prevoiced [p] – [b]	2;0–3;0	Eimas (1975b)
		6;0	Aslin et al. (1981)
Oral vs nasal vowel contrast by English-acquiring infants	[pa] – [pã]	1;0–4;0	Trehub (1976)
Stridency contrast in the onset consonant by English-acquiring infants	[řa] – [za]	1;0–4;0	Trehub (1976)
Hindi retroflex/dental by English-acquiring infants	[ʈa] – [t̪a]	6;0–8;0	Werker et al. (1981)
Nthlakapmx glottalised velar/uvular by English-acquiring infants	[ḱi] – [q́i]	6;0–8;0	Werker & Tees (1984)
German round/unround vowel by English-acquiring infants	[dʊt] – [dʏt] [dut] – [dyt]	4;0	Polka & Werker (1994)
Zulu contrasts by English-acquiring infants	Lateral fricative voicing	6;0–8;0	Best (1991)
	Plosive vs implosive	6;0–8;0	Best (1995)
	Velar voiceless aspirated vs velar ejective		
Rhotic/lateral by Japanese-acquiring infants	[ra] – [la]	6;0–8;0	Tsushima et al. (1994)
Thai tone contrasts by English-acquiring infants	Rising vs falling tone Rising vs low tone	6;0	Mattock & Burnham (2006)

either in production or perception since the Japanese liquid inventory only contains one rhotic, Tsushima and his colleagues (1994) found that at 6–8 months monolingual Japanese infants could distinguish the lateral and rhotic liquids. This case is not unique at all. In fact, in addition to 'difficult' sounds, young infants are actually capable of perceiving speech contrasts that are not found in their target languages, as can be seen in Table 4.2.

It is not our purpose here to list every single human language contrast that is perceivable by infants, but Table 4.2 should adequately reveal that infants up to the age of eight months seem to be capable of discriminating segmental contrasts in any language. It is as if they are receptive to any potential human language, thus making them 'universal learners' at the initial stage, especially since their perceptual capacity is not limited to distinguishing segmental contrasts: Syllables are perceived as units by 2-month-old infants (Bertoncini & Mehler 1981) as well as newborns (Bijeljac-Babic et al. 1993); newborns are capable of discriminating differences in linguistic rhythm (Mehler et al. 1988; Nazzi et al. 1998; Ramus et al. 2000). Bearing in mind that it takes the average adult learner, who has reached cognitive maturity, more than a year to achieve native-like perception in a foreign language, the passive learning that is taking place in the infant during the pre-production stage is extremely speedy and dynamic.

What underlies this incredible capacity? If it is the case that infants are born with the ability to perceive speech in terms of phonemes, as claimed by the earliest perceptual studies, the initial state of the phonological grammar will have to contain all the features that phonological theories refer to. Consequently, development will have to take the form of unlearning whatever is absent from the ambient language. In the light of development being considered as a building process, viewing the pre-production stage of acquisition as unlearning denies the possibility of any development taking place during this stage, which is counter-intuitive. If it is the case that infants do not start by perceiving phonemes, then an alternative explanation for their discriminative ability would be that they are extremely sensitive to acoustic differences in sounds in general, in which case it would mean that this sensitivity may not be specific to speech sounds or even to humans. An examination of subsequent perceptual studies and those investigating older infants as well as non-humans may reveal more about this issue. But first, we need to ascertain whether the perceptual capacity demonstrated in the studies of very young infants can be equated to the ability to perceive phonemes. In order to do this, it is imperative to have a clear understanding of the correspondence between phonemes, abstract linguistic units, and acoustic features that make up phonetic segments, which is not always apparent in the literature. Hence, before proceeding with further perceptual studies, we will now embark on our next mission, which is to disentangle some of the ambiguous terminology contained in much of the literature.

4.3 Phonetic units and phonemic categories

The relationship between phonetics and phonology is generally considered complex. This is largely due to the fact that the interdependent relationship between them (they are dependent on each other for manifestation) makes it extremely difficult to draw a clear boundary between the two domains. As a consequence, it is not always straightforward to distinguish one from the other, thus resulting in the use of the terms being ambiguous or interchanged every now and again. We do not need to go further back than the beginning of this (current) chapter, where infant perceptual studies investigating voicing contrasts in the early 1970s were mentioned, to see how easily interchangeable the terms phonetic and phonemic can be: It may have been confusing to find some studies treating voicing contrasts of stops being phonemic while others were phonetic. Although the terms were used correctly then, erroneous usage of these terms does occur in the literature from time to time.

When investigating the mechanisms behind language acquisition, it is of the utmost importance to be able to make a clear distinction between phonetic units and phonemes, since phonetic mastery should be differentiated from phonemic acquisition. In terms of speech production phonetic mastery involves the development of articulatory skills and in perception, it is linked directly to acoustic signalling of speech (written between square brackets), while phonemic acquisition does not involve motor skills directly. Phonemes are abstract speech units found in the lexicon (written between slashes), used for semantic interpretation in both production and perception, and acquired as a function/result of one or more cognitive mechanism. In order to understand the difference between phonetic units and phonemes, let us formulate a hypothetical state of affairs. No matter how far it may seem to be from real life, we will formulate an extremely simple hypothesis to demonstrate clearly not only the difference between phonetic units and phonemes, but also how easily confusion between these two terms can arise. We will take writing paper as our example and make the following assumptions:

1. The world consists of only three countries, countries X, Y and Z, each of which is isolated.
2. All the paper in the world is produced by human hands.
3. All paper is produced using the same tools and come in sheets of uniform size.

4. For all countries, although there is only one quality and one colour of paper, there are 1,000 different thicknesses, each of which are numerically coded starting from 1, with 1,000 being the thickest.
5. There are three categories of paper in the world, where not all paper can be used for writing: Only 201–600 are categorised as writing paper, as 1–200 are too thin and 601–1,000 are too thick for this purpose.
6. Only four types of writing products exist in the world, all of which are used for writing (including books) and only differ in the thickness of the paper used. They are memo pads (M), books (B), notebooks (N), and diaries (D), which are all made by binding the same number of blank sheets of a particular thickness. Although there is variation within each product class, there is no single product consisting of mixed paper thicknesses.
7. Not all four writing products exist in every country: While all four products exist in country X, diaries do not exist in country Y and memo pads do not exist in country Z. See Table 4.3 for an overview.
8. The range of the paper thickness used for a certain product differs according to country: In countries X and Y, memo pads and books are made using the same paper thickness, 201–300 and 301–400, respectively; country Z, where there are no memo pads, uses 201–400 for making books; notebooks in country X are made using 401–500, in country Y using 401–600, and in country Z using 401–540; and while country X uses 501–600 for making diaries, country Z uses 541–600.

While statement numbers 1–7 should be adequately straightforward for any reader to imagine, the content of number 8 may obscure the simple picture. Hence, Table 4.4 is given in order to counteract any such effect and to provide a visual illustration of our hypothetical world.

What is implied in our hypothesis above is that any paper thickness that does not fall within the range of 201–600 will not be recognised as

Table 4.3 Paper product distribution

Country	Product M	Product B	Product N	Product D
X	✓	✓	✓	✓
Y	✓	✓	✓	–
Z	–	✓	✓	✓

Table 4.4 Paper setting

<table>
<tr><th>Thickness number</th><th>Category/Function</th><th>Products of Country X</th><th>Products of Country Y</th><th>Products of Country Z</th></tr>
<tr><td>1</td><td>Thin paper (1–200)</td><td></td><td></td><td></td></tr>
<tr><td rowspan="4">2
3
↓
98
999</td><td rowspan="4">Writing paper (201–600)</td><td>M: (201–300)</td><td>M: (201–300)</td><td rowspan="2">B: (201–400)</td></tr>
<tr><td>B: (301–400)</td><td>B: (301–400)</td></tr>
<tr><td>N: (401–500)</td><td rowspan="2">N: (401–600)</td><td>N: (401–540)</td></tr>
<tr><td>D: (501–600)</td><td>D: (541–600)</td></tr>
<tr><td>1,000</td><td>Thick paper (601–1,000)</td><td></td><td></td><td></td></tr>
</table>

M = memo pads; B = books; N = notebooks; D = diaries.

paper suitable for writing by any human in any country. As for the correlation between paper thickness and the different products, it is specific to each country. Bearing in mind that books are handwritten and all products are made of binding the same number of sheets of blank paper, brand new products would be indistinguishable from each other except for their various thicknesses. Based on the assumption that there is no interaction at all between the three countries of the world, a product made of paper thickness 540 would be sold as a notebook in countries Y and Z, but not in country X, where the natives label it as a diary. It will be explained very shortly how this relates to phonetic units and phonemes. However, before that, let us stretch our imagination a bit further by supposing now that a thickness 600 product, sold in countries X and Z as a diary, is presented to a native of Y. Recalling that diaries do not exist in Y where there are more types of notebooks than in the other countries, the native of Y will obviously think that the gift is a notebook. The reverse of this situation is when a native of Z presents a thin type of book (paper thickness less than 300) to a native of X or Y, who will never doubt that the gift is not a memo pad. The point here is that the perception of a paper product is naturally based on the standards of your own native country.

It may be difficult to imagine that all the paper in the world differs from one another in only one way, which is measurable and identifiable in terms of thickness. However, grouping them based on whether they can be used for writing bears a realistic sense when you consider that sounds made by the human mouth can be categorised into speech and non-speech sounds. In the same way that some paper is simply too thin for writing and some too thick to be bound together to turn into products, not everything that is produced by the human mouth is suitable for speech, such as a certain acoustic token found in a human sneeze. Hence, the first categorisation is universal, which, in the realistic case of speech sounds, occurs in accordance with certain universal restrictions on articulation and acoustics defining possible and impossible sounds for humans to produce and hear.

The situation where all writing paper thicknesses were grouped according to product type and certain variation is allowed within each product type also reflects real life. The different product types (memo pad, book, notebook or diary) can be equated with phonemes, since every language has a phonemic inventory and languages differ in what phonemes are included in their inventories. The numbers indicating paper thickness can be equated with actual speech sounds used for expressing phonemes. Just as the mapping between product type and actual products is not one-to-one (for example, there are 100 different thicknesses of notebooks in country X), each phoneme surfaces in various acoustic forms. This is because not only do native speakers of a language differ in which acoustic signals they use for a particular speech sound, but also speech acoustics can vary within each person depending on mood, health conditions or other factors. Accordingly, the acoustic range that is assigned to each phoneme is not universal, but specific to each language, just like the range of paper thickness of a product varies according to country.

We can now exploit the parallelism we have just drawn between speech and our hypothetical paper scenario to see how phonetic units relate to phonemes by considering another simplified hypothesis. We base the new one on speech sounds and place the two scenarios next to each other in Table 4.5, in which the assumptions of the paper setting set out earlier have been abridged for convenience.

Apart from there being only three languages and four phonemes in the world, which were both necessitated in order to simplify as much as possible, the speech sound setting above may seem to mirror the relationship between speech sounds and phonemes. However, in real life there is another level between phonemes and the raw acoustic signals, namely the phonetic level, imposed by the fact that humans cannot perceive every measurable difference in the raw acoustic signals (*cf.* Liberman et al. 1967). In other words, the mapping between a phoneme and its acoustic specification is not one-to-one.

We refer to our paper setting once more to facilitate our

Table 4.5 Paper setting and speech sound setting

	Paper setting	Speech sound setting
1.	The world consists of only three countries.	There are only three languages in the world.
2.	All the paper in the world is produced by human hands.	Sounds are produced by the human mouth.
3.	All paper is produced in the same way.	All mouths have the same structure.
4.	All the paper in the world differs only in thicknesses, coded 1–1,000.	All sounds, audible to the human ear, can be given an acoustic value, coded 1–1,000.
5.	Only 201–600 categorise as writing paper, as 1–200 are too thin and 601–1,000 are too thick for this purpose.	Only 201–600 categorise as speech sounds, as not all sounds that the mouth can produce are used for speech.
6.	Only four writing products exist in the world.	Only four phonemes exist in the world.
7.	Not all four writing products exist in every country:	Not all four phonemes exist in every language:

Country	Product			
	M	B	N	D
X	✓	✓	✓	✓
Y	✓	✓	✓	–
Z	–	✓	✓	✓

Language	Phoneme			
	/m/	/b/	/p/	/pʰ/
X	✓	✓	✓	✓
Y	✓	✓	✓	–
Z	–	✓	✓	✓

8. The paper thickness for each product differ according to country: | The phonetic realisation of phonemes differs according to language:

<table>
<tr><th>Products of country X</th><th>Products of country Y</th><th>Products of country Z</th></tr>
<tr><td>M (201–300)</td><td>M (201–300)</td><td rowspan="2">B (201–400)</td></tr>
<tr><td>B (301–400)</td><td>B (301–400)</td></tr>
<tr><td>N (401–500)</td><td rowspan="2">N (401–600)</td><td>N (401–540)</td></tr>
<tr><td>D (501–600)</td><td>D (541–600)</td></tr>
</table>

<table>
<tr><th>Lang. X phonemes</th><th>Lang. Y phonemes</th><th>Lang. Z phonemes</th></tr>
<tr><td>/m/ [201–300]</td><td>/m/ [201–300]</td><td rowspan="2">/b/ [201–400]</td></tr>
<tr><td>/b/ [301–400]</td><td>/b/ [301–400)</td></tr>
<tr><td>/p/ [401–500]</td><td rowspan="2">/p/ [401–600]</td><td>/p/ [401–540]</td></tr>
<tr><td>/pʰ/ [501–600]</td><td>/pʰ/ [541–600]</td></tr>
</table>

understanding. Although our assumption so far is that all humans in all countries can distinguish the different product types, nothing has been said about the correspondence between the actual products and paper thicknesses; whether it is one-to-one, in which case memo pads, books, notebooks, and diaries, for example in X, come in 100 identifiable thicknesses each. If we assume that humans are not capable of distinguishing more than 20 different thicknesses of any product type, it would make sense that there is another level and that each product type consists of 6–20 subtypes. Under such assumption, there will be ten different books, B_1–B_{10}, in Y and twenty in Z, B_1–B_{20}, and so on. Although the measurable differences in paper thickness will remain the same universally and anyone should be able to distinguish the different native product types and its subtypes, the paper thickness difference within any sub-type will not be distinguishable to any native of any country.

This is similar to how speech sounds are processed in real life. Although we make use of acoustic differences in speech sounds, not every measurable difference is utilised in the same way or even perceived by the human ear. Since the acoustic outcome of a phoneme is variable, the phonetic level is necessary to filter out the non-perceivable differences and distinguish perceivable differences that are within the range defined by the phonemic system of that language. A perceivable difference could, for example, be near the upper or lower border in one person, somewhere in between in another person, and not even remain constant in one place in a third person, and so on. The phonetic level allows us to acknowledge any perceivable differences, without compromising the ability to distinguish phonemes.

Speech production and perception is speedy (rapid speech can contain up to 30 phonemes per second according to Liberman et al. 1967) and relies on auditory memory. Even if the acoustic manifestation of phonemes does not vary according to the surrounding segments, if every acoustic difference were perceivable and each word stored by memorising each acoustic signal that the word is made up of, it implies that any differences between and within each speaker must also be memorised. Without the phonetic level, where noises can be filtered out as well as inter- and intra-speaker differences recognised, but more importantly neutralised, the cognitive burden on the information-processing resources of having to store all raw acoustic forms will be far too heavy, not to mention how much more processing time it would take to convert the phonemes into acoustic

Table 4.6 The phonemes of languages X and Y

<table>
<tr><th>Language X</th><th>Language Y</th></tr>
<tr><td>/m/
[201–300] → $[m_1]$ – $[m_{10}]$</td><td>/m/
[201–300] → $[m_1]$ – $[m_{10}]$</td></tr>
<tr><td>/b/
[301–400] → $[b_1]$ – $[b_{10}]$</td><td>/b/
[301–400] → $[b_1]$ – $[b_{10}]$</td></tr>
<tr><td>/p/
[401–500] → $[p_1]$ – $[p_{10}]$</td><td rowspan="2">/p/
[401–600] → $[p_1]$ – $[p_{20}]$</td></tr>
<tr><td>$/p^h/$
[501–600] → $[p_{11}]$ – $[p_{20}]$</td></tr>
</table>

signals in production and vice versa in comprehension. Therefore, it makes perfect sense for there to be a mapping between acoustic signals and phonetic representations before and after accessing the phonemic level.

Thus, we now add the phonetic level into our hypothetical speech setting by assuming that ten acoustic signals can be grouped into a sub-type. Take for example language X, in which /p/ can be produced phonetically between $[p_1]$ and $[p_{10}]$. Supposing that this phoneme is used for verbs to signify the present tense and $/p^h/$ the past tense, and a speaker trying to articulate a verb in the present tense, happens to produce an acoustic token that measures [501] for some reason, such as blocked airway in the nose. The acoustic signal will be mapped onto $[p_{11}]$ and then to $/p^h/$, resulting in the verb being understood by others as being in the past tense, provided that there are no other cues than the acoustic ones. Take a look at Table 4.6 illustrating the phonemic systems of X and Y from number above, to which a phonetic level has been added. What phonological difficulty will a speaker of Y confront when starting to learn X?

The picture should be very clear in that there will be no obstacles for the learner with regard to /m/ and /b/ and the only task is to learn that speech sounds $[p_{11}]$ – $[p_{20}]$ should not be equated with /p/, but with a new phoneme. This is equivalent to a native of country Y moving to countries X or Z and having to learn to think, every time he or she sees a diary, that it is not a notebook. For the learner of X to achieve the same linguistic competence as its native speakers, learning involves both the phonetic and phonological levels, since changes must be made to the mapping between the phonemes and its different phonetic forms. Leaving aside the question of whether it is possible to make changes at both levels, the mastery of the new phoneme(s), which in our case leads to distinguishing /p/ and /pʰ/ in production as well as perception, is indeed a difficulty often discussed in the second language acquisition literature.

Now that we have drawn a clear line between phonetics and phonology within our speech scenario, we can turn our simple settings towards reality. Without adding further dimensions to them, but just by supposing that there are more than four different products or phonemes in the world (we can go as far as 400 within each setting), consider how this will this change our simple pictures. Now think about additional dimensions for our paper setting, such as colour, size, function, and production method. It should not be necessary to repeat these steps for our speech sound setting to envisage how complicated the situation is with speech sounds in real life.

With many more than three languages and four phonemes, sound inventories of the world's languages differ along numerous phonological dimensions, such as distribution between consonants, vowels and glides, phonotactics, pitch, and tone, and so on. The large variation in the number and combination patterns of the phonemes means that there is also variation in their acoustic manifestation in the sense that the relevant acoustic dimensions depends on the structure of the inventory. Certain dimensions may be relevant only if there are certain segment(s) and/or other dimension(s) present in the system. In other words, the same segment in two different languages may not have the same dimensions in terms of number and/or property. For example, while instrumental analysis of voice onset time (VOT, the measurable time-lag in a stop consonant production between the release of the articulatory closure and the vocal cord vibration) is generally used for categorising speech sounds and also considered very reliable for measuring the voice feature of stop consonants in the literature, two studies on the acquisition of stops in English and Spanish by Macken and Barton (1980a,b) revealed that this is not always the case.

Macken and Barton (1980a) showed that VOT was useful in revealing the developmental stages of acquiring voiced stops, [b, d, g], in English-speaking children. However, when the same authors investigated the same voiced stops in Spanish-speaking children, the phonetic feature [continuant] turned out to be a better measure for these children (Macken & Barton 1980b). It was claimed that this was due to the spirant allophones of the voiced stops, [β, ð, ɣ] occurring more frequently than the stops in Spanish, thus resulting in the spirants with their continuant feature being more basic and also acquired earlier than the VOT feature by children. This is a very good example of the intricate nature of human speech sounds and how the multi-dimensional properties of acoustic signals can complicate the mapping between the phonetic units and phonemic categories for researchers.

Hence, while the acoustic level is universal and the phonemic one language-specific, we cannot always ascertain at which end of the spectrum the phonetic level lies. On the one hand, the practice of classifying and identifying all speech sounds of the world in terms of phonetic units by using some kind of universal measures makes the mapping between acoustic signals and phonetic units seem universal. On the other hand, when you consider the multi-dimensionality of real speech sounds, whether all the dimensions are present in all languages, and the possibility of dependency between them, not to mention the possibility of certain dimensions not being measurable by current technological tools, the universal status of phonetic units may seem to wobble. The blurred status of phonetic units is shadowed further by the ability of humans not only to distinguish between speech and non-speech sounds (seen in infants as young as newborn; Vouloumanos & Werker 2007), but also to hear non-speech sounds as speech sounds and vice versa under certain conditions (Remez et al. 1981).

By making use of simplified hypothetical settings, we have been able to demonstrate the phonetic units – phonemes correspondence and most importantly, establish why they cannot be equated with each other. Although this distinction is not always clear in the literature, we should now be able to distinguish between the phonetic capacities of infants, observable through perceptive or productive performance, and the mental representations of speech sounds in the phonological grammar. Phonemes are the basic linguistic units used to differentiate the meaning of words, testable in minimal pairs. For example, consider the words 'pie' and 'buy' in the phonology of English. Although it is not obvious from their spellings or even their phonetics forms, [p^{h}aɪ] and [baɪ], the phonological representations of these words form a minimal pair, /paɪ/ – /baɪ/, differing only in the voice feature. Although the aspirated onset voiceless labial, [p^{h}] in 'pie' is distinct from [p] in 'spy' on the surface, the aspiration is not contrastive at the underlying level in the English grammar, since /spaɪ/ surfacing as [sp^{h}aɪ] does not incur any semantic changes.

Thus, while the differences between speech sounds can be phonetic, some of them are also phonemic if they are used contrastively (contributing to word meaning) in a language. Accordingly, phonemes exist within languages and it is only the features that make up the phonemes that are universal. When young infants were tested on different speech sounds in early perceptual studies and they discriminated native and non-native contrasts without prior experience, it was claimed that infants have an innate capacity for perceiving human speech. Considering that contrasts refer to phonemes, which can be categorised as native or non-native, it is not surprising that such findings led researchers to assume a biological predisposition to perceiving phonemes of all languages. However, with a clear distinction between phonemes and phonetic units, we can now speculate that the ability of the infants shown in early studies is phonetic and proceed with our examination of the pre-production stage of acquisition.

4.4 Perceptual development

As we saw in section 4.2 above, the remarkable perceptual ability exhibited by infants as young as newborn make them seem like universal learners by virtue of their ability not being restricted to any (specific) language. In our current task of investigating the initial state of the phonological grammar, it is only natural to ask whether this universal nature of earliest perception has any correlation with the notion of Universal Grammar (*cf.* Chomsky 1965; Pinker 1994): Is it the case that the learner is equipped with innate abilities that is specifically designed for perceiving speech sounds of any language? If so, acquiring a language would involve 'unlearning' the sounds that do not belong to the ambient language. However, from the intuitive point of view that some kind of *learning* is taking place in the infant through linguistic exposure and from what we have just illustrated about phonemes in the previous section, it is more plausible to view infants as being capable of perceiving all possible phonetic differences that is audible to the human ear. Referring back to Table 4.6, it could be that at the initial state infants can perceptually distinguish all 40 phonetic tokens of the world's languages without the any knowledge of phonemes. We will leave the issue of innateness of this ability for later and now take a look at studies of older infants to see how perception develops.

When Werker her and colleagues (1981) documented the ability of 6–8-month-old English-acquiring infants to discriminate the retroflex vs dental onsets in Hindi, adult native speakers of Hindi and English were also tested on the same contrasts. As predicted and reported by prior studies investigating adult perception, such as Miyawaki et al. (1975) reporting on Japanese speakers' inability to discriminate the two-way liquid contrast [r] – [l] present in English phonology, but not in Japanese, the adult speakers of Hindi perceived the contrasts as belonging to two different phonemic categories, while the native speakers of English failed to do so. With a clear indication that the infant discriminative ability does not last into adulthood, the next step was to ascertain when changes appear in the infant perceptual ability. Thus, Werker and Tees (1984) examined the discriminative ability of Hindi as well as Nthlakapmx (or Salish, a language of native Indians in Canada) by English acquiring infants at 6–8 months, 8–10 months and 10–12 months. While adults were tested again and their discriminative inability with non-native segments confirmed, the infants could discriminate the non-native distinctions with 95 per cent accuracy at 6–8 months; 60–70 per cent at 8–10 months; and only 20 per cent at 10–12 months.

The gradual decline in the discriminative ability was concluded as the effect of increased native language experience with age and that infants at around the age of 8–10 months start to attune to the native speech sounds. Subsequently, more studies investigated infants acquiring other languages using other distinctions and confirmed the finding by Werker and Tees (1984) that the infant perceptual performance for non-native phonetic differences declines with age (Best & McRoberts 2003; Best et al. 1995; Mattock & Burnham 2006; Tsushima et al 1994; Werker & Lalonde 1988). Such studies are further supported by findings of perceptual bias for the native language in infants during the second half-year of their life. For example, Jusczyk and his colleagues found that 9-month-olds prefer nonsense words with native language stress patterns (Jusczyk et al. 1993a) as well as phonotactics (Jusczyk et al. 1993b).

Although various pivotal studies thus led to a firm general consensus that a gradual decline in discriminating non-native speech sounds commence at around eight months, no study attempted to clarify whether the initial discriminative ability of the infant's *native* contrasts is maintained, as implied by any assumption of innate abilities, or improves with age during the second half of the first year. Kuhl and her colleagues (2006) addressed this substantial research gap: With the hypothesis that the perception of speech sounds belonging to the native language is facilitated through linguistic exposure, American and Japanese infants of two age groups, 6–8 months and

10–12 months old, were tested on the English [r] – [l] distinction. The finding was that while the perceptual performance on the liquid distinction was the same for American and Japanese infants of the younger age group, the older American infants performed significantly better than their younger peers and the older Japanese infants showed a decline, as predicted. Similar findings have been reported in Tsao et al. (2006) for native speakers of English and Mandarin tested on the Mandarin affricate–fricative contrasts.

The symmetrical perceptual development for native and non-native sounds revealed in these studies is more in line with the notion that development is constructive, since a decline for non-native sounds without enhancement for the native ones cannot avoid being associated with shrinking knowledge. In fact, these studies undermine the view that infants are born with the ability to distinguish all speech sounds. It is not so much in the sense of perceptual development being regarded as losing the ability to perceive non-native distinctions, since this occurs due to lack of exposure, but the implied assumption of native distinctions being maintained through native language exposure falls apart, since it simply does not allow any changes in the native language perceptual abilities at any age. Furthermore, any assumption of an innate universal phonetic inventory that shapes according to linguistic experience would be weakened if any of the non-native speech sounds are excluded from the declining process, in spite of non-exposure.

In actual truth, not all non-native speech sounds contrasts are lost in spite of lack of exposure and few studies have failed to find a decline in the ability to distinguish some non-native contrasts. A study by Best and colleagues (1988) evidenced that 6- and 14-month-old English-acquiring infants did not show any decline for Zulu clicks, which were also discriminated by adult English speakers. Another study by Polka and Bohn (1996) tested 6–8- and 10–12-month-old English- and German-acquiring infants as well as adults on English and German vowels and found that both infants and adults of the two languages could differentiate the non-native vowels fairly well. Furthermore, when Polka and co-workers (2001) investigated the perceptual performance of English- and French-acquiring infants using the English [d] – [ð] contrast, the two language groups did not differ at 6–8 months or 10–12 months of age. No matter how few they are, the fact that certain sounds remain distinguishable without exposure undermines the view that the discriminative ability for native sounds is facilitated through exposure and non-native ones reduced through non-exposure. Does this mean that there is no phonology or phonetics at the initial state and infants are merely sensitive to the acoustic properties of speech sounds?

When we consider the intricate nature of speech perception, it is hard to believe that young infants are discriminating speech sounds based on acoustic differences. Development in speech perception involves word segmentation and extracting words from fluent speech is an extremely difficult task, since there are no spaces between words, not to mention the difficulty of detecting boundaries between two segments due to coarticulation. Words are seldom produced as single-word utterances and even when mothers are asked to teach single words to their children, it is only in 20 per cent of the time that they appear in isolation (Woodward & Aslin 1990). Furthermore, the variability of speech signals between speakers due to factors such as differences in the shape of the mouth, voice, pitch, and within speakers in terms of speed and mode, means that there is no absolute set of acoustic properties for speech sounds, even when coarticulation is discounted from the equation (for more details, see Jusczyk 1997/2000: 493–5). Nevertheless, in addition to all the differences between languages of the world that infants have been tested on, newborn infants can distinguish speech from non-speech and even display preference for listening to speech than other stimuli (Vouloumanos & Werker 2007), which means that speech has a special status in relation to other sounds.

Furthermore, Mattock and Burnham (2006) investigated the perception of speech (lexical tone) vs non-speech (violin sound) tones by 6- and 9-month-old infants acquiring Chinese, a tone language, and English, a non-tone language. Their finding regarding speech tones is consistent with earlier studies as far as speech tones are concerned: The discriminative ability of 6- and 9-month-old Chinese-acquiring infants and 6 month-old English-acquiring infants was the same, but deteriorated in the English-acquiring infants by nine months. However, what is noteworthy is that the English-acquiring infants' ability to distinguish different non-speech tones did not decline at nine months, which led the authors to conclude that the perceptual reorganisation taking place at this time must be linguistic. Although this may suggest that something must be prompting the infant learner to listen to speech in a manner different to other sounds in the environment and that speech perception involves more than the general auditory abilities, the various perceptual studies of the older preverbal infants that we considered in this section do not provide any evidence about what the infant learner brings to the task of language learning. This is because, although we know about what infants can and cannot do in terms of discriminating aspects of speech, little is known about the contributory factors in the linguistic environment to the perceptual enhancement that takes place during the second half of the infant's first year.

With no clear evidence whether the infants' perceptual abilities for discriminating various differences in human speech sounds are innate, we may be inclined to assume that phonetic units are acquired before phonemes and that phonological acquisition is based purely on working out the sound distribution in the native language. Such an assumption implies that the initial state is no different for human infants than for non-human species. As a matter of fact, when Vouloumanos and her colleagues (2009) investigated the reason behind the perceptual bias for speech that they found earlier in newborn infants (Vouloumanos & Werker 2007), they reported that it cannot be rooted in prenatal experience, since the infants also showed equal bias for vocalisations of the rhesus monkey. This contests the assumption that there are two levels of representation in infant perception, one for speech and the other for non-speech. Is it the case that speech perception develops into perceiving phonetic differences in the 'speech mode', but at the initial state only general auditory mechanism is available for perceiving speech, as for non-human species?

On the one hand, when we consider that language is thought to have evolved from the need to communicate and that communication is not specific to humans, since we know that certain non-human animals also have ways to communicate with each other (for example bird songs, bee dancing, whale songs, dolphin signature whistles, prairie dog calls, etc.), it is quite natural to infer that the ability to learn language is not unique to humans. We are not equating human languages, which contain grammar, with communication systems of non-humans with no grammar, but merely regarding the learning path. On the other hand, when we look at how impossible it is, even for adults with mature cognitive capacities, not only to understand a language that we have never encountered before, but to simply try to figure out where words begin and end, it does not take a linguistic analysis to sense the complexity involved in the task of decoding human speech. Hence, it not at all far-fetched to assume that the incredible ability of human infants is aided by a language-specific cognitive function that is unique to humans. This is a subject matter that lies at the heart of a long-term debate on the language ability and is still ongoing due to lack of evidence that can be considered sufficiently clear-cut, mainly owing to non-humans not being testable on human speech production as well as limitations set by ethical issues in the methodology of studying infant cognition.

Under such circumstances, how are we to uncover the truth about what the human infant brings to the task of language learning? If we suppose that only humans are born with language-specific learning mechanism, we would expect to find some difference between the perceptual capacity of human infants and that of non-humans. No matter how subtle it may be, a comparative investigation might suggest that while non-humans perceive human speech using a purely auditory mode of analysis, human infants analyse speech in another, perhaps phonetic, mode. However, if there is no difference at all between human infants and other species, it would imply that language is not specific to humans, thus invalidating any phonological theory assuming innate language ability. We shall now turn to comparative studies of human vs non-human speech perception to see whether the initial state is the same for humans and non-humans.

4.5 Human infants and non-humans

Starting with a study by Kuhl and Miller in 1975 (see also Kuhl 1981), who reported that chinchillas are capable of discriminating and categorising voicing contrasts, just like humans, other studies followed. In 1978, the same authors demonstrated that chinchillas could also perceive different places of articulation in stop consonants. Kuhl and Padden (1982) showed categorical perception, which was assumed to be specific to humans, of voicing contrasts by macaque monkeys in 1982 and of place of articulation contrasts in stop consonants in 1983. These place of articulation contrasts were also perceived by trained Japanese quails (Kluender et al. 1987). When Hienz et al. (1981) trained and tested blackbirds as well as pigeons in detecting tones in 1981, they found that the perceptual capacity of pigeons, but not blackbirds, was similar to cats and humans. Two other avian species, budgerigars and zebra finches, were also found to have discrimination performance for English /r/–/l/ boundary that was similar to humans (Dooling et al. 1995). In 2001, Sinnott and Mosteller compared how Mongolian gerbils process vowels differently from consonants, which they found to be similar to humans.

All these studies seem to indicate that speech perception may not be specific to humans, since non-human species can also discriminate a variety of human speech sounds. This does not only confirm that the tasks in earlier human infant perceptual experiments did not involve phonemic discrimination ability, but it also leads to a serious doubt about the idea of specialised speech-processing mechanisms. However, one could argue against rejecting language being specific to humans based on two reasons. First, although human infants are not discriminating phonemes during the earliest perceptual stage, they may be equipped with innate phonetic abilities for discriminating speech sounds. Second, the non-human species used in the experiments were all trained prior to the actual experiments, whereas the perceptual studies of newborn humans did not involve any training at all. On the whole, it is difficult to know, at least for segmental differentiation, whether speech processing in human infants start out in the same way as human speech is perceived by non-human species or similar perceptual discriminability results are achieved by humans and non-humans through different mechanisms. Consequently, we might suppose that better clues can be found by comparing the non-segmental perceptual capacity of human infants with nonhumans that had not been trained in the experimental procedures. Ramus, Hauser, Miller, Morris & Mehler 2000 is such a study.

Ramus and his colleagues came to a ground-breaking conclusion regarding the issue of whether the mechanisms enabling the perception of prosody are unique to humans, which had never been investigated before. Languages can be classified into three rhythm types (Pike 1945; Ladefoged 2001): *stress-timed* (for example Arabic, Russian, Thai, and most Germanic languages), *syllable-timed* (for example Turkish, Yoruba, and most Romance languages), and *mora-timed* (for example Japanese), (see Chapter 6 for further discussion of timing and the mora). Studies have shown that newborns can discriminate languages with different rhythms (for example French vs Russian and English vs Italian, in Mehler et al. 1988; English vs Spanish, in Moon et al. 1993; English vs Japanese, in Nazzi et al. 1998), but not languages belonging to the same linguistic rhythm group (for example Dutch vs English and Spanish vs Italian, in Nazzi et al. 1998). Ramus et al. (2000) tested the discrimination of Dutch vs Japanese using the same habituation-dishabituation task for 32 French newborn infants and 13 non-trained tamarin monkeys. Similarities and differences between the monkey and the human auditory systems were studied through head-orientation responses to natural speech (twenty sentences in each language) production by four speakers played forward and backward as well as synthesised (computerised) speech, in which all speech cues other than rhythm were removed. The conclusion was that since both newborns and tamarins were able to discriminate Dutch and Japanese in forward natural and synthesised speech, but both groups failed to do so in backward natural and synthesised speech, newborns and tamarins process speech in the same way. This claim was extended by Toro and co-workers (2003), who replicated this work using rats.

Studies showing that non-humans can discriminate languages with different rhythms without any training may force us to give up the idea that language is unique to humans. However, we should ask one important question before throwing out the baby with the bathwater: Is it feasible to compare human infants less than one week old with adult non-humans? To answer this question, we need to consider two significant differences between the two groups, namely cognitive maturity and linguistic exposure.

Although it is common practice to calculate the cognitive capacity of non-human primates in terms of human child age, we ought to question whether the cognitive difference between an adult monkey and a newborn child may go beyond what can be considered a reasonable comparison. Underscored by a study that found left hemisphere dominance for processing vocalisations in the brain of adult, but not infant, rhesus monkeys (Hauser & Andersson 1994), we can be certain that cognitive difference exists even between adult and infant monkeys. If some part of speech perception relies on general learning principles and there is a connection between general learning principles and cognitive maturity in the sense that learning is easier for the cognitively mature, then a comparison of completely immature human newborns and cognitively more mature adult tamarins may not be as revealing as one might wish.

As for the difference in linguistic exposure between human newborns and non-humans, while humans were considered to have no exposure by definition, it is difficult to know the exact condition for the non-human species. If born in captivity, the amount of exposure to human language can vary greatly. Since it is difficult to imagine that the caretaking routine is the same in all facilities, not to mention possible differences within a facility, it can be anything between minimal exposure under controlled condition and maximal exposure through daily interaction with their human captors. Furthermore, it is important to note that although the untrained non-humans were untrained in the sense that they had not heard the utterances prior to the specific experiments, we must take their experience in terms of participation in previous (perhaps even similar) experiments into consideration. For example, of the four Japanese macaques used in a speech perception study by Sinnott and Gilmore (2004), two of them were fifteen years old, each with twelve years of experience with various speech perception studies, while the other two were only three years old and had only one prior experience.

The above critique should not be taken as arguing for specialised speech-processing mechanisms, nor is it refuting the findings of comparative perceptual studies. It is only aimed at the implicit claim of the commonality of newborn human infants and non-humans, as we should be sceptical about comparison conditions and simplified interpretations of the difference between the two groups. Although further studies may move us closer to resolving the issue of whether human infants' initial representations are merely acoustic representations shared with other species or they go beyond that, what we can gather so far from behavioural studies of earliest perception is as follows:

1. The initial representations in the human infant seem to divide speech sounds into categories.
2. During the earliest pre-production stage, the infant is a 'universal learner', evidenced by the discriminative ability to perceive speech sounds of all languages.
3. The ability to discriminate non-native speech sounds starts to decline after the first 6–8 months, during which time the infant tunes into the phonology of the ambient language.
4. Some non-human species show similar capacity for perceiving certain speech contrasts.

Thus, although the perceptual capacity demonstrated by infants is so incredible that it may suggest that humans are born with innate mechanisms specific to speech-processing, as opposed to general auditory processing, there is no convincing evidence for this. In fact, behavioural studies seem to indicate that there is no phonology during the earliest stages of perceptual development. However, since development takes place in the perceptual capacity of the human infant in the form of tuning in to their ambient language, as we saw earlier, and such development is not known to take place in non-humans, we cannot simply assume that the non-phonemic perception of human speech by non-humans and human infants during the earliest stage is the same. In other words, since similar performances in perceptual discrimination tasks by human infants and non-humans do not necessarily imply that the same cognitive mechanisms are used, we still have no clear evidence whether language is unique to humans. However, there is one last resort that we can turn to, before we suspend our investigation as to whether human speech processing is the same in humans and non-humans. Since many brain studies have uncovered an unmistakable left hemispheric cerebral dominance for language in humans, thought to be specific to our species, we will now examine the field of neuropsychology that studies the structure and function of the brain.

4.6 The infant brain

Studies in neuropsychology using neuro-imaging have repeatedly confirmed both structural and functional asymmetries between the right and left hemispheres in the adult brain and found left-hemispheric predominance in most right-handed normal adults when processing their native language, as was first suggested by Broca in 1861 (see Dehaene-Lambertz et al. 2008 for the description of physiological details). What is currently known about speech perception in adults is that the neural network involved in phonetic representation is located predominantly in the left-temporal lobe, whereas the network for acoustic processing is bilateral (Näätänen et al. 1997) and that phonetic representation is calculated in addition to that for the acoustical features of the stimulus in sensory memory (Dehaene-Lambertz 2000).

Hoping that the technological advance in brain imaging methods may provide the missing link between behavioural observations of infants and their underlying brain mechanisms, a few studies have turned to the obvious question of whether the infant brain also has left hemisphere (LH) dominance for speech, as in the adult. The planum temporale, the cortical area situated behind the auditory cortex, is the most asymmetrical structure in the brain: More than half the population appears to have a more developed left planum temporale (only one in ten people has a more developed right planum temporale) and its size can be more than five times larger on the left than on the right (Bear et al. 2006: 630–2). In terms of structure, since the anatomical asymmetry of the human brain in the planum temporale is already detectable in the foetus, as early as even before 31 weeks' gestation (Wada et al. 1975), it is not surprising that the gross anatomy of the infant brain is strikingly similar to that of the adult from birth (for example Peña et al. 2003). The functional similarity, however, has not been as straightforward to uncover.

Electrophysiological studies using a high-density geodesic net of sixty-five electrodes recorded higher voltages over the LH than the right hemisphere (RH) in 2–3-month-old infants listening to syllables (Dehaene-Lambertz & Dehaene 1994; Dehaene-Lambertz & Baillet 1998). Since the greater left-hemispheric activation could either be due to asymmetries in the brain morphology or a genuine advantage involved in phonetic processing, Dehaene-Lambertz (2000) tested 4-month-old infants on acoustic vs phonetic stimuli. Her results then did not show a clear lateralisation difference for phonetic and acoustic processing in the infants. However, when she tested 2–3-month-old infants again with her colleagues (Dehaene-Lambertz et al. 2002), functional magnetic resonance imaging (fMRI) was used, since it was considered more useful in studying the functional organisation of the infant brain than event-related potentials (ERPs), which have an excellent time resolution, but do not provide spatially accurate information on the active brain areas. When the team recorded brain activity evoked by normal speech played forward and in reverse to exclude auditory stimulation, they found that left-lateralised brain regions, which are not confined to primary auditory cortices, were already active in these infants.

What followed was a cutting edge study of 12 newborns by Peña and colleagues in 2003 using a 24-channel optical topography device to assess changes in the concentration of total haemoglobin (brain activity) in response to normal and reversed speech in twelve areas of the RH and twelve areas of the LH. Their results were quite similar to the fMRI results obtained with older infants (Dehaene-Lambertz et al. 2002) and showed significantly more activation in LH temporal areas when exposed to normal speech than to reversed speech or silence, thus leading to the conclusion that human infants are born with an LH superiority to process specific properties of speech. Studies of the infant brain is generally not committed to resolving the debate of whether the association of language with the LH may reflect an innate disposition of certain areas of the brain for language or this association may arise as a consequence of language acquisition. Interestingly, however, the finding that was singled out by Peña and colleagues (2003) was that their study provides evidence that the neonate brain already responds specifically to normal speech within a few hours of experience with speech signals outside the womb.

Although it is not the case that the lateralisation recorded in infants is exactly the same as that in adults (Holland et al. 2001), studies show that what is going on in the brain regions of infants is quite similar to adults. Furthermore, with studies showing fewer structural asymmetries in speech-impaired or written-language-impaired children (Plante 1991) and the same regions of the LH being involved in sign languages as in oral languages (Sakai et al. 2005), we could be convinced that the human brain is structurally and functionally organised to process speech in the LH from birth and that this capacity is indeed unique to humans. However, the question is whether non-human animals possess the same brain asymmetries as humans.

Regarding the question of whether non-humans also have structural asymmetries, although the human brain is structurally more complex than that of other primates, it seems that chimpanzees and great apes actually have structural dominance of the LH to some extent (*cf.* Dehaene-Lambertz et al. 2006). As for functional asymmetries, Petersen et al. (1978) found that the neural lateralisation in the LH is also found for signal processing in Japanese (adult) monkeys. Hauser and Andersson (1994) reached the same conclusion when they tested adult rhesus monkeys. Based on the assumption that in any species, orienting the right ear to species-specific vocalisations indicates an involvement of the LH – this was seen in mice (Ehret 1987), harpy eagles (Palleroni & Hauser 2003) and sea-lions (Boye et al. 2005) – Heffner and Heffner (1986) found that adult macaques can still discriminate two specific forms of their own vocalisation after a lesion in the RH, but not if it is in the LH. This was confirmed by Poremba and colleagues (2004) when they conducted a positron emission tomography (PET) study of adult monkeys being exposed to the vocalisations of their own species and showed LH activation. However, since this asymmetry was not found in infant rhesus monkeys (Hauser & Andersson 1994), infant sea-lions (Boye et al. 2005) or infant harpy eagles (Palleroni & Hauser 2003), the LH dominance for vocalisations in non-humans is considered to develop with exposure.

While it seems that the link between the structural asymmetry and meaning behind vocalisations in the non-human brain is not yet understood, more recent comparative studies of speech processing are showing differences between humans and non-humans regarding various linguistic capacities (Dehaene-Lambertz et al. 2006). Although further studies are needed in order to determine whether signal processing in non-humans can be equated with speech processing in humans, whether human speech perception by non-humans involves phonetic processing, and whether non-segmental speech perception (such as linguistic rhythm) by human infants involves something more than general auditory processing, we can safely conclude two points from the above. The first is that the non-human infant brain is different from those of the non-human adult, the human adult as well as the human infant, thus implying a neurological difference between the human infant and the non-human infant. Second, while we must be cautious regarding the extent to which neural lateralisation corresponds with cognitive mechanisms and bearing in mind that the focal point of research in such studies is neural activity, and not what cognitive mechanisms underlie human speech perception by different species, we can also take neurological studies to confirm the finding of infants' perceptual bias for speech by behavioural studies. Nevertheless, we still have no definite answers as to the exact nature of initial representations in the human infant or whether the human infant initially uses the same cognitive mechanisms as adult non-human species in speech perception.

4.7 Nature or nurture

To summarise what we have seen so far, infant perceptual studies show that human infants have a bias for speech and that infants as young as newborn are capable of discriminating speech contrasts in any human language. In the early days of behavioural studies on infant perception in 1970s, the incredible capacity of infants starting out as universal learners tended to be interpreted as our biological predisposition to distinguish the universal set of phonetic contrasts. There were two reasons for this. First, the assumption that all the basics for speech perception are already in place at birth fitted in perfectly with the mainstream phonological theory, which was based on the notion of Universal Grammar (Chomsky 1959). Second, most infant perceptual studies only involved segmental discrimination. Since the mapping between phonemes and their physical manifestation is not one-to-one (in fact far from it, as we saw in section 4.3) and the task of perceiving a phoneme, therefore, involves neutralising any differences in the acoustic signal, the specific postulation that the infant is capable of phonemic discrimination had to assume the infant perceptual capacity to be at least as developed as that of the adult, if not more, especially since very young infants are also capable of discriminating non-native contrasts not distinguishable by adults.

However, the nativist view that human species is genetically programmed to acquire language was seriously questioned and considered implausible by many researchers in the area of child language since it leaves no room for development to take place in the infant or for the role played by experience in acquisition. As a natural consequence, infant perceptual studies were extended to scrutinising the developmental stages of the universal learner and found that the infant perceptual capacity gradually ceases to be universal as it is shaped according to the ambient language at around nine months of age, which can evidently only occur as a result of exposure to the native linguistic environment. At approximately the same time, behavioural experiments with non-humans species showed that some adult non-humans perform in a similar way to human infants in the discrimination of certain speech contrasts. All this led many researchers to assume that early infant perception is based on general auditory processing and abandon the idea of an innate or specialised speech processing mechanism. Nevertheless, the debate on whether it is nature or nurture is still ongoing. Why?

The so-called nature-nurture issue started when the American behaviourist psychologist B. F. Skinner in his, perhaps now infamous, book *Verbal Behavior* (1957), expounded the view that language, like any other aspect of animal learning, was developed through external reinforcement. This view was challenged by the linguist Noam Chomsky (1959) in a very influential review in the journal *Language*. Under Skinner's hypothesis, no innate information was required; indeed, the acquisition of language was a normal process of learning. He based his theories on laboratory experiments with rats (that could be) trained to press a bar in order to be rewarded with a food pellet, a form of external reinforcement. Chomsky castigated Skinner for this over-simplistic approach to the sophisticated process of language acquisition on the basis of laboratory experiments. From this followed the innateness hypothesis proposing that human infants are born with the capacity to acquire language through a 'language acquisition device' or LAD, which is encoded with the knowledge of universal grammar and universal phonetics that allows them to acquire language quickly and accurately without instruction or stimulus.

Chomsky later went on to argue for the 'poverty of the stimulus'. This argument revolves around the observation that children acquire the grammar of their language with limited input. Since the input does not contain enough information for the learner to work out the grammar of the target language, some part of the grammatical knowledge must be innate. It is thus easy to see how perfectly this could be tied up with the initial ability of the infant to perceive distinctions in all languages of the world. On the other hand, when we consider that it is through exposure to the ambient language, rich in phonological information that shapes the initially universal perceptual capacity of the infant into one that that is more language-specific or restricted, we can see that the poverty of the stimulus argument is weakened dramatically.

The conflict between 'nature' and 'nurture' has created a theoretical battlefield in many different disciplines. For language acquisition, the importance of resolving the relative contributions of innate predisposition and environment is paramount. However, in linguistics, the tendency has been to focus on the innate mechanisms and environment- and learning-based accounts of language acquisition have been secondary to the principles of Universal Grammar (UG), while in non-linguistic approaches to child language, the focus has been on the similarities between human infants and non-human species. One way to interpret what we have seen so far is that some of the linguistic principles, which were assumed to be responsible for particular elements in language acquisition, are aspects shared by other faculties than language and by other organisms. This interpretation is, in fact, consistent with Chomsky's more recent view of the extremely restricted language faculty expressed in the influential paper by Hauser and colleagues (2002). If it is the case that the faculty of language is extremely narrow, this could answer the question why we are still searching for what is specific to language: Linguistic theorists have underestimated the role played by other faculties in acquisition and by the input.

Linguistic theory has certainly moved on since Chomsky's initial proposition, and it is no longer the case that UG alone is believed to be responsible for language acquisition or that language faculty is an autonomous module that is independent of other cognitive components. The notion of the innate linguistic capacity now refers to the mechanisms underlying the infant's speech perception and the debate is about whether the incredible perceptual capacity exhibited by young infants without prior exposure is general to auditory perception or specific to speech perception.

Although newborn human infants and adult non-humans may differ too much in terms of cognitive maturity and linguistic exposure to sustain the claim of commonality between the two groups, the fact is that behavioural and neuropsychological studies of very young infants show no concrete evidence for a specialised speech-processing mechanism. However, this is not the same as saying that speech is processed by the human infant in the same way as non-human species or that phonetic processing of speech by the infant has nothing to do with innate mechanisms specialised for language. In fact, studies using brain imaging techniques have confirmed perceptual bias for speech in the human infant. Thus, the general picture that emerges from various infant perception studies in different fields is that they appear to indicate that language is not specific to humans, but, at the same time, they do not provide sufficient evidence to deny this idea either: an analogy can be made between language learning and infants learning to walk – just as all normally developing infants are born with legs that they cannot use for walking until a time that is biologically determined, the human infant may well be equipped with innate language learning mechanisms which develop according to a pre-determined time schedule and environmental conditions; the difference is that while legs are physically visible, cognition is not. It may be that development must take place in the infant before we can hope to find any evidence for specialised speech-processing mechanisms. Hence, the conclusion that we can draw regarding the earliest pre-production stage of acquisition is that what human infants show in discrimination tasks of segments in perceptual studies is the ability to perceive phonetic differences and not the ability to discriminate phonemes, as was wrongly claimed in earlier studies.

We can suppose that the remarkable perceptual performance exhibited by the youngest infants is a result of an innate ability to perceive all phonetic differences, since they have no meaningful words to represent in terms of phonemes. It would then make sense to assume that although there is a mapping between acoustic signals and phonetic representations, infants do not perceive any phonetic difference as being contrastive, which is why they can perform equally well with speech sounds of all languages during the first six months of life. During the very early pre-production stages of acquisition, the infant is a passive learner acquiring phonetic representations without converting the phonetic values into phonemes. Exposure to the native language, and the discovery that words are encoded with meaning, compel the infant to distinguish the native sounds from others, which start to become organised in terms of categories at around eight months. Towards the end of the first year, since similar sounds that are not contrastive in the native phonology are treated as belonging to one category, they are no longer distinguishable, although they may be contrastive in other languages and were previously distinguishable. In this scenario, attuning to the native language means gradually learning to categorise the phonetic representations into the phonemes of the native language. Accordingly, the more the sounds are different from those that are contrastive in the native language, the longer they remain distinguishable, since they do not obtain phonemic status. However, this assumption does not answer the question that we asked at the beginning of this chapter, which is whether the infant learner has a biological predisposition to perceive speech.

If we are to get closer to answering the fundamental question of the extent to which humans have an innate capacity to comprehend and produce speech, we need to be extremely cautious about our assumptions by taking into consideration the role played by extragrammatical factors. Since the ability to perceive segmental contrasts can be explained through phonetic categorisation based on acoustic and articulatory properties, which is not unique to humans, we now turn to non-linguistic explanations of language acquisition in the next chapter to see whether there is a need at all to assume anything to be innate.

5

NON-LINGUISTIC PERSPECTIVES

As we saw in the previous chapter, perceptual studies suggest that the human infant may not, indeed, be predisposed to acquire language since the incredible abilities demonstrated even by newborn infants could be replicated in non-human species. During perceptual development, before infants can produce words, they are learning about the sound distribution of their ambient language in a multi-dimensional acoustic space. By the time the infant is 10–12 months old, attunement to the native language seems to be complete, since this is when word meaning emerges in the infant (Werker & Lalonde 1988) and speech contrasts are used for distinguishing meaning. Although the question still remains as to how children learn language so easily and quickly, if there are no innate constraints or representations that the learner can make use of, language learning can only rely on the information provided by the input. To put it crudely, language is learned through imitation. However, since human children do not reproduce adult language accurately like parrots, there has to be more to language learning than pure imitation.

The non-linguistic approach to language acquisition supposes that language learning is experience-based since the input from the ambient language contains a statistically tractable distribution of language elements. The mechanisms responsible for language acquisition would then be computational resources that categorise speech sounds and organise them into the phonemic inventory defined by the linguistic input. However, in this setting, acquisition is not straightforward computation, since the difficulty is found not only in the fact that mapping between the physical properties of the signal and language-specific phonemes is not one-to-one, but also speech segmentation involves the ability to categorise in spite of speaker, speech rate, and phonetic context variability in the input. This, unlike for computers (for example Waibel 1986), is not a problem for the human infant (for example Eimas & Miller 1980a; Kuhl 1979a,b; Kuhl 1983).

The aim of this chapter is to provide an introduction to how language acquisition can be explained without assuming any innate knowledge of language along the lines of Universal Grammar (UG). Since there are various non-linguistic perspectives on how children acquire language both from the point of view of perception and production, both of which can be considered to be separate areas, not to mention the fact that the study of phonological acquisition is spread across several research disciplines, we can only skim through the vast amount of studies where our focus will be on the fundamental difference in the basic assumptions of non-linguistic and linguistic theories of acquisition, rather than a comparison of non-linguistic approaches.

5.1 Learning theory

The consequence of the observed similarities in the perceptual capacity between human infants and non-humans is to view the underlying mechanisms of language acquisition as being domain-general, as opposed to being specific to language. However, for any theory of language acquisition to be plausible, it needs to explain how infants arrive at the language-specific elements through exposure to the ambient language. Recently, Kuhl (2000) proposed a new learning theory in which language input is mapped in detail by the infant brain. There are three instances in the process of neural commitment by the infant: Pattern detection in the input, exploitation of the statistical properties of the input, and alteration of infant perception. Needless to say, exposure is essential to this theory, but also it assumes that the absence of exposure produces a life-long effect on the language ability.

Infants have demonstrated outstanding abilities in pattern detection tasks. For example, they seem to be capable of sorting vowels in spite of variability in terms of speaker and context (Kuhl 1979a,b, 1983) as well as sorting syllables based on the initial consonant, such as grouping words starting with nasal consonants versus stop consonants (Hillenbrand 1984). As we saw in the previous chapter, the ability to detect patterns is not restricted to phonetic units; newborn infants can discriminate languages with different linguistic rhythm, which requires the skill of detecting stress and intonation pattern, and by the time they are nine months of age, infants seem to have acquired the phonotactic knowledge of their input language (Jusczyk et al. 1993b). Thus, even when words are not recognised by very young infants, they are able to recognise patterns in the language input. But how is it possible to extract patterns when there are no breaks between words in running speech?

A study of 7-month-old infants by Goodsitt and co-workers (1993) showed that infants are capable not only of detecting, but also exploiting the statistical properties of the language before they know the meaning of words. The infants in this study were tested under three conditions on their ability to discriminate [de] and [ti] syllables embedded in trisyllabic utterances in which the two other syllables, the context syllables, were [ko] and [ga]. In the first condition, the context syllables always appeared as [koga]. The transitional probability (the odds that one unit will follow another) between the syllables [ko] and [ga] in this condition is 1.0, and the target syllable appeared before or after these, as [dekoga], [tikoga], [kogade] or [kogati]. In the other two conditions, the transitional probability was reduced to 0.3 by varying the order of the context syllables, as [koga] or [gako], and by reduplicating, as [koko] or [gaga]. Since the infants showed significantly more accurate discrimination of the target syllable in the first condition in which the transitional probability was higher than in the other two conditions, it was concluded that infants exploit transitional probabilities in perception.

The third instance of neural commitment to which Kuhl's learning theory refers, the alteration of perception, is based on the proposal that human infants are equipped with a perceptual magnet, prototypes that act as a phonetic magnet for surrounding sounds. The suggestion that language input sculpts the brain to create a perceptual system that highlights contrasts used in the ambient language and de-emphasise those that are not is reflected in numerous studies showing how infant perception tunes in to the target language, some of which were presented in the previous chapter. For example, infants acquiring Japanese that does not distinguish between [r] and [l], as English does, can discriminate these liquids at six months, but fail to do so at twelve months.

Prototypes are exceptionally good representatives of a phonetic category, for which an effect known as the magnet effect has been observed through responses in tests of speech perception that was different from those of non-prototypes (Kuhl 1991). What is meant by the magnet effect is that a prototype enhances the ability to generalise other stimuli within the category. Kuhl and her colleagues (1992) tested 6-month-old American and Swedish infants on two vowel prototypes using stimuli that were exactly the same for the two groups. Since the American infants showed the magnet effect for the American English /i/ vowel prototype, but not for Swedish /y/ vowel prototype, and Swedish infants showed the reverse pattern, distortion of vowel perception caused by language experience in infants was considered to have taken place before the age of six months. Based on these observations Kuhl proposes a model accounting for the development of infant perception from a universal state to one that is language-specific called the Native Language Magnet (NLM) model (Kuhl 1994, 1998, 2000).

The essence of the NLM model is that at birth, infant perception partitions acoustic space distinctions in a language-universal way and that experience, which is assumed to be stored in the memory, activates the language magnet effects at around six months of age, so that the original natural boundaries are altered according to the ambient language. The NLM model suggests that learning involves the creation of mental maps for speech achieved through the magnet effect and assumes that acquisition goes through three phases. In the first phase, the infant is a universal learner and differentiates between all sounds of human speech. These abilities are derived from general auditory mechanisms. During the second phase, the infant's sensitivity to distributional properties of linguistic input produces phonetic representations based on the distributional modes in the ambient language. This experience is described as 'warping' perception and produces a distortion that decreases perceptual sensitivity near the boundaries of categories. As experience accumulates prototypes begin to function as perceptual magnets, increasing the perceived similarity between members of a category. In the final phase when neural commitment has taken place, language is perceived through a language-specific filter, thus producing facilitation in native and a reduction in foreign language phonetic abilities, which makes second language learning difficult.

Vocal learning by the infant through imitation of ambient language patterns provides the link between perception and production in the NLM model. It is assumed that the development in speech production is guided by perceptual representations of speech stored in memory before the infant could recognise words. Although it is not exactly clear how these perceptual representations are stored, they are claimed to be not specified in motor terms, and the link between perception and production is thought to rely on domain-general capabilities where an essential role is played by visual cues and 'motherese'. Motherese is also called 'parentese', child-directed or infant-directed speech (IDS). We will return to the topic of IDS later, but for now we should note that it is the universal speaking style used by caretakers when speaking to infants. IDS is characterised by alterations that are made at the phonetic as well as prosodic levels, which is thought to facilitate perception and learning of the ambient language phonology. As for the role played by visual cues, it has been recognised for some time now that it is very important. This is dramatically demonstrated in the so-called McGurk effect (McGurk & MacDonald 1976). When subjects in an experiment were presented with the auditory information about /b/, but the visual information that was presented at the same time was that of /g/, they reported the impression of the intermediate /da/ or /θa/. Furthermore, a study by Kuhl and Meltzoff (1982) reported that by 18–20 weeks, infants can recognise auditory-visual correspondences to speech similar to lip reading, since they looked longer at a face matching a vowel than one that did not.

The NLM model was later expanded to the NLM-e model (Kuhl et al. 2008) to better accommodate the continuity between speech perception and later language abilities, which is, in fact, a topic that has not been researched much. The NLM-e model also makes specific references to social interaction as an important factor during phonetic learning, based on a study in which children showed better L2 learning when the input was provided through human interaction (a teacher) than a video or audio recording (Kuhl et al. 2003), and to how early phonetic learning in L1 affects L2 acquisition later in life. Tsao and colleagues (2004) observed a relationship between speech perception and later language skills when they tested infants at six months of age and then also at thirteen, sixteen and twenty-four months. Their finding suggests that infants, who remain open to non-native linguistic possibilities for longer, will not progress so quickly towards the target language. A similar behavioural study of 7–30-month-old infants by Kuhl et al. (2005) confirmed that the infant's early speech perception performance predicts later language abilities (also, Rivera-Gaxiola et al. 2005), whose results were replicated in Kuhl (2008) using ERP and extended the observed patterns to a link between speech perception and language impairment. Thus, using both behavioural and brain measures, Kuhl and her colleagues showed that better native phonetic abilities predict faster advancement in the native language, while better non-native phonetic abilities predict slower development.

In answer to the question why language learning is easier for children than adults with superior cognitive skills, Kuhl's learning model refers to the critical period hypothesis which views language learning as being constrained by time or other factors that lie outside the process of learning. Accordingly, first language (L1) acquisition (in children) is thought to involve the creation of mental maps for the native language, which is a neural commitment that interferes with second language (L2) learning. This is supported by brain studies showing the same processing for native and non-native contrasts at six months of age, but not at twelve months (Cheour-Luhtanen et al. 1995), by difficulties in learning contrasts in L2 that are not found in L1, and by fMRI studies of bilingual adults showing a difference between those who acquired both languages early in life and those who did not (Kim et al. 1997).

Thus, the overall claim made by the NLM model is that language is innately discoverable, but not innate in terms of UG. Interestingly, however, the magnet effect is only found in human infants and not in other species, although they also show sensitivity to transitional probabilities (Kuhl 1991), thus suggesting that the perceptual magnet is innate only in humans. In terms of perception, we may wonder how the concept of the innate perceptual magnet differs from the UG notion of certain aspects of language being specific to humans, and in terms of production, the assumption that it follows from imitation can be considered rather vague. Nevertheless, since there is no doubt that the influence of the ambient language during the early stages of acquisition is far greater than assumed hitherto, we shall now take a closer look at the role played by statistical learning in acquisition.

5.2 Statistical learning

In view of the fact that perceptual development precedes production in infants and numerous observations from production data that the tendency is to acquire speech sounds that are more frequent than those that are less frequent in the ambient language, it makes sense to assume that infants are sensitive to distributional regularities in the speech input. It is only in the last couple of decades that infant perceptual studies have documented the large extent to which infants are influenced by their ambient language. In addition to the findings that 6-month-old infants are attuned to the vowel system of their native language at the cost of losing their ability to distinguish non-native vowels (Kuhl et al. 1992), that by ten months of age infants can no longer distinguish non-native consonants (Werker & Tees 1984), and that 9-month-old infants can distinguish sound sequences that occur frequently vs less frequently in the native language (Jusczyk et al. 1994), experiments have shown that infants can make use of distributional regularities in the input with extremely limited exposure (Gómez & Gerken 2000; Saffran et al. 1996).

Although not all non-linguistic approaches to language acquisition assume that every aspect of the computation of information in the language input is based on abilities shared with other species, the initial perceptual abilities and statistical learning, the ability to discover the distributional frequency of sounds within a language, are not thought to be unique to humans. The basic assumption of statistical learning is that the language input provides information about the distribution of linguistic units that differs from language to language and that infants, through their sensitivity to the stochastic (probabilistic) patterns in the input, can work out the acoustic dimensions that are relevant for categorising native speech sounds. Since there do not appear to be any acoustic cues for word segmentation that are common to all languages, statistical learning mechanisms, rather than an innate knowledge of language (UG), are considered to underlie language acquisition.

Based on the likelihood of one sound (or syllable) being followed by another is higher within words than across word boundaries (such as the phrase *pretty baby* in English, the probability of *pre* followed by *ty* is considerably higher than *ty* followed by *ba*), Saffran and colleagues (1996) conducted an experimental procedure to test the ability of 8-month-old infants to perform word segmentation in synthesised nonsense syllables. The subjects were presented with a two-minute continuous speech stream consisting of four trisyllabic words for the purpose of familiarisation, for example [tibudo] and [pabiku] with flat stress. The subjects were then presented with a continuous stream of syllables with no boundaries where the only word boundary cues had to be extracted from transitional probabilities between syllable pairs. While the probability that [bu] follows [ti] in [tibudo] is 1.0, just as the likelihood of [do] following [bu], the probability of a particular syllable following the last syllable across word boundaries is only 0.33. What followed was a presentation of repetitions of the four trisyllabic strings, two of which would coincide with words presented during familiarisation and two of which did not, for example [dopabi]. Based on the assumption that infants listen longer to novel items in a speech stream, the listening preferences of the infants indicated that they distinguished ‘words’ since they listened longer to 'non-words'. Thus, it was extrapolated that infants use transitional probabilities between syllables to detect word boundaries in fluent speech.

It is not only the transitional probability of syllables that is thought to be applied in statistical learning by infants. Mattys and colleagues (1999) examined whether phonotactic cues were used by infants to learn the statistical distribution in the input. They tested 9-month-old infants with two types of consonant cluster CC in CVCCVC sequences; one with a CC that occurs frequently at word boundaries and another that occurs frequently word-medially. While infants listened longer to word-medial CCs, when a 500ms pause was inserted between words, their preference changed to CCs that appeared at word boundaries, thus indicating that infants are also sensitive to statistical distribution of phonotactics.

At the segmental level, the first study to provide evidence that infants use the statistical distribution of phonetic variation in the ambient language was undertaken by Maye and co-workers (2002). The basic assumption is that two different categories are formed if a certain acoustic property of two sounds is informative enough to exhibit contrast to form a bimodal distribution of values of the relevant acoustic dimension, and if the acoustic property is not contrastive, a unimodal distribution will be formed. Thus, while a bimodal distribution indicates that a contrast has a linguistic value, a unimodal distribution results in an acoustic property being ignored due to it being uninformative for phonetic categorisation within that language. Given that the attunement to the native language has already started in 6-month-old infants (at least for vowels), 6–8-month-old infants were tested on voiced unaspirated vs voiceless unaspirated stops, [d] and [t], which is a contrast that infants have shown to distinguish (Pegg & Werker 1997). Novel speech stimuli were arranged in accordance with the systematically different distribution patterns. One group of twenty-four subjects was presented with a bimodal frequency distribution, in which stimuli near the endpoints of a sequence appear more frequently than those in the centre, and another group of twenty-four subjects was exposed to unimodal distribution of the same stimuli, in which the most frequently occurring stimuli were in the centre.

The prediction was that infants exposed to bimodal distribution would be better at discriminating the contrast, as a result of a two-category representation, than those exposed to unimodal distribution, regardless of whether or not there was any meaning attached to the sound sequences. The results demonstrated the infants' sensitivity to the phonetic frequency distribution in the language input. Interestingly, however, none of the infants exposed to a unimodal distribution could discriminate the [d] – [t] contrast, as opposed to a previous study by Pegg and Werker (1997). Thus, an effect of reducing discriminative ability was suggested for unimodal distribution. While it was mentioned that similar experiments using an artificial paradigm could show statistical learning in infants younger than six months of age, the fact that it takes more than ten months of exposure for infants to form a complete phonetic categorisation from the input was suggested as being due to the qualitative difference in the input between artificial (experiment) and natural conditions. Furthermore, it was put forward that the reason behind why vowel categorisation occurs earlier than that of consonants in infant perceptual development is because not only are there fewer vowels, but also they occur more frequently, than consonants.

There seems to be ample evidence that infants are indeed sensitive to transitional probabilities in the speech input at several levels and apply distributional information in order to categorise speech elements of the ambient language. However, since the range of statistical correlations found in natural language is immense, such as the probability of syllable shape co-occurrence (for example closed vs open syllables) and of vowel types in adjacent syllables (for example the probability of a nasalised vowel appearing in two adjacent syllables), and so on, we need to ask what the relevant unit of information is that infants attend to and to what extent statistical learning uses transitional probabilities in actual learning. In fact, studies show that human learners also use statistical cues to segment non-speech input, such as musical tones (Saffran et al. 1999) and visual patterns (for example Fiser & Aslin 2001). Furthermore, as Hauser and his colleagues (2001) replicated the study by Saffran et al. (1996) on cotton-top tamarin monkeys and obtained similar results, it seems quite clear that statistical learning abilities are not confined to any domain or species.

Nevertheless, we know that only humans are capable of reaching the final state of language acquisition, evidenced by a comparative study of the statistical learning in cotton-top tamarin monkeys and humans by Fitch and Hauser (2004) who found that the statistical learning applied by tamarins was more limited and that humans have far greater abilities to abstract hierarchical structure from input stimuli. Therefore, we might suppose that infants either innately know what type of statistical information to look for or they make use of a learning ability other than the statistical one. In point of fact, Jusczyk (1999) argues that multiple cues are necessary to extract words from fluent speech and questions the reliance on statistical learning alone, since he found that infants are capable of utilising allophonic cues by the time they are 10½ months old, but not at nine months of age.

Furthermore, Marcus et al. (1999) conducted experiments using strings of syllables on 7-month-old infants to see whether mere statistical learning could account for rule learning. After the subjects were 'taught grammars' through a familiarisation procedure of the form ABA or ABB (for example *ga-ti-ga* or *ga-ti-ti*), they were presented with new 'words' consisting of different phonetic material, but with the same ABA and ABB patterns (for example *wo-fe-wo* or *wo-fe-fe*). Half of the new words would be of the pattern (ABA or ABB) consistent with those presented during familiarisation. Care was taken that the infants should not be able to extract phonetic cues, such as voiced and voiceless consonants in the sequence, or transitional cues such as those in the experiments by Saffran et al. (1996). While Marcus et al. (1999) did not in any way deny the existence of statistical learning mechanisms, as proposed by Saffran et al. (1996), since the majority of the infants showed a preference for the 'inconsistent' pattern by looking longer at a flashing light, it was concluded that infants can extend their pattern learning to unfamiliar syllables and suggested that algebraic abilities are applied by infants to extract rules.

Subsequently, Saffran and Thiessen (2003) asked the question whether infants find some phonotactic regularities that are easier to acquire than others. Three experimental conditions were designed. In the first experiment, the infants were subjected to two different syllable patterns containing the same set of phonetic material during familiarisation, either CVCV (for example *boga*, *diku*) or CVCCVC (for example *bikrub*, *gadkug*) and showed preference for the familiarised pattern when presented with a continuous stream of syllables. This preference was also seen in the second experiment when the stimuli, instead of syllable shape, differed in the consonant voicing, such that it took the form of [-voice] – [+voice], as in *todkad*, *tigpod*, *kigtod*, or reverse, as in *dakdot*, *dopgit*, *dotgik*. However, when the voicing of the stimuli had no consistent pattern, no distinct advantage for the conditioned stimuli was found over the non-conditioned, indicating that certain types of sound patterning are more difficult to learn. It was thus concluded that statistical learning is constrained to regularities that are consistent with the patterns found in the world's languages.

From what we have seen so far, we can conclude that infants are indeed sensitive to statistical distribution of sounds and patterns in the input language, which they use to work out how sounds combine to form words and perhaps even how words combine to form phrases and so on. The fact that statistical learning in language acquisition is not domain- or species-specific, but assumed to be constrained in order to relate to the undeniable similarities observed across languages, has been tied with the view that cross-linguistic similarities are the result of constraints on learning and not due to innate knowledge (Saffran 2003). Although such a statement may remind us of the 'chicken-or-the-egg' problem and arguments can be made in its defence, there are still questions that remain unanswered, such as what exactly is the nature of the constraints on learning through statistical computation and the mechanisms behind such constraints, how does statistical learning interact with other learning abilities, what are the perceptual units that infants use to build up the sets of assumptions to arrive at the complexity of what is finally acquired, and how do children know what type of information to look for in the input? We must hope that future research will be aimed at providing answers to these questions, but for now it should be acknowledged that there is already adequate evidence that the influence from the ambient language has been underestimated far too much and far too long in phonological acquisition studies.

5.3 Experience-based production

5.3.1 Connectionism

The discussion in the previous sections has concentrated on how children develop their native language perceptually. Those studies do not address production, except perhaps, obliquely. A model of production which has been proposed by Stemberger (1992) based on work by McClelland and Rumelhart (1981) in the context of reading is known as a 'connectionist model'.

The connectionist view of development is discontinuous, taking place in stages and emphasising the role played learning through experience so that development is gradual, thus infants start with nothing, unlike the nativist approach based on Universal Grammar (UG), discussed in Chapter 4.

The architecture of this model, as we shall explain below, is a type of web of connections between different units, each able to influence the others. Stemberger's main objection to the type of assumption that was prevalent at the time (see in particular Smith 1973 or Menn 1971) was that the burden placed on the learner was too great and attributed to the learner a number of procedures which mapped out the relationship between input from the adult and the child's own productions. It is Stemberger's main contention that the procedures assumed cannot have any psychological status. Instead the type of model he proposes is based on general learning principles and on contextual cues.

Connectionism assumes that any information acquired by the child is encoded in 'units with an activation level' (Stemberger 1992: 168). If the activity in a given unit is high then the unit is being produced and if it is low, then the unit is inactive, and the unit's resting level is where it remains when out of use. Units with high resting levels can be activated more rapidly than those with low resting levels. The resting level of a unit would normally be dictated by frequency, thus frequently heard material will be more easily accessible than less frequently encountered. The units are arranged on different planes; semantic, word, phoneme or feature. Connections exist between the various levels so higher level (say semantic or word) information will 'cascade' down to connect with material at a lower level (say segment or feature). The information activated at the lower levels will then feed back to influence the higher level.

One feature of this type of model is that there is an overlapping of representations at the various levels – although not, apparently at the lexical level. So, connections are in all directions creating the web referred to above. Crucially, Stemberger assumes the child's representations to consist of segments rather than syllables and these segments are composed of features on a different level. The features feed back into the segments. To use Stemberger's own example, the features of /b/ partially overlap with those of /v/, which could lead to /b/ being activated when the target is /v/, since these two sounds share two features, and errors can occur in feedback. This would also help to explain some substitutions. Although deletions from consonant clusters are more common, connections between features can lead to coalescence, termed 'fusions', such as we witnessed in Gitanjali (see Chapter 2) who having a preference for the labial, presumably because of its relatively high frequency, was inclined to activate the labial feature from an input cluster and combine it with some feature(s) of a sound in a shared cluster. Thus, /sm/ (in *smoke*) combined the manner feature [+continuant] from /s/ with the place [labial] from the /m/ yielding [fok].

The resting level will determine the degree of accuracy with which a given form, be it feature, segment or word, is produced. Thus, a form with a high degree of activation in the input will be more likely to be produced accurately, whereas one with a low level will be very unlikely to be produced correctly. This means that the role of frequency in the input must be paramount, since this will provide high levels of activation in particular domains and in turn lead to an increased degree of accuracy. We shall see, in due course, another type of theory that depends on frequency in the input.

Stemberger claims to be able to account for various types of error (or 'warps' as he terms errors). Many such errors will be induced by interference. These include the very prevalent cases of consonant harmony which were discussed in some detail in Chapter 2. His solution here is that harmonisation will target segments with a low level of activation which have, perhaps, recently appeared in the system. Observing that place of articulation harmony most commonly affects sounds of a similar type – for example perhaps stops /p/ and /t/, which share many features, at the beginning and end of *pot* or *top* and when one of these two is activated feedback can also pass some activation to the other segment. /p/ and /t/ in initial and final position should inhibit the activation of the same consonants in final and initial position. Another fact about this process is that it is generally initial sounds that are attacked by final ones (what we have described as regressive harmony). If this is the position of the target segment but the activation level of the non-target segment is greater, then the chances are that harmony will result. Thus we might expect to find [tɒt] for *pot* or [pɒp] for *top*.

This explanation looks plausible enough until we remember that, although we encounter a number of different harmony patterns in children, some of these patterns are more prevalent than others. In Chapter 7 we shall return to the pattern exhibited by Trevor (Pater & Werle 2003). Trevor exhibited both progressive and regressive harmony activated by either labial or dorsal input but no harmony activated by coronals. We find that, in particular among English acquiring children, the coronal is rarely the trigger of harmony. Thus, the second of the two examples in the paragraph above, [pɒp], is far more likely to emerge than the first, [tɒt]. According to the explanation presented, this would imply that /t/ has a lower activation level and, since the coronal is likely to be very common in the child's input, this fact is hard to explain. In the case of Trevor's development, other forms of harmony than regressive dorsal targeting coronals died out of his production by the age of two but this last form persisted, as indeed it did for Amahl, for some further time (again, see Pater & Werle 2003 and Chapter 7). This pattern would imply that the coronal has a generally low activation level and the dorsal a very high one. We shall discuss below another type of explanation that relies on the frequency of certain sounds in the input. Stemberger rounds up his discussion by suggesting that most phenomena present in child output can be attributed to 'on-line changes based on the adult form as the child perceives it'. They are merely the result of errors of access.

Other inhibitions in production, according to this type of theory have to be attributed to physiological factors so, at this point, it might be appropriate to digress a little and consider the path followed by the infant in the early production stage; that is before the development of a phonemic inventory.

5.3.2 In the direction of production

At birth, the child's vocal tract resembles more that of a primate than a human adult's. Clearly the child's vocal tract is considerably smaller than the adult's (a difference in resonator length), leading to much higher frequencies in the resonance of vowels. Apart from that, the infant has 'a broader oral cavity, a shorter pharynx, a gradually sloping oropharyngeal channel, a relative anterior tongue mass, a closely approximating velum and epiglottis and a relatively high larynx' (Kent 1992). Figure 5.1 shows a comparison between the infant and adult vocal tracts. The development of the ability to produce speech requires changes in the vocal tract and in the nervous system (see Kent & Miolo 1995 for the changes which take place in the musculoskeletal and nervous systems). By four months the vocal tract more or less resembles the adult's.

Most of our concentration in this book has been on the articulation of consonants as they appear to present a greater challenge and, indeed, in the earliest stages of vocalisation the ratio of vowels to consonants is a great deal higher than subsequently; even in the latest stage of the first year it is around 50 per cent, which is far higher than adult speech. This ratio, of course, gradually decreases from 4.5 at 0–2 months; 3.6 at 2–4 months; 2.8 at 4–8 months down to 2.0

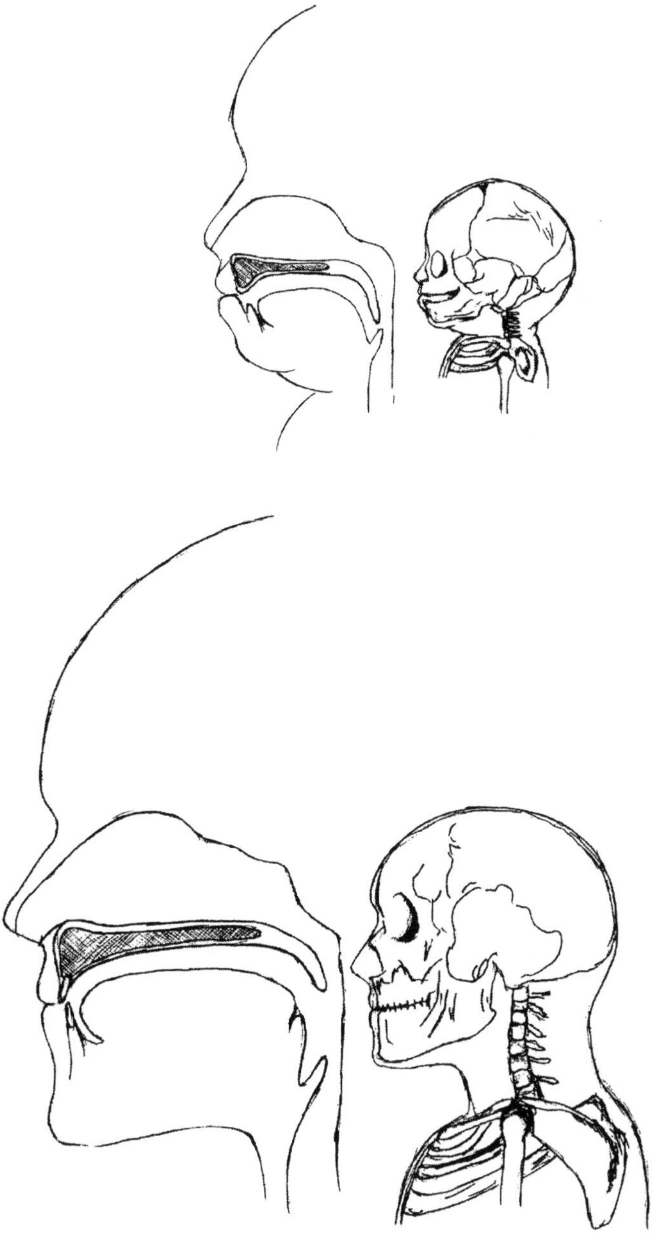

Figure 5.1 *Infant and adult vocal tracts. (Illustration by Kazuma Kato)*

at 8–12 months. At the early stages the non-high front and central vowels [ɛ ʌ ɪ] predominate and even by twelve months, because of the frequency of 'grunt-like' vocalisations, [ə] and [ʌ] together account for about half of all vocoids produced, these are followed by low vowels [ɑ] and [æ] at 21 per cent and 8 per cent, respectively. Vocoids tend to be heard as mid-low front, central or mid-low back with high vowels [i] and [u] infrequent. If Jakobson (1941) was correct, we would expect these two vowels, which, with /a/, form the quantum set of acoustically distinct vowels, and which are claimed to occur in some approximation in all the languages, to be among the earliest to appear. The fact that they are not, casts a number of doubts on the markedness account relating acquisition to typology.

At the earliest stage, most of the consonants produced are laryngeal [ʔ h] accounting for some 87 per cent of all those produced, followed by velars [k g] at 11.6 per cent. If we consider the limitations of the infant's tongue, this is easily explainable. Laryngeal sounds do not require any dexterity of the tongue and velars do not require manipulation of the blade of the tongue. Of the remaining block, all but [ç] and [χ] occur in the English phonemic inventory. By the next stage [ʔ] has fallen to 15.5 per cent while [h] at 59 per cent still dominates. At four months, the only consonant sounds not produced are [m f z]. By the fourth stage [h ʔ] have fallen to a combined 50 per cent. Meanwhile, there is a rise in lingual and labial articulations, dominated by the voiced stops [d] and [b m]. There are no fricatives in babbling articulations and no liquids, in spite of the fact that all languages appear to have at least one of each.

Syllables first appear around three months but at this stage, they fall into the category of what Oller (2000) describes as 'marginal'. That is to say that a combination of some consonant-like sound with some vowel-like sound begins to occur. The canonical syllable, the basic constituent of 'canonical babbling' appears around the seventh month. Canonical babbling relies on a unit which is 'similar to the syllable in adult speech'. Such babbling is largely repetitive in nature (for example [bʌbʌbʌbʌ], etc.), but gradually variegated babbling is introduced where the nature of the consonantal element changes (for example [bada], etc.)

In the period 5–13 months, the proportion of syllable type sequences is as shown in (5.1):

(5.1) V (60%) > CV (19%) > CVCV (8%) > VCV (7%) > VC (2%)
CVC (2%)

Notice that this scale reflects the overall proportion of vocoids produced relative to consonants. Codas are relatively rare (as anticipated by markedness considerations) but onsetless syllables form the bulk of vocalisations (contra markedness considerations). It should, of course, be remembered that this period starts relatively early at the point before the appearance of the canonical syllable. Favoured syllables, from cross-linguistic data gathered by Vihman (1992) seem to be as shown in (5.2):

(5.2) [da] > [ba] > [wa] > [də] > [ha] > [hə]

The main features seems to be that vocoids are generally low-back or central and consonants are front articulated (bilabial or apical) or glottal. The supraglottal sounds are voiced. Vihman comments on the fact that French children produce /h/ in spite of the fact that this is the stage when the child is homing in on the ambient language and French does not have /h/ in its inventory.

A further observation one could make that the supraglottal consonantal articulations all appear to be voiced – a fact that must prove problematic to a markedness account, since it is generally claimed that voiceless obstruents are less marked than voiced ones (see for example Stampe 1972). One caveat here, however, is that these findings may be the product of the transcription. Transcriptions are bound to be somewhat subjective and the 'voiced' sounds may simply be non-aspirate sounds.

These patterns, which are not language-specific, reflect the physiological rather than phonological development of the child and cannot be said to have any influence from input. So there is a clear disjoint between the development of production and perception, while frequency in the input seems to be informing the recognition patterns in perception, production output is not so obviously influenced by the ambient language.

5.3.3 Input-based acquisition

None of this denies a role to the input, however, and we shall consider another study which we could categorise as 'experience-based'. Zamuner (2003) tested a hypothesis that the nature of the input, rather than universal principles, determines the order of a child's acquisition. In particular, she looked at the acquisition of English codas in infants in order to test the Universal Grammar Hypothesis (UGH) and the Specific Language Grammar Hypothesis (SLGH).

The first of these hypotheses is based on markedness in the cross-linguistic Jakobsonian sense. You will recall that markedness theory suggests that children acquire language based on innate properties of language, which guide their acquisition of phonology. The second hypothesis proposes that children acquire language based on the patterns of the input language, which drive their acquisition of phonology.

Zamuner (2003) set out in particular to investigate the acquisition of codas in American-English-acquiring children based on the hypothesis that frequency of certain forms in the input would influence the children's acquisition. She, therefore, assessed the predictions that a UG hypothesis would make and set this against a prediction that might be made on the basis of input frequency in a particular language.

Evidence from UG suggests that the least marked place of articulation and, indeed, the least marked coda position is coronal. For example, in the Australian language, Lardil, codas are restricted to placeless nasals, that is to say nasal consonants that acquire their place of articulation from the following consonant, and to apical coronals (sounds produced by the tip of the tongue – alveolar and retroflex). Placeless nasals can, of course, generally occur word internally and there is ample cross-linguistic evidence of this. Indeed, cross-linguistic statistics reveal that the coronal coda is significantly preferred, although it has to be admitted that there is a group of languages where the unmarked place of articulation appears to be dorsal. Cross-linguistically, therefore, labial is the most marked place of articulation.

A further feature of cross-linguistic preference is for a more sonorous syllable ending – that is to say that the preferred syllable ends in a final vowel , this means that the CV syllable has to be the most favoured, however where CVC occurs, the preferred coda is a sonorant – either a nasal or a liquid (see Clements 1990). Thus sonority troughs are onsets, not codas. Examples to back this up include Japanese and Italian, where non-geminate codas are restricted to sonorants; Japanese allows only nasals while Italian allows /l, r/ as well (see Îto 1986). Beijing Mandarin only allows /n ŋ ɹ/. The implicational universal is that if languages allow obstruent codas, they also allow sonorant ones, but not vice versa. Zamuner's analysis of thirty-five languages appear to bear out this prediction, although not so convincingly, perhaps, as the place of articulation predictions above.

Taking these facts together, the UGH for coda acquisition must predict that coronals (/t d s z ʃ ʒ ʧ ʤ θ ð n l r/) would be produced by children more than non-coronals and that sonorant codas (/m n ŋ l r/) more than obstruents. A little weeding out needs to be done with this list, however, since affricates, for example, would not be expected to occur in young children's inventories because of the articulatory difficulties inherent in their pronunciation. Other sounds have inherent difficulties and might also be expected to be excluded. For example, although Zamuner does not exclude this sound, it would be unlikely to find /r/ even, as we can witness from children acquiring rhotic dialects, such as American-English. However, this sound is included in the list. The simplified version of this prediction is that children can be expected to produce coronal codas (t d s z n l r) and sonorants (m n ŋ l r) more than obstruents. It might be possible to collapse these two strands of the hypothesis by suggesting that the most favoured coda might be a sonorant coronal /n/ (although it could be suggested that both /l/ and /r/ would also qualify, being even more sonorous). On the other hand, we know that voiceless codas seem to be preferred over voiced (see the languages mentioned in Chapters 1 and 2) so, Zamuner argues, we would have to suggest that something like /n̥/ would be the most likely. This, of course, would be extremely unlikely since voiceless sonorants are highly marked and few languages include them in their basic inventory.

In her investigation of frequency of codas in monosyllabic words of English, Zamuner compiled results from four databases: two dictionaries, Random House and Webster, and two databases containing tokens from child-directed speech.

Over the four databases, both adult and child, in the ten most frequent codas are /t d l n k m r s/ and within the least frequent are /b ŋ ʤ ð ʒ/. The input data chosen as the base for the predictions is based on token counts from CDSC (Child Directed Speech Corpus), which provides the closest approximation to children's input between ages nineteen months and twenty-eight months and token frequency has been shown to predict acquisition more accurately than type frequency. The language specific patterns that emerge in order of frequency from this particular corpus are as shown in (5.3):

(5.3) t > r > n > d > z > k > s > l > m > v > ʃ > g > o > θ > ŋ > ʧ > f > ʤ > b > ʒ ð

Therefore, the SLGH for coda acquisition will be that children produce the same ranking for codas in word-final position, and to some extent, the prediction of the SLGH is similar to that of the UGH, that is to say that coronals rank highly under both hypotheses and, in particular sonorant /n/ and /r/. Not all the predictions are the same, however, since /k/ has a high frequency in English, in spite of the fact that it is neither coronal nor sonorant.

The predictions of the two hypotheses are, however, somewhat different. The UGH makes general predictions about coronals and sonorants, while the SLGH specifically picks out the hierarchy above, making the prediction that the most frequent codas in the child data will have the same ranking.

In order to test her hypothesis, Zamuner obtained data from three different sources. Her rankings shown in (5.4) come from (a) number of published studies (b) from the CHILDES database (MacWhinney 1995) and (c) from an experiment conducted by the author. The first two were considered in what was termed an 'independent analysis', which counted codas initially produced, regardless of their faithfulness to the adult target. One particular point of note here is that the /k/ appears to rank relatively highly in the frequency list, although not, in general as high as the coronal /t/ or /n/ in either (a) or (c). Then they were subjected to a relational analysis where codas were produced accurately. Zamuner's own experiment involved the use of images on a screen.

(5.4) a. t > n > k > d, m > ʔ > p > ʧ, l > b, f, F, ŋ, r, s
b. k > t > n > d, s > b, f, l, ŋ, p, r, z
c. r > ʃ > t, n, k > p > n > θ > v > ŋ, g

These findings, according to Zamuner, seem to point to the SLGH. However, it could be suggested that there are some problems, both with the methodology and with the conclusions.

For the most part, the overall ranking from the three sources appears to be fairly similar, in particular with respect to /t, n, k/, but the exception is the presence of /r/ and /ʃ/ in (c). It will be noted that /ʃ/ does not appear at all in (a) or (b) and that /r/ is relatively low in both of these. There are two possible interpretations that could be placed on this finding. The first is that the nature of the items used in the experiment might have had the effect of skewing the results – Zamuner does comment that the study was based on single word types and the results leading to the ranking of /r/ may well have been influenced by the fact that the word *bear* was the testing item; she suggests that if the words had been more varied, the result could well have been different. The second possible explanation could have to do with the transcription. As we have seen, /r/ is a sound that is mastered very late by most children, whether they are acquiring English or most other languages. Substitutions are made for initial /r/ and English final /r/ is generally not produced at very at an early stage. It is, indeed, very improbable that /r/ truly occurs in the coda at all even in dialects such as that being acquired by Zamuner's subjects. It has been suggested on the basis of distribution that the /r/ is part of a rhoticised vowel in the adult language (see Ladefoged 2001; Harris 1994; Green 2001). We have to ask whether, in fact, this /r/ was produced or whether it occurred as a corresponding [ə] with which it shares acoustic properties.

Another flaw in the methodology was that stimuli were not controlled for the influence of surrounding consonants, so Zamuner subsequently considered such an influence on certain misarticulated codas.

(5.5) [tʌk] *cup*
[bæf] *bath* (twice)

She suggests that these may be due to the presence of a sound sharing the same place of articulation in the word (type of harmony). This may possibly be the explanation for the first of these, but target /θ/ is highly likely to be produced as [f] and we have no evidence of what the response would have been had a stimulus with a different initial consonant (for example *cloth*) been used instead. Thus, the conclusion that high probability and frequency predict early coda production, while reasonable as a hypothesis, does not seem to have been proven. We return to the role of frequency in the next section.

5.4 Frequency effects in the ambient language

The question we asked in the previous chapter was what role is played by the innate knowledge of language that is assumed by phonological theories. In search for an answer, we examined behavioural and brain studies of early perception. Having seen how sounds present and not present in the native language shape the perceptual system of the infant, we saw that speech perception is, indeed, crucial for word learning. Apart from the brain study that observed structural and functional similarities between human infants and adults, as well as between human infants and non-human adults to a certain extent, but a difference between non-human infants and the others (humans and non-human adults), we found no concrete evidence for speech perception abilities exhibited by infants to be specific to language or humans, which led us to question whether there is any need to assume any innate abilities assumed by phonological theory. Hence, we examined non-linguistic approaches to acquisition in this chapter. Now that we have seen how infants make use of statistically tractable distribution of elements in their language environment, there is no way of denying the magnitude of influence of the language environment on the infant learner. However, the question that we need to ask further is how large a role does language experience play in phonological development. Is it the case that mere exposure to the ambient language is all that it takes for an infant to acquire language? Can we equate language acquisition with the computation of the distributional facts of the native language by applying various non-domain-specific learning mechanisms?

While it seems that infants are incredibly sensitive to quantitative information in the input language, which influences them in a way that such experience contributes to changes in the linguistic system, the main problem with non-linguistic accounts is that whether it is statistical learning, algebraic learning, connectionist approach, or even computer modelling, they are all based on occurrence frequency of various linguistic units and patterns in the input, and anything that cannot be accounted for in terms of the input will have to attributed to other extra-linguistic factors, such as physiological constraints or poor motor control. Since language learning is based purely on experience, patterns that emerge in children must be attributed to the distributional properties of the input, which can be equated with occurrence frequency. Since various studies have shown that children acquiring different languages do differ in the same way as the world's languages differ from one another, what problems are associated with a frequency-based approach to acquisition?

Probably the most discussed challenge for experience-based models is the U-shaped curve of learning, which is also known as over-regularisation, commonly demonstrated using the example of the English regular vs irregular past tense morphology of the verb 'to go'. It is commonly observed among English-speaking children that when they acquire the concept of past tense, they often start out with producing the correct irregular form, *went*, but go through a period of over-regularising it as *goed* before *went* becomes stable (development takes the shape of 'U'). In phonology, what is often cited is the single case of Hildegard's *pretty* initially produced just like the adult form, but became [pɪtɪ] at one point (Leopold 1947). However, Poole

(1934) also reports this phenomenon for the acquisition of /s/. He observed that /s, z/, produced accurately by the group of children aged 5;6, disappeared in older children, and reappeared again at the age of 7;6. While over-regularisation errors never predominate, if occurrence frequency is provided as the reason why child production forms differ from adult forms, it is problematic to explain any observation of a correct form preceding the form that is in accordance with the regularities within that language. It has been suggested for English morphology that since irregular patterns are stored in an associative memory while regulars are not, over-regularisation occurs whenever children's memory traces are not strong enough and retrieval fails, thus resulting in the past tense affixation rule applying to the irregular verb stem (Marcus et al. 1992). Although it could perhaps be argued for Hildegard's initial form to involve imitation, the argument along the line used for morphology cannot be applied plausibly for Poole's observation, since the sibilants that underwent the U-shaped learning are neither the most nor least frequent consonants in English.

Another problem for explaining child patterns in terms of occurrence frequency lies in the difficulty of identifying what is frequent in the input. We can easily imagine that working out language-specific frequencies is not as simple as counting how many times a particular unit of speech appears among all the words found in that language. For example, while /ð/ is one of the most frequent fricatives in English due to its high occurrence frequency in words such as *the*, *then*, *that*, *they*, *there*, and so on, it is very rarely found in the early segmental inventory of English-acquiring children (for example Hodson & Paden 1981). Naturally, this is because segments seldom appear on their own and frequency needs to be accessed by taking the environment into consideration. One good example of a contextual analysis was presented in the previous section.

A further problem for frequency-based approaches is found in its inadequacy in explaining the observed cross-linguistic patterns, since their explanation is limited to the language to which the learner is exposed. We can take the unmarked place of articulation as an example. Maddieson (1984) provides the following (5.6) figures for stops and nasals based on cross-linguistic occurrence frequency:

(5.6)	*Stop consonants*	*Nasal consonants*
	99.7% coronal	99.7% coronal
	99.4% dorsal	94.3% labial
	99.1% labial	53.0% dorsal

As is apparent from the figures in (5.6), there is a cross-linguistic tendency for coronal to be the most frequently occurring place of articulation, which is consistent with the claim that coronal is the universally unmarked place of articulation (e.g. Paradis & Prunet 1991) and, more specifically, that for languages which allow only a single nasal segment in the coda position, this is most often the coronal nasal for example in Japanese and Gilbertese (Blevins 2004). However, there is little agreement among phonologists on the unmarked place of articulation across languages. For example, the unmarked place has been claimed to be coronal for Spanish, labial for Japanese, dorsal for Swedish, and for English, all three places have been claimed as the unmarked place (Hume 2003).

This situation seems to hold for child languages as well. While it has been suggested that any place of articulation may surface as unmarked in consonant harmony, we showed in Chapter 2 that cross-linguistic child data appear to give coronal a special status, since consonant harmony in children tend to target coronals. We also showed in Chapter 2 that children have a tendency to front velars to produce coronals in their place, but we cannot ignore the fact that children acquiring languages such as Japanese, in which dorsal consonants are more frequent than English, tend rather to back consonants instead (Yoneyama et al. 2003). Indeed, this may seem to fit well with the prediction by frequency-based approaches to acquisition that child languages differ to the extent that adult languages differ. However, there is no way of accounting for cross-linguistic tendencies, unless the reason behind such observations can be based on what is more or less natural for human speech production, such as ease of articulation. In the case of the observation on coronals, although one could in fact argue against the unmarked state of coronals in terms of aerodynamics, since tongue tip gestures in coronals are faster than tongue dorsum gestures in dorsals and lip gestures in labials, which gives rise to higher velocity (= energy) of articulation for coronals, there is no compelling reason why any one of the three places of articulation should be articulatorily more complex than another (Jun 1995). Thus, the difficulty for frequency accounts is that without phonetic grounding, since any asymmetry between the different places of articulation will have to be based on observations of their behaviour in other domains, such as phonological processes.

Perhaps the most serious problem with accounting for child patterns based on occurrence frequency is that we do not know what the infant uses as the perceptual unit for linguistic analyses: phones, syllables, words, or even phrases. One way to view development is that analytical abilities are used for computing frequency patterns in order to acquire the phonetic categories that are specific to the ambient language, which then develop into the language-specific phonemic inventory used in lexical representations. Thus, infants must acquire phonetics, before they can segment and then later build words. However, based on a study that showed that newborns are better at discriminating CVCs than CCCs (Bertoncini & Mehler 1981) and that they are sensitive to the number of syllables, but not to the number of phonetic segments (Bijeljac-Babic et al. 1993), it has been suggested that infants do not have a detailed representation of speech sounds. In a study by Jusczyk and colleagues (1999a) 9-month-old infants were made to listen to nonsense words of monosyllabic CVCs and showed sensitivity (longer listening time) to words with the same onset than those with the same rhyme. Their conclusion was that infants are more sensitive to the onset than other constituents of the syllable. While this finding was confirmed by Goodman and co-workers (2000) who tested older infants and reported that both 9- and 18-month-old infants respond better to prefixes than suffixes, the saliency of the word-final position for language-learning has also been suggested by Slobin (1973) and Echols and Newport (1992). More recently, Swingley (2008) tested the knowledge of onset and coda consonants in 14–22-month-old infants and found that 1½-year-olds have accurate encoding of consonants in both syllabic positions even in words they cannot yet produce.

Thus, although we can be certain that frequency effects play an important role in acquisition, without a general consensus as to what linguistic unit is used in perception by infants, it is extremely difficult to see to what extent occurrence frequency can account for child language. Consequently, in addition to language learning accounts based on distributional analyses and occurrence frequency not being able to explain how these are linked to the acquisition of phonemes that are used for encoding word in memory, they would predict all children acquiring the same language to exhibit more similarity in production than they do. For example, while the development of syllable structure in Dutch-acquiring children seems to follow frequency patterns (Levelt et al. 2000), regarding the acquisition of /s/-obstruent vs obstruent-sonorant clusters by Dutch children, it turns out that some children start by producing the less frequent /s/-obstruent clusters (Fikkert 2007). Hence, it appears that it is not only occurrence frequency and physiological constraints that are influencing variation in child production.

Stites and co-workers (2004) investigated the possibility that variation in production will be increased for phenomena that are highly frequent across the world's languages, the unmarked, but are of low frequently within the ambient language. They fully acknowledged that occurrence frequency in the ambient language plays a considerable role in acquisition. For example, they claimed that English-acquiring children tend to produce coda clusters before onset clusters (Kirk & Demuth 2003) is due to their high occurrence frequency over onset clusters and that English-acquiring children produce coda consonants before Spanish-acquiring children learn to do so, since coda consonants occur in 25 per cent of syllables in Spanish, but 60 per cent in English. However, since many child language phenomena within various languages tend to coincide with cross-linguistic tendencies, for which they predict more efficiency and less variation, the subject matter of their investigation was stop consonants in the coda position in English, which is highly frequent within the language, but cross-linguistically most marked.

The input to the child data was drawn from two sources of child-directed speech (adult speech samples spoken to children between 0;11.25–5;1.6) and compared with child production data which consisted of 284,976 words from three children in CHILDES database (MacWhinney 1995) and 136,214 words from additional two children between the ages of one and two years (own corpora). There were 184,220 words with singleton codas in word-final stressed syllables with the distribution in (5.7), in approximate percentage.

(5.7)	affricates	0.95
	liquids	18.65
	nasals	16.30
	fricatives	20.78
	stops	43.31

The liquids, /l/ and /r/, were excluded from consideration, because children rarely acquire these accurately at this early stage and also, /r/ could not be expected as the children in the study are from non-rhotic Massachusetts and Rhode Island. Also, affricates were excluded due to its very low occurrence frequency in the input. Since they found that certain segments were produced in the onset, but not in the coda when the two children's onset consonant production was compared with that of the coda, physiological or motor control constraints could be excluded. During the study period, the girl subject N targeted 1,115 codas (including twenty-two plural morphemes) and the boy subject W targeted 629 (including twelve plurals and a copula). Since Child N from 1;2.3 targeted 80 per cent of stops, at 1;3.7 nasals started to appear but were not 80 per cent accurate until two months later, and fricatives were 80 per cent accurate at 1;2.12, she was considered to have a preference for frequency over markedness. Child W, on the other hand, increased his production of nasals and fricatives during the first three sessions, which showed a consistent 80 per cent accuracy, but produced stops with more variation, and was therefore considered to prefer markedness over frequency. In fact, Zamuner (2003) also investigated these two strategies and also found that children acquiring the same language differ in which strategy they adopt.

While experience-based models of phonological acquisition deny any role to innateness in the child learner, approaches assuming that markedness plays a role, however small it may be, have never denied the influence of the ambient language on child patterns since it is thought that the input triggers the default settings to be set or re-set. As we saw how experience-based learning alone cannot account for the observed strategies utilised by children acquiring the same language where cross-linguistic tendencies seem to play a role, we will examine linguistic models that take ambient language influence into consideration. But before that, since we can now acknowledge the impact of the linguistic input on child patterns, we will briefly examine to what extent children are affected by adult speech directed at them.

5.5 Sources of input

We have been considering the way in which children might acquire language through exposure to the ambient language, where frequency in the input may be considered to play a significant part. In this section, we shall return to other aspects of the input that must play an important part in enabling the infant to extract the necessary information from the input in order to aid his or her progress to the acquisition of phonology.

Earlier in our discussion, we pointed out that other factors than mere exposure to language were important in helping the learner to establish a phonological system. The two aspects, in particular, that were highlighted were the role of motherese or, as it is frequently referred to as infant-directed speech (IDS), and the importance of visual cues to aid acquisition.

You will recall from Chapter 4 that Chomsky has argued that humans must be innately programmed to acquire language, at least having innate knowledge of universal phonetics and universal grammar since the child's task is to decode the incoming signal and to identify the patterns in it and that that signal is imperfect – this argument is known as 'poverty of the stimulus'. This argument is not perhaps as cogent as might at first be supposed. For one thing, as we shall see, the stimulus is considerably richer than Chomsky claimed and for another, the child, as he or she develops over the first year of life, has ample exposure to the ambient language.

Whichever theory regarding the processes involved in moulding the learner's mind to the patterns of the ambient language, the child's task is made considerably easier by the nature of the input. The observation has been made that the type of speech addressed to infants differs significantly from that addressed to adults.

The importance of child-directed speech has been emphasised time and again. Children are not exposed to the same input as adults. Child-directed speech, infant-directed speech (IDS), or motherese (these terms will be used interchangeably as we progress), is used by adults and older children when addressing infants. It differs in many ways from adult-directed speech: the prosodic structure involves higher pitch, slower tempo and exaggerated intonational contours, while the semantic and syntactic structure are simplified. A test of child-directed speech from the US, Russia and Sweden found that although these are very different languages, all exhibited a stretching of the acoustic space relative to adult-directed speech. A stretched vowel triangle makes speech easier to discriminate for infants (Kuhl et al. 1997).

Fernald (1985) suggested that the intonation pattern of motherese attracts the infant's attention in a way in which the more modulated patterns of adult-directed speech does not. She observed that, in samples tested acoustically, the F_0 range for IDS was considerably greater than for adult-directed speech, the former being in the range 90–800Hz and the latter 90–300Hz. Fernald and Kuhl (1987) performed three experiments on 4-month-old infants using synthesised auditory stimuli in order to test three different potential features that differ between IDS and adult direct speech, fundamental frequency modulation (pitch), amplitude modulation (loudness) and duration. The results of the three head-turning experiments indicated that it was only the pitch variation that had any significance for the subjects.

In English, of course, the pitch pattern does not have any lexical or grammatical implications, unlike tone languages such as Mandarin and Thai. Given the frequency enhancement inherent in IDS, there must be a question as to whether these patterns override and obscure the lexical tones of these languages or whether such tones are obscured. Mattock and Burnham (2006) report that, although perhaps not so clearly identifiable as in adult-directed speech, they still remain identifiable in IDS, which implies that tone perception may well not be affected by the pitch patterns of IDS.

Similarly, Fais et al. (in press) discovered that IDS does not obscure the vowel devoicing that occurs in adult Japanese, giving the impression of surface consonant clusters. They found that adults continue to devoice in IDS at more or less the same rate as in adult directed speech. This, they suggest, makes adult language accessible to learners and aids their development of the feature. Thus, the purpose of IDS seems, not only to be to aid perception but also allows the infant to access features of the language to aid their production.

The other source of input which helps to enhance the infant's acquisitional abilities is found in what are what we referred to above as 'visual cues'. As we mentioned there, experiments by McGurk and MacDonald (1976) showed that being able to read the speaker's lips greatly enhances the listener's understanding. Their experiment with adult subjects was briefly described but this type of effect can be found in infants.

Child psychologists, concerned about that speech of young nursery school children have commented on the effect that the outward facing buggy may have on speech development. The observation is that, when babies were wheeled in upright prams facing the pusher they would receive continual face-to-face language input. If the child is facing the world instead of the pusher, the story goes, then a valuable source of phonological enhancement is lost.

One example of the influence of the visual cue is provided by Yildiz (2006) based on a study of Turkish children and adults learning English. The main purpose of the study was to study age effects on learners and the subjects were divided into four groups, children beginners aged 4–6 years, children intermediate learners aged 7–8 and two groups of university students of beginner and intermediate level. The /r/ of Turkish is a trill and, in common with acquirers of many such languages, the normal substitution form in acquisition is

[j]. The interesting finding, however, is that the youngest age group only, when attempting repetition tasks for English tended to substitute [w], in much the same way as we discovered with Gitanjali and Julia in Chapter 2. It was clear that the children had detected the labiality in the English approximant. It was particularly significant that they were inclined, in particular, to produce this result when they were being presented with a model in the form of the researcher pronouncing the sound. Yildiz suggests that the reason for this substitution was that the children were picking up on the visual cue of lip rounding, which is the most salient feature of this particular sound.

Clearly, however, while visual cues must play an important part in aiding the child to recognise and reproduce sounds, we have to be cautious about the extent to which such overt patterns influence the transcriber. It may be that children are also targeting the lingual gesture but that the transcriber only picks up on the labiality. Not all children target this particular aspect of the /r/ and it is well to be cautious when making claims about the child's analysis.

The perspectives presented in this chapter have not attributed any active processes to the learner. In the next two chapters, we will look at how phonologists have attempted to explain the processes applied by the child.

6

TOWARDS PRODUCTION

While we saw how large a role is played by the ambient language in the previous chapter, we also saw that frequency-based explanations alone cannot account for child patterns observed within a child, among children acquiring the same language or across the world's child languages. It was thus suggested that, never forgetting that the role played by the grammar is much smaller than assumed hitherto, we need to refer to linguistic concepts to explain phonological acquisition. On the other hand, most (of the earlier) grammatical accounts of phonological acquisition in the literature treat perception as a cognitive process that is somehow already well-developed and completely separate from the production grammar. As an obvious consequence, phonological models of acquisition tend to disregard perception and focus on how to account for the discrepancy between adult and child production forms.

Over the recent years, however, the role played by the ambient language through perception has been acknowledged adequately, so that there is no longer any disagreement between researchers studying language acquisition from any viewpoint that development takes place in perception as well as production and that these are not processes that are totally independent of each other. Infant perceptual development towards language-specific phonology is thus viewed as a stage of phonological development that feeds into the production grammar. Since phonology operates between the mental representation of words associated with meaning and their manifestation (speech), an assumption about the mental representation acquired from the input is imperative. Therefore, we can assert the importance of phonological grammar models in accommodating the link between perception and production, which is the topic of this chapter.

6.1 Relating the input to the child output

The perception-production link would be simple if it were the case that children only possess the mental representation of words they can understand and produce. But we all know that children are capable of comprehending many more words than those they can produce more or less accurately. The ability to perceive phonetic differences is not the same as the ability to perceive phonological contrasts, as we saw in Chapter 4, where newborn infants were perceptually capable of distinguishing almost any speech contrast in the languages of the world. However, since the experiments were not specifically designed to investigate the infants' ability to perceive phonemes, the semantically vacuous contrasts were not phonological. Language is not an arbitrary system. As phrases and sentences are composed of words that surface according to language-specific rules on their order and/or structure, words are composed of speech sounds that also surface in accordance with language-specific rules. It is the knowledge of these grammatical rules, the link between form and meaning, that the native speakers of a language have in common and that the learner needs to acquire.

A large set of words uttered by adults (or older children) is naturally available in the linguistic environment to serve as the input to the learner's grammar. It is from this superset that the learner acquires lexical items that are thought to have some form of mental representation. The learning of new words in terms of phonology is: when a connection gets established in the child's long term memory between a word and its meaning, it is the phonetic adult surface representation (SR) that creates the new lexical entry and becomes encoded with phonological or underlying representation (UR) for storage. While comprehension involves a mapping from the adult SR to the child UR, in word production it is the other way around; the learner needs to retrieve the UR of the word in order for it to surface through the child's mouth as SR, which obviously tends to exhibit deviance from the adult SR the younger the child is. Figure 6.1 illustrates the phonological path from the input to the output in the child. It is between the level of UR and SR in the child that we see child phonology in action at various developmental stages.

$$[\text{Adult SR}]_{\text{INPUT}} \longrightarrow /\text{Child UR}/ \longrightarrow [\text{Child SR}]_{\text{OUTPUT}}$$

Figure 6.1 *The phonological path from the input to the output in the child.*

/Child UR/
↙ ↖
[Child SR] [Adult SR]

Figure 6.2 *The adult SR is also accurately reflected in the child UR.*

The two types of SRs in Figure 6.1, one produced by the adult and the other by the child, reflect what is observable in terms of raw production data. Yet what goes on between these two SRs, designated as the child UR, is not at all straightforward to access. In fact, not much is known about the lexicon, in spite of it being studied using language data, behavioural experiments, computer simulation, and mathematical modelling, stretching across a number of disciplines in cognitive science, such as phonology, speech science or phonetics, computational linguistics, and psycholinguistics. Nevertheless, some assumption of the child UR is necessary, since what the learner acquires through linguistic exposure is the UR that is manifested in production. In view of the fact that children show accurate comprehension of words they know, it would be reasonable to assume that the adult SR is also accurately reflected in the child UR. The question is then whether the child uses the same UR for production and comprehension, like adults do and as shown in Figure 6.2.

The assumption that the same UR is used in production and comprehension by the child implies that simplification strategies only apply in production and that no transformation goes on between the adult SR and the child UR in comprehension. On the one hand, this could be justified by the fact that comprehension precedes production in development. On the other hand, the assumption of the child UR in Figure 6.2 further implies that (in theory) the child is using one grammar for comprehension and another for production, which poses a problem for a theory of the phonological grammar. The explanatory burden of phonological theory is on the mapping between UR and SR. The mapping between UR and SR in the adult is accounted for with a set of assumptions about the UR, which is formulated as one (adult) grammar, and the discrepancy between SRs in the adult and the child is explained as another (child) grammar that is based on another set of assumptions. In other words, one grammar can only account for one set of UR. Since accurate comprehension means that adult SR can be equated with child UR, child UR differs from adult UR only as much as adult SR differs from its UR, explainable with an adult grammar. This means that there are two grammars at work in Figure 6.2: In addition to the adult-like grammar accounting

/Child UR/$_{\text{PRODUCTION}}$	/Child UR/$_{\text{COMPREHENSION}}$
↓	↑
[Child SR]	[Adult SR]

Figure 6.3 *Two sets of UR?*

for child UR being accessed through adult SR in comprehension, it is necessary to posit a child grammar to account for the greater degree of divergence between child UR and child SR in production than in comprehension (between adult SR and child UR). Hence, the problem is in justifying how two grammatical accounts can be given with only one set of URs, which leads to the question: Could it be that the learner has two sets of URs, one for comprehension that is equivalent to the adult SR and another, perhaps an impoverished one, for production, as in Figure 6.3?

Whether the same child UR is used for both production and comprehension, as in Figure 6.2 or there are two sets of UR, as in Figure 6.3, we need to examine the plausibility of the assumption of the input to the child's grammar before we can contemplate the child UR. The evidence that we saw in Chapter 4 for the infant perceptual capacity to start tuning in to the language-specific phonemic system before the appearance of first words may give us good reason to equate adult SR with child UR in comprehension. However, since the above figures do not substantiate an accurate phonological mapping between the input and the child UR, we will now take a brief look at concrete claims of child UR being acquired accurately from adult SR in the input.

6.2 Assumptions about the input

The most cited evidence for the accuracy of the input to the child's grammar is an incident reported by Berko and Brown (1960), which has come to be known as the 'fis phenomenon'. It is referred to as demonstrating the phonemic accuracy in perception that is lost in production, since a child producing [fɪs] for an inflatable plastic fish being asked '*Is this your fish* [fɪs]?' answered in the negative and agreed '*Yes, my* [fɪs]' only when the question asked was '*Is this your fish* [fɪʃ]?' One of the first phonological accounts to assume the accuracy of the child input is Smith (1973), whose analysis is based on generative phonology. The input to the child's forms was taken to be the adult SR, which is stored in the lexicon and undergoes the application of a series ordered rules in production. Smith's claim for an accurate child UR is based on two observations. First, not only

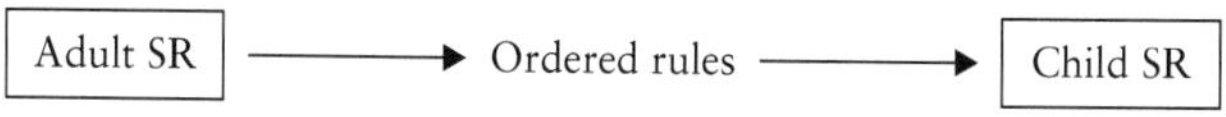

Figure 6.4 *Smith's 1973 model.*

did Amahl's comprehension far outstrip his production, but also, there was an incident that was similar to the fis phenomenon. When Smith asked Amahl what else is [sɪp] than *sip* at a stage when Amahl was producing this output form for both *sip* and *ship*, Amahl did not show any mapping to *ship*. Second, the accuracy of the child UR is based on the way in which he proposes the child's phonological grammar to be restructured during development: When the child discovers the discrepancy between his or her own SR and that of the adult and as a consequence changes a rule, the change applies to all of the child SRs subject to this rule in an 'across the board' manner, as soon as the rule is established. Thus, Smith (1973) proposed a child phonology model in which the adult SR serves as the child UR, as illustrated in Figure 6.4.

Macken (1980) re-examined what has become known as the 'puzzle-puddle-pickle' phenomenon in Smith's work and identified the problem as being partially misperception. The phenomenon takes the form of a chain shift (see also Dinnsen & McGarrity 2004). Amahl's words in the *puddle* class (words such as *kettle, middle,* etc.) are subject to a velar rule which causes alveolar stops to be manifest as velars when they precede the dark (velar) /l/ (or indeed its vocalised variant). Thus, *puddle* would be pronounced [pʌgl], placing it in the same set as other velar + /l/ words such as *pickle*. However, by a stopping rule, through which fricatives become stops, *puzzle* is rendered as [pʌdl]. The relative ordering is crucial to Smith's system since, were the order to be reversed, or were the rules to be unordered, *puzzle* would be susceptible to the velar rule. We leave aside the problem of the child's system being burdened with more rules than that of the adult and becoming progressively less complex as its phonological system develops in this model, since our focal point is on the assumption of the child's UR. The fact that the *puzzle* words demonstrate that it is not an articulatory difficulty that prevents the *puddle* words from being correctly pronounced would seem to indicate that these puddle words may have been misperceived as *pickle* words.

This point was made by Macken who backed up her argument by noting that the velar rule becomes optional after the stopping rule is deactivated, while there are no *puzzle* forms coming in the ambit of the velar rule in the intervening period. She further pointed out that, while the operation of the stopping rule is exceptionless, there are several lexical exceptions (and even variable pronunciations) (see Macken 1980: 10) in words undergoing the velar rule. Furthermore, at the point when the velar rule becomes optional, words in the *pickle* set are engulfed in the affected set (that is, *puddle* → [pʌdəl]; *pickle* → [pɪtəl]). It was thus suggested that the inconsistent behaviour of the *puddle* set, in contrast to the consistent behaviour of the *puzzle* set might be that the *puddle* words are indeed misperceived, explaining why not all forms are affected.

On the other hand, since all fricatives and affricates were replaced by stops in the child SRs, the invariability of the *puzzle* words could be due to articulatory limitations of the child. This would lead to the conclusion that fricatives are perceived correctly and stored in the child's lexicon in identical form to adult SR, but cannot be produced accurately, whereas the misperceived *puddle* words are stored in his lexicon in the way in which he perceives them, namely as [pʌgəl], hence the exceptions, which may have been correctly perceived. Smith subsequently incorporated a perceptual filter into his model in 1978. This inclusion was prompted by the need to explain cases where no other explanation could be offered beyond misperception. Consequently, Smith's model was modified into child phonological rules applying to the adult SR after passing through a perceptual filter, as illustrated in Figure 6.5.

In spite of the incorporation of a perceptual filter into the model, the UR of the learner is still considered to be much the same as the adult SR in not only Smith's new model, but also in more recent OT accounts of child phonology. While Smolensky's (1996) paper is often referred to as claiming for the accuracy of the child input forms, the first claim for this in OT terms was made by Gnanadesikan (1996) through Gitanjali's use of her dummy syllable [fi-] in words containing more than two syllables (which was demonstrated so comprehensively in Chapter 3 that we do not need to repeat it here).

In summary, if we discount cases of misperception, child production data seem to justify the assumption that the adult SR in the input serves as the child UR, since, in addition to accurate comprehension of the adult SR, they also indicate that they contain details

Figure 6.5 Smith's 1978 model.

of the adult SR that is not always used in production. However, neither Smith nor Gnanadesikan offers any concrete explanation as to how the adult SR is mapped onto the child UR for the obvious reason of their explanatory adequacy being limited to production. In other words, how can the grammar that can account for an accurate mapping between the adult SR and the child UR in comprehension also account for the transformation occurring in the mapping between the child UR (or the adult SR for that matter) and the child SR? Since the reality is that the younger the children, the greater the gap they show between comprehension and production forms, the biggest problem for such phonological models is in formalising how the learner can comprehend words that they cannot say. But as we asked earlier, how are we to know what the child UR is and whether there is only one set of UR all throughout the developmental stages? Indeed, although extremely small in number, there are proposals that attempt to answer these questions. We now turn to discussing models within OT that assume a single set of child URs, as in Figure 6.2, and an alternative approach assuming two sets of child URs, as in Figure 6.3.

6.3 Assumptions about the underlying representation

Within the framework of OT, Smolensky (1996) was the first to propose a model accounting for both production and comprehension in child language. While it is assumed that markedness constraints are contrast-neutralising and faithfulness constraints are contrast-inducing (Davidson et al. 2004: 325), the question is how the contrasts contained in the auditory stimuli can be distinguished in perception if the relevant faithfulness constraints mapping such contrasts are lower ranked than markedness constraints. In other words, with a ranking of Markedness >> Faithfulness, the only way that the infant can distinguish between two similar speech tokens in perception is through other channels than those provided by the grammar, since the child's grammar is contrast-neutralising.

Acknowledging that infant perceptual capacities reflect fairly accurate comprehension, thus ranking Faithfulness highly, but that the inaccurate production reflects the reverse, Smolensky (1996) argues that what distinguishes production from comprehension is that structures sharing the same underlying form compete in production and structures sharing the same surface form compete in comprehension. For instance, taking a child producing *cat* as [ta], the grammar must rank the markedness constraints, NoCoda disallowing closed syllables and *Dors disallowing segments to have the feature [dorsal], higher than Faithfulness, as shown in the simplified version of Smolensky's original tableau (Tableau 6.1).

Tableau 6.1 Production grammar

Candidates		Grammar	
Input	Surface form	Markedness	Faithfulness
☞ /kæt/	[ta]		*
/kæt/	[kæt]	*!	

In comprehension, the child uses the same grammar to analyse [kæt] as /kæt/ where the decision of the winning candidate is left to the relevant faithfulness constraints, as shown in (Tableau 6.2), where '→' indicates the winning candidate and '¡*' a fatal violation.

Tableau 6.2 Comprehension grammar

Candidates		Grammar	
Input	Surface form	Markedness	Faithfulness
→ /kæt/	[kæt]	*	
/skæti/	[kæt]	*	¡*

Smolensky's single grammar model combines production, (Tableau 6.1), and comprehension, (Tableau 6.2), into Tableau 6.3, in which both the underlying form candidates and the surface form candidates are generated by the grammar, thus accounting for highly unfaithful output forms and relatively faithful input forms in child language.

Tableau 6.3 Production and comprehension grammar

Candidates		Grammar		Functions	
Input	Surface form	Markedness	Faithfulness	Production	Comprehension
/kæt/	[ta]		*	☜	
/kæt/	[kæt]	*!			←
/skæti/	[kæt]	*	¡*		

Although the single grammar model outlined above is capable of reflecting the fact that comprehension is a prerequisite to production, what is most problematic in Tableau 6.3 is that not only is it assumed that the initial state ranking is still maintained by the child at the onset of production, but also, since faithfulness constraints alone decide the winning candidate in comprehension, the mapping between the perceived surface forms and their underlying representations is guaranteed to always be perfectly faithful (Hale & Reiss 1998; Pater 2004). Taking the production side first, the MARKEDNESS >> FAITHFULNESS ranking in Tableau 6.3 does not technically allow earliest child production to contain any marked forms, even if such forms are of high occurrence frequency or of high phonotactic probability within the language being acquired. However, we have already stipulated that the onset of speech cannot be equated with the initial state of the grammar. As for the perceptual side in Tableau 6.3, it predicts an accurate mapping between adult surface forms and their corresponding underlying representations in the child grammar at all times, since FAITHFULNESS alone determines the choice of the underlying representation for each surface form. While possible misperceptions can never be ruled out in child language (Macken 1980), there is no way for this model to account for cases of misperception, however rare they are, since faithful perception implies that all contrasts are accurately encoded in the underlying forms.

Furthermore, Smolensky's approach runs into problems when a single output form is mapped onto two underlying representations, of which a correct underlying representation will have to violate FAITHFULNESS, as in the case of final devoicing in German and Dutch where /rad/ and /rat/ surface as [rat]. Moreover, Smolensky's model assumes development in comprehension to be completed, since the underlying forms are perfect from the beginning, thus implying that any development which takes place must be external to the grammatical system. This may suggest after all that perception and production should be treated as two separate linguistic subsystems with a set of URs in each system. Pater (2004), on the other hand, argues against this separation by claiming that early perception is similar to later development in production and proposes an alternative single grammar model in which perception-specific FAITHFULNESS is employed to account for perceptual development.

Pater (2004) draws on numerous experimental studies exhibiting parallelism between perception and production in order to justify the same set of constraints applying to both domains, but with a time lag between them. First of all, to account for the presence of the accurate contrasts in underlying representations, which are lost in production, faithfulness constraints are indexed to the two domains (perception and production) with relevant markedness constraint(s) ranked between them. Although the same markedness constraints apply in production and perception, faithfulness constraints are specified as FAITH(LS) applying to the Lexical-to-Surface (child UR to child SR) mapping in production or FAITH(SL) applying to the Surface-to-Lexical (adult SR to child UR) mapping in perception.

The notion of domain-specific FAITHFULNESS is based on 'non-uniformity' of constraint application (Prince 1993, cited in Pater 2004) which is a phenomenon of a higher ranked constraint being violated under certain circumstances. Non-uniformity is like a mirror image of the emergence of the unmarked: while it is the generally violated markedness constraint which can sometimes be obeyed in the emergence of the unmarked, it is the generally obeyed constraint which is sometimes violated in non-uniformity. In order to maintain the highly ranked position of MARKEDNESS in child language, the only way for MARKEDNESS to be violated in child language in perception is to posit production-specific and perception-specific faithfulness constraints through non-uniformity. This is demonstrated in Pater 2004 using a truncation example of the American-English word *garage*, which is comprehended as [gəráʒ], but produced as [gáʒ] by Trevor (Pater 1997). The relevant constraints are given in (6.1).

(6.1)	WORDSIZE	A word is made up of a single trochee
	MAX(LS)	If the input is a lexical form, every segment of the input has a correspondent in the output
	MAX(SL)	If the input is a surface form, every segment of the input has a correspondent in the output

The markedness constraint WORDSIZE is based on the data of English- and Dutch-acquiring children who delete unstressed initial syllables in disyllabic words, but produce initially stressed disyllables accurately, and on an interpretation of a perceptual study of 7½- and 10-month-old infants, by Jusczyk and colleagues (1999b) that trochees are acquired before iambs. Consequently, it is assumed that words are limited to a single trochaic foot in comprehension and production. The faithfulness constraint MAX(SL) evaluates underlying or lexical representations, which are labelled with 'L', and prohibits any deletions between what is perceived and its lexical representation. Production-specific faithfulness constraint MAX(LS) evaluates perceived surface forms, labelled with 'S', and prohibits any deletions to occur between the lexical representation and its corresponding surface form in production. The interaction of these three constraints in the domains of perception and production in child as well as adult languages is illustrated in Tableau 6.4.

Tableau 6.4

Child language		MAX(SL)	WORDSIZE	MAX(LS)
Perception	L_1 $[[gáʤ]_{Ft}]_{PrWd}$	**!		
	☞ L_2 $[gə[ráʤ]_{Ft}]_{PrWd}$		*	
Production	☞ S_1 $[[gáʤ]_{Ft}]_{PrWd}$			**
	S_2 $[gə[ráʤ]_{Ft}]_{PrWd}$		*!	
Adult language		MAX(SL)	MAX(LS)	WORDSIZE
Perception	L_1 $[[gáʤ]_{Ft}]_{PrWd}$	**!		
	☞ L_2 $[gə[ráʤ]_{Ft}]_{PrWd}$			*
Production	S_1 $[[gáʤ]_{Ft}]_{PrWd}$		**!	
	☞ S_2 $[gə[ráʤ]_{Ft}]_{PrWd}$			*

The top half of Tableau 6.4 shows that in child language, segmental complexity is reduced in production but maintained in perception and the bottom half shows the accurate production and perception in the adult grammar as a comparison. The difference between the child and adult grammars is the ranking of the constraints. Although Pater's model is based on Smolensky's model, the crucial improvement is that FAITHFULNESS distinguishes between different representations. By taking into account child language research suggesting impoverished early lexical representations and phonetically rich perception of such representations by the child, whose task in acquisition is the lexical encoding of complexity followed by development in production, Pater posits four levels of representations that are claimed to be elaborated during the course of development, with three types of mapping between them, as shown in Figure 6.6.

The first level of acoustic representation is supposedly free from any ambient language influence and characterised by the perceptual ability to distinguish any phonetic detail of the world's languages in infants before the age of six months. The second level is reached after adequate exposure to the ambient language triggering language-specific perception and characterised by the ability to perceive the adult SR. Only when the adult SRs are paired with their meaning can

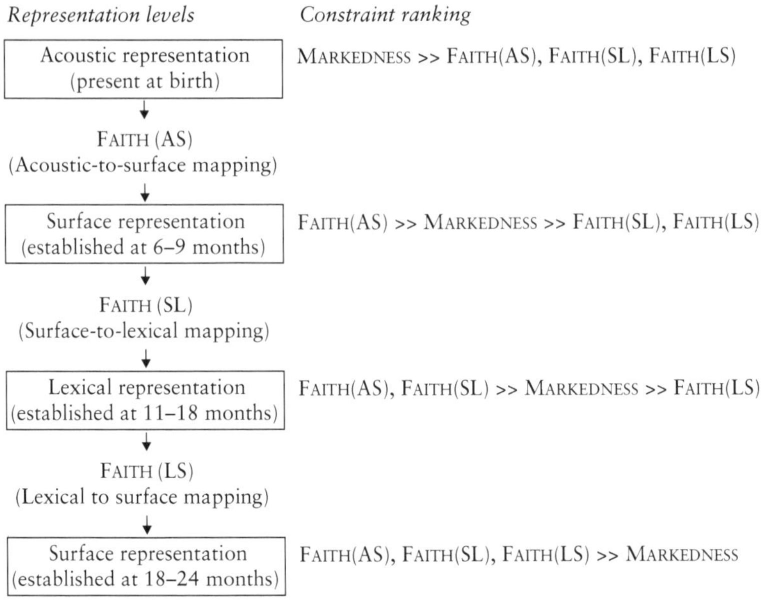

Figure 6.6 *Pater's four levels of representations.*

the third level of lexical representation be elaborated where the child UR appears, and the final level of surface representation is reached when the learner can maintain lexical contrasts in production.

The four developmental stages, mirrored as four constraint rankings on the right side in Figure 6.6, depict what is generally assumed regarding the relationship between perception and production in language acquisition: perception, which precedes production and which is initially based on phonetics, gets tuned into the phonological system of the target language, where the broad picture of phonological development is the internalisation of phonetic values according to the language-specific system of phonological contrasts in the two domains. Thus, Pater's proposal neatly ties together perception and production through the notion of domain-specific Faithfulness which accounts for the child perceiving distinctions that he or she cannot produce. However, since it is only Faithfulness that is domain-specific in order to account for precocious perception relative to production and Markedness does not differentiate surface forms from lexical forms, Pater's (single grammar) model faces a dilemma in accounting for the child who produces unmarked SRs at the same time as marked output forms not coupled with meaning.

Such a case would be DF, a 5-year-old boy studied by Bryan and

Table 6.1 Pre-therapy assessment of DF

Real words			Non-words	
Target	Repetition	Naming	Target	Repetition
pig	[bi]	[bɪn]	/pæg/	[pæg]
soap	[dəʊʔ]	[dəʊʔ]	/sæp/	[sæp]
money	[baɪ]	[maɪs]	/mɒnɪ/	[bɒnɪ]
elephant	[eɪɫ]	[eɪvə]	/ʌlɪfɒnt/	[ʌlɪfɒʔ]
butterfly	[bʌbaɪ]	[bʌfaɪ]	/bɒtəfleɪ/	[bədəfeɪ]

Howard (1992), who exhibited phonological disability in the repetition of real words and picture-naming tasks, but was able to repeat non-words with reasonable accuracy. Although DF had a delay in the acquisition of vocabulary for comprehension in addition to his phonological disability, he was of normal hearing and other aspects of his development were within normal limits. Since DF was able to match spoken words with their correct pictures, there was no evidence of perceptual impairment. What is noteworthy is that DF was able to produce non-words, not only with reasonable segmental accuracy, but also with syllabic accuracy, as the examples in Table 6.1 show.

Compared to Smolensky's model, in which the perceptual grammar is equated with the productive grammar, Pater's model seems to provide a better account of the attested gap between production and perception. It also distinguishes between representations that are coupled with meaning and those that are not by making a provision for phonetics in the perceptual grammar. However, the problem is that the constraint ranking for this provision is only seen during the first developmental stage. Thus, Pater's model is able to provide a neat account for DF's perception of real words and his production of disyllabic and trisyllabic real words being reduced to monosyllables and disyllables, respectively, due to the higher ranked markedness constraint, WordSize. However, DF's production of non-words, particularly the syllabic accuracy of di- and trisyllabic non-words is problematic for Pater's model, since the dominant WordSize would prohibit such forms to emerge in production.

Although our investigation is on normal phonological acquisition, it is important to acknowledge that child data from non-disordered phonological cases is not the only source for validating phonological theory and that disordered phonology provides a further insight to the theory by triggering questions that may not have been asked otherwise (see Dinnsen & Gierut 2008, for many more cases of disordered phonology). DF's production of non-words makes Pater's model appear to display an asymmetry in its incorporation of phonetics, since it suggests that a phonetic provision is also needed for production. However, this is not called for by DF's data alone or any other disordered phonology for that matter, since it is not unusual for both children and adults to be able to repeat novel or non-words more or less accurately. Hence, we will now examine the possibility that there are two sets of URs in the child by studying a phonological model that assumes two grammars.

6.4 Two grammars

Following Menn (1983) (see also Menn & Matthei 1992), Spencer (1986) re-analyses Smith's data and proposes a linguistic model incorporating two grammars: one for production and another for comprehension. Although Spencer also assumes the same accuracy in terms of child URs as Smith, his dual lexicon model inevitably assumes two sets of URs in the child, since it is based on autosegmental phonology. By utilising the notion of underspecification, he applies 'realisation rules' between two sets of URs; one for the input, which is more or less an accurate form of the adult SR after passing through the perceptual filter, and the other for the output, to which 'pronunciation rules' are applied before surfacing in production. This is shown in Figure 6.7.

The theory of underspecification assumes that not all feature specifications that make up phonological segments, but only those that are necessary for distinguishing one meaning from another within a phonological system are present. For example, while the phonological system of a language that has two nasal segments, the alveolar /n/ and the labial /m/, needs these to be specified with features [nasal; alveolar] and [nasal; labial], respectively, at the underlying level, a system with the alveolar nasal as the only nasal does not need its phonological system to specify more than the feature [nasal] for it to be distinguishable from other segments. In the same way, since the child

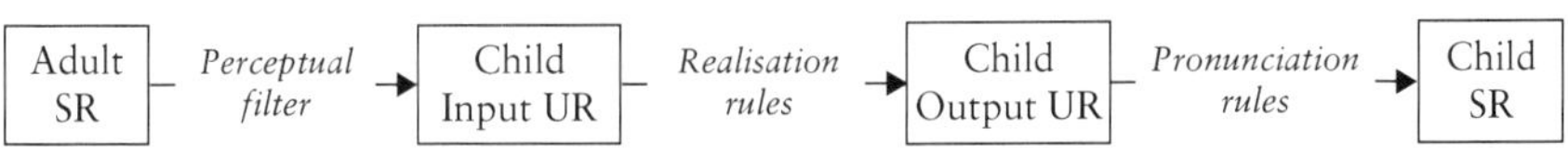

Figure 6.7 Spencer's 1986 model.

SR differs from that of the adult, the child's system of URs is considered to be less specified than the underspecified adult system. For comprehension to take place accurately, however, the child UR must be specified more or less in the same way as the adult system. Thus, the varying degree of underspecification necessitates the child input component to be split up into two, the 'Child Input UR' with adult-like specification for comprehension and the 'Child Output UR', the more underspecified for production. The link between the two sets of child URs is realised through processes that de-specify after receiving the input and re-specify after retrieving it for production.

Besides bypassing the aforementioned problem of attributing a more complicated grammar to the child than to the adult, the advantages of assuming two sets of child URs are demonstrated through reanalyses of various cases of consonant harmony and phonological structures, which we will briefly show below. The case of lateral harmony, which causes targets /j, r/ to surface as lateral [l] where there is another token of /l/ in the same word is one of the most persistent processes, both in Amahl's speech and in developmental phonology generally (6.2).

(6.2) *lorry* /lɒri/ → [lɒli]
yellow /jɛlo/ → [lɛlo]

Smith accounts for this by applying Rule 18, by which /l, r, j/ are neutralised to [l] whenever /l, j, r/ are the only consonants in the adult SR. In Spencer's model, the segments of the child UR of such words are placed on a CV-tier with feature specification of Cs (consonants) and Vs (vowels) where the targets /l, r, j/ are given C slots specified as [+sonorant; +coronal; –nasal] but unspecified for the lateral feature, [±lateral], and the feature [+lateral] is unassociated or 'floating'. Figure 6.8 illustrates the child UR for *lorry* /lɒri/.

Although the child is thought to have an adequate articulatory representation of these words, since he or she is only aware of the presence of /l/ without specific information, the Association

		[+lateral]		
CV-tier:	C	ɒ	C	i
	[+sonorant] [+coronal] [–nasal] [±lateral]		[+sonorant] [+coronal] [–nasal] [±lateral]	

Figure 6.8 *The child UR for lorry.*

Figure 6.9 *Slots in the CV tier.*

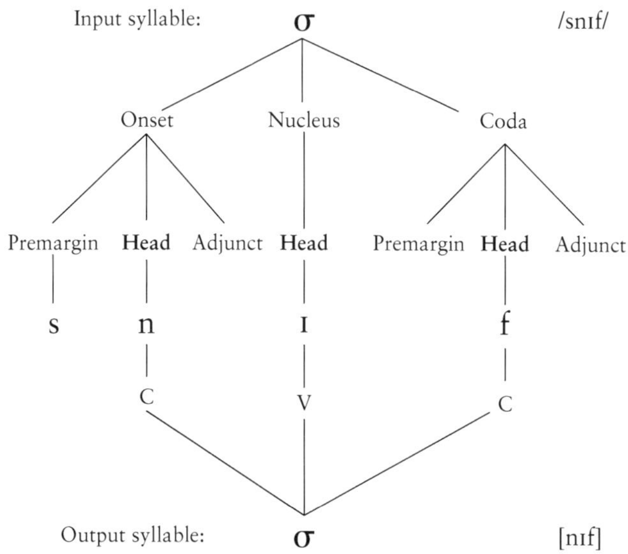

Figure 6.10 *The deletion of stray segments in the word sniff /snɪf/ → [nɪf]*

Convention requiring unassociated features to associate from left to right with segments that can bear them (Clements & Sezer 1982) causes the association of the floating feature with the appropriate slot in the CV tier (Figure 6.9).

In addition to certain segment structure conditions that are necessary for positing the autosegmental approach, Spencer's model assumes that syllable structure conditions account for the child's consonant cluster reduction patterns through the mapping of input representations onto a CVC syllable template, modelled on Cairns and Feinstein (1982). It is only the heads of syllable positions that are filled, thus leaving unassociated material to be deleted (see Îto 1986 for details on 'Stray Erasure'). Figure 6.10 shows the deletion of stray segments in the word *sniff* /snɪf/ → [nɪf].

Data of children who delete /h/ in the onset, as in the case of Amahl, are not uncommon and challenge the syllable template in Figure 6.10. Spencer argues that onset-/ss/ deletion could be accounted for as /ss/ being outside the scope of the syllable structure convention because it lacks supralaryngeal features that it requires for onsets. However, it is not always /s/ that is deleted in Amahl's consonant deletion in /s/-clusters, as shown in (6.3).

(6.3) Amahl's /s/-clusters:

	Adult SR		Child SR
a.	*sleep*	/sliːp/	[liːp]
	slide	/slaɪd/	[laɪd]
	slug	/slʌg/	[lʌg]
	snake	/sneɪk/	[neɪk]
	sniff	/snɪf/	[nɪf]
	snow	/snəʊ/	[nuː] → [noː]
b.	*star*	/staː/	[daː] → [tʰaː] → [tsaː] → [saː]
	steam	/stiːm/	[tiːm] → [siːm]
	step	/stɛp/	[dɛp] → [sɛp]
	stick	/stɪk/	[gɪk] → [tʰɪk] → [sɪk]
	stop	/stɔp/	[bɔp] → [dɔp] → [tʰɔp] → [tˢɔp] → [sɔp]

While the syllable template in Figure 6.10 would predict for development to go in the direction from retaining only syllable position heads towards retaining other constituents of the syllable positions, Amahl's development for /st/-clusters in (6.3) shows some peculiarity: /s/ starts out as being deleted due to its premarginal status in the syllable template in /st/-clusters, as in /sl/- and /sn/-clusters, but ends up in the onset head position. Perhaps the main issue for the dual lexicon model is not with the syllable template, as it also has problems in accounting for processes which operate across words (Menn & Matthei 1992). Nevertheless, compared to a single lexicon model, Spencer's model does overcome a number of serious problems caused by the dubious status of the rules behind the labial harmony process (owing to the application of autosegmental theory).

In order to account for Amahl's pronunciation of *quick* /kwɪk/ surfacing as [kɪp], Smith has to apply three strictly ordered rules: Rule 7, a pre-consonantal *s* deletion rule, is required to exclude *s*C clusters from triggering harmony. Then the progressive labial assimilation rule is applied to account for the coda becoming a labial by Rule 8, which transfers the labiality of a post-consonantal glide to the next consonant. Finally, Rule 16 deletes the /w/ in the onset. Spencer combines all these three into a realisation process. /w/ is deleted through its non-head status in the syllable template, leaving

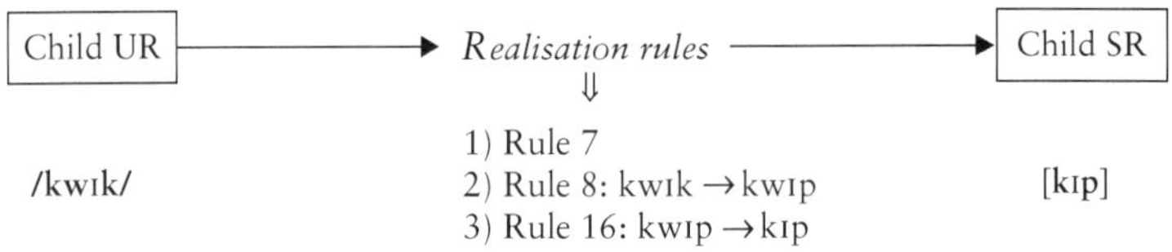

Figure 6.11 *Smith's model.*

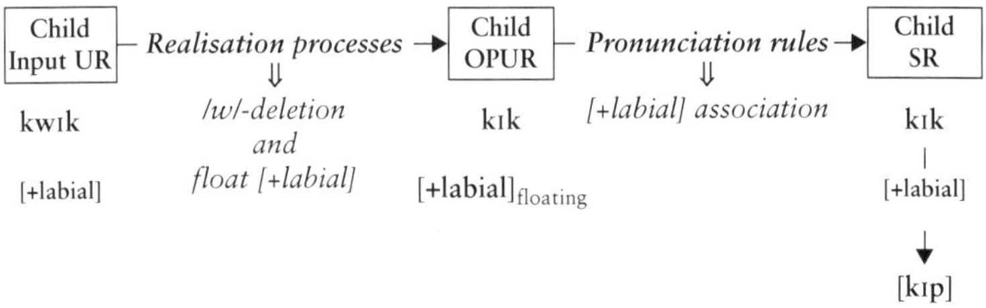

Figure 6.12 *Spencer's model.*

its [+labial] feature to float as residual knowledge, and this is associated with the coda by a pronunciation rule. See Figures 6.11 and 6.12 to compare.

While Smith's model has no way of explaining why [kwɪp] does not surface in an intermediate developmental stage between [kɪp] and [kwɪk] since the three rules used to derive [kɪp] are independent, the assumption of /kwɪk/ and /kɪk/ as the child URs is able to handle this development by simply accounting for it as a development in the syllable template: the [+labial] feature is no longer floating. Furthermore, the problem of bi-directionality in cases of velar harmony that Smith's model encountered due the independent status of the rules is also overcome in Spencer's by giving them the same autosegmental harmony treatment as lateral harmony.

Going back to the disordered phonological case of DF, Spencer's model seems to provide an explanation that was not possible for a single grammar model. Before being referred to Bryan and Howard (1992), DF's previous therapy was aimed at improving his articulation and his production of phonemic contrasts, which showed no effect. This is not surprising, since his disability cannot be considered to be in production or the mapping between the lexicon and the output surface representation, evidenced by DF's reasonably accurate production of non-words. Given that DF was able to perceive real words, the impairment cannot be in the mapping between the perceived surface form and the lexical representation either. However, if perception and production are assumed to be two separate

Table 6.2 Post-therapy assessment of DF

Real words			Non-words	
Target	Repetition	Naming	Target	Repetition
pig	[bɪg]	[bɪg]	/pæg/	[bæg]
soap	[səʊp]	[səʊp]	/sæp/	[sæp]
money	[mʌgɪ]	[mʌdɪ]	/mɒnɪ/	[mɒɪn]
elephant	[eɪfəfənt]	[ɛlɪvɪv]	/ʌlɪfɒnt/	[ʌdɪvɒnk]
butterfly	[bʌbəfwaɪ]	[bʌbəfaɪ]	/bɒtəfleɪ/	[bædəfeɪ]

components, the perceived phonetic form can be distinguished from the phonological form used in production and two types of underlying representations can be posited; input UR for perception and output UR for production. The connection between perception and production grammars in phonological acquisition would then be that input URs function as the basis of developing lexical representations. As a consequence of the formal distinction between phonetics and phonology, DF's production can be differentiated between real words and non-words. Thus, Bryan and Howard's therapy for DF was based on Spencer's (1986) dual lexicon model and consisted of improving his lexical representation by extending the phonological analysis of non-words to real words. Table 6.2 shows the result of the treatment after only fourteen weeks.

As can be seen in Table 6.2, DF's phonological production of real words and non-words came very much closer. By distinguishing between all sound contrasts that the child can perceive and produce, DF was diagnosed as not being able to update his UR in his productive grammar in accordance with the development in his perceptual grammar, thus using defective UR for production. Interestingly, it is data such as these that weaken the position that 'mispronunciations' by children occur due to poor motor control or physiological factors.

One way that a single grammar model can overcome the problem posed by DF's case is to posit temporary input representations for non-words. However, leaving aside the implausibility of assuming temporary input representations, a single grammar model cannot account for novel words in acquisition that enter the lexicon through phonology without elaborating a mechanism that not only distinguishes between real words and non-words, but also connects these two types of words in terms of development. For an OT single grammar model, such connection between perceptual UR and productive UR causes further problems, since it would impose some sort of restriction on the UR, which goes against the basic principle of OT, the richness of the base.

As for Pater's single grammar model in which DF's non-words are problematic, since markedness constraints do not distinguish between real words and non-words, one could explore the possibility of MARKEDNESS being indexed to two types of production, just as faithfulness constraints can apply to either perception or production. In fact, Pater briefly mentions the possibility of positing domain-specific MARKEDNESS. Although there is no reason why an OT model should not be able to posit different kinds of constraints within a single hierarchy or multiple sub-hierarchies, if MARKEDNESS is also made to operate domain-specifically, it would render a two-grammar model.

The difficulty in extending the application of MARKEDNESS to non-words for a grammatical model is that it goes against the standard practice of distinguishing between phonetics and phonology. As the underlying representation in phonology is by definition coupled with meaning, since meaning is distinguished by phonological contrasts within a language, postulating underlying representations for phonological structures without meaning is problematic. The fact that phonological constraints must be indexed to two different domains, when perception is taken into an account, may suggest that perception and production are two different systems, in spite of the strong connection between the two domains. The main stumbling block is that when perception is formally incorporated into the grammar, it is difficult to do so without referring to more concrete units, such as raw phonetics. This obviously relates to the question of to what extent phonetics should be included in a phonological theory.

In comparison with Smith's SPE (*Sound Pattern of English*, Chomsky & Halle 1968) model, the dual lexicon model may appear to be an innovative approach to child phonology that overcomes problems created by phonological rules being independent of each other. However, the difference between the two models exists only in the techniques used to describe a theory of child phonology. Thus, where Smith's model embodies all derivational rules for the child SR in one realisation process, we can also view Spencer's model as applying one process between adult SR and child SR, since it is his application of autosegmental phonology and the concept of underspecification that necessitates the two steps of de-specifying the input for it to be re-specified for production. Since despecification and respecification together make up the realisation process and adult

SR in the input is assumed to be perceived more or less accurately, there is no fundamental difference between the two models. Thus, Spencer's model is not a two-grammar model and it assumes phonological accuracy in the child's perception of adult SR, which presupposes full specification of phonological features at the underlying level, even though not all feature values may be present.

The assumption that the child UR is fully specified implies that all features are given innately and development does not take place in this area of phonology. This implication should be questioned, since Pater's proposal and DF's case reveal that full specification cannot be assumed for earliest lexical representations. But how are we to know what exactly the child is extracting from the adult SR and storing in the form of UR for the purpose of comprehension? Since the child's comprehension of an adult SR only implies an accurate mapping of it to the meaning, we might consider the possibility that an accurate comprehension of adult SR does not necessarily lead to it being 100 per cent equal to the child UR. Just as adults are capable of comprehending each other in a telephone conversation under sub-optimal conditions, such as high noise level, it is not unreasonable to assume that the mapping from SR to meaning in the child is possible as long as the speech signals of the adult SR contains enough information for the child to match it the UR. Indeed, a study by Pater and colleagues (1998) found that voiced–voiceless consonants could not be perceptually distinguished by 14-month-old infants when the stimuli consisted of words coupled with their meaning, which suggests that the complexity in featural composition is something that develops in the child. We will now move on to investigating the perspective that the initial representation does not contain all feature specifications.

6.5 Underspecification

We saw that Spencer (1986) was assuming a theory of lexical information being underspecified for various features which could be predicted by default rules. This model was based on work by Archangeli (1984). The discussion below is based on a somewhat later developed theory.

6.5.1 A theory of distinctive features

Theories of perception make few predictions about how the child will proceed into speech production. As we have seen, they will tend to concentrate on the acquisition of language-specific features and the elimination of non-native features, concentrating on the role of the input. They effectively deny any role to Universal Grammar (UG), since the predictions made by UG depend on assumptions about what is unmarked in language. Similarly, Stoel-Gammon and Cooper (1984) suggest that UG-based assumptions stemming from Jakobson's work attribute only a passive role to the learner. As we discussed in Chapter 3, from their study of the path of acquisition of three children from a month before the onset of meaningful words to the fifty-word stage, they suggest that each child has its own unique pattern of development. Their study concentrates on the variability found in acquisition, and attributes this not to the variability in the adult forms targeted but rather to the children's own 'choices' at the various stages in the path towards a settled inventory. In this section we shall be considering how the universal pattern might be accommodated to the apparently infinitely variable and child-specific pattern.

The idea of 'markedness' is fundamental to the theory of underspecification as discussed in this section. As we saw in Chapter 3, Jakobson's theory insofar as it concerned acquisition, was based on the acquisition of contrasts, in other words the establishment of a phonemic inventory. The theory presupposes only a minimal ability at the onset of speech. The first contrast established, according to Jakobson, is that between consonant and vowel and then the child gradually acquires place of articulation contrasts alongside those of oral vs nasal. However, the learning path is not uniform across infants and equally, infants exhibit considerable variability in the course of their acquisition. In some sense, this insight is modelled in a feature theory expounded by Rice and Avery (1995) and Rice (1995, 1996). We can view this approach as an extension of the theory of phonological features proposed by Avery and Rice (1989).

Avery and Rice make the initial assumption, that was being developed at the time, that segments are not composed of unordered bundles of features, but are hierarchically organised into what has become known as 'feature geometry' (for example Clements 1985; Sagey 1986). This is an assumption that has now become standard and we will not explore further the various other models on the market. In the model we show in Figure 6.13, adapted from Rice and Avery (1995), the segmental structure contains four major elements dominated by a root node. As with other feature theories, the root must contain sufficient information to tell us whether we have

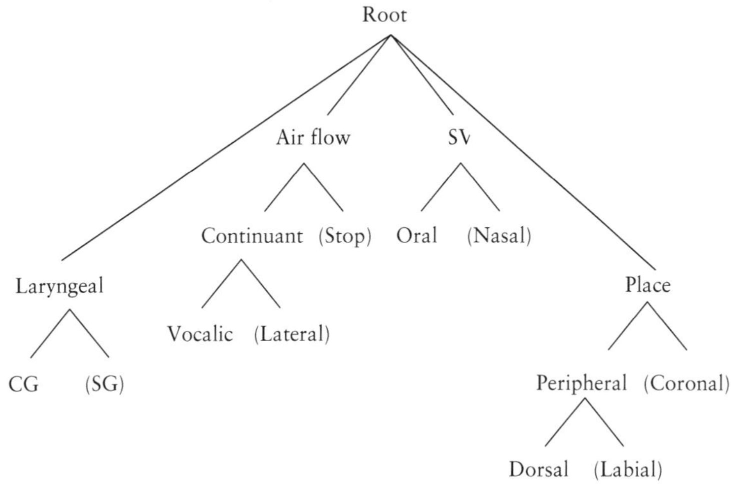

Figure 6.13 *Feature Hierarchy (from Rice & Avery 1995).*

a vowel or a consonant. The major nodes involved are those which provide us with information about the features of the sound in question and each of the elements has two choices, one of which is the default setting and the other might be construed as marked. In each case, the default setting is shown in brackets.

Let us examine each of these elements independently.

The laryngeal node organises the laryngeal features such as voicing, the two labels CG meaning constricted glottis and SG meaning spread glottis. Remember that in adult speech, only obstruent consonants are generally reckoned to show a laryngeal contrast, sonorants are consistently voiced. In early acquisition infants may not exhibit similar contrasts in all positions. Rice (1995) points out that, according to Smith (1973), in the early stages of his acquisition, Amahl had the following inventory of sounds /b d g m n ŋ w l/, although these were subject to allophonic variation. He exhibited no real contrasts in laryngeal features. That is to say that, generally speaking, his initial consonants are all lenis, voiceless, unaspirated; his medial obstruents are lenis and voiced and his finals are fortis voiceless and may or may not have been aspirated. (Fortis: high overall muscular tension (usually voiceless); Lenis: low overall muscular tension (usually voiced)).

Let us look at some examples in (6.4):

(6.4) Amahl
[b̥ɛk] *peg*

[g̊up] *cube*
[ɛbu] *apple*
[b̥eːbi] *baby*
[b̥ʌgit] *bucket*
[b̥ɒgu] *bottle*

However, we can assume that the child had not acquired these as true contrasts, nor necessarily as predictable allophonic variation, since we do encounter some variability, even at Stage 1, for example intervocalic /k/ in *chocolate* can be manifested as both [g̊ɒgi] and [g̊ɒki] and *thank you* exhibits a voiceless lenis unaspirated intervocalic stop in medial position [g̊ɛg̊u]. Although we have more limited data available for them, at the stage at which we encounter their productions, both Gitanjali and Julia seem to have acquired the contrasts in initial and final position (see (2.10) and (2.11) in Chapter 2). Gitanjali also appears also to have acquired the distinction intervocalically, although we have to be circumspect about making such a claim from these few data. Not so Julia, who still produces [pɪdɪ] for *pretty.*

The air flow node offers the choice of continuant and stop, the latter being the default. As we saw in Chapter 2 and as we shall discuss in greater detail in Chapter 7, if we examine Amahl's early utterances, he does not produce any fricatives and so can be said to have no contrast at the air flow node. It is not true to say, however, that he universally replaces fricatives with stops, again as we saw in Chapter 2.

The place node is organised as shown in Figure 6.14.

The implications of this figure is that the first place contrast acquired by the child, in line with Jakobson's predictions, will be between coronal and labial and, subsequently, a three-way contrast will be acquired – labial ~ coronal ~ dorsal. We shall elaborate on this in due course when we consider how the model assumes segment structure to be acquired.

The final node is sonorant voice (sometimes also referred to as

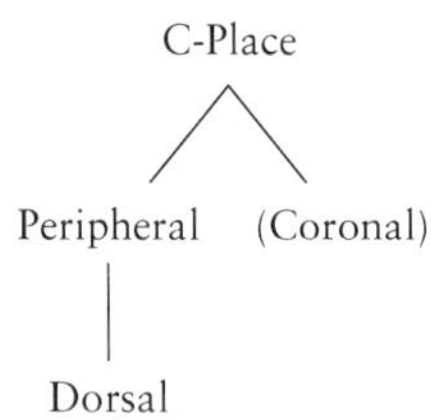

Figure 6.14 *The C-Place node.*

'spontaneous voice'). Effectively, this is the manifestation of the feature 'sonorant' in other theories. As we can see, unlike other theories, sonorant is not a root feature. The two branches, shown in Figure 6.13, are the nasal default and the approximant which can be further specified as lateral or non-lateral, the former being the default.

6.5.2 Structure building

The fundamental premise of this theory is that the child initially has minimal structure beyond the simple contrast between consonant (some sort of oral obstruction) and vowel (no obstruction). Structure has to be built and this is achieved 'monotonically' – one step at a time.

Let us look at the process of structure building. At the first stage, there is merely a place node – this might be any place and will be subject to variability since the child has not yet developed a fixed place contrast. If we were to follow Jakobson's predictions, then this first place might generally manifest itself as labial but it could equally be coronal or dorsal, the theory makes no absolute predictions here. The stages through which the child goes to build up the contrasts in place follow an incremental path, so that when the first contrast appears the peripheral node is activated. As we can see from the model in Figure 6.13, it might be expected that the first such contrast is between the coronal (universal default place) and the labial. According to Rice (1996) there now develops a contrast between coronal or dorsal and labial. The addition of a dorsal node to the peripheral gives a three-way place distinction. Figure 6.15, taken from Rice (1996), shows the progression.

The prediction made by this model, from the cross-linguistic point of view, is that if a language has a dorsal place, then it will also have a labial and a coronal. We will not pursue this cross-linguistic

	i. Single place	*ii. Two distinctive places*	*iii. Three distinctive places*
	Place	Place Place | Peripheral	Place Place | | Peripheral Peripheral | Dorsal
Possible realisations	Any place	Either coronal–dorsal, coronal–labial or dorsal–labial	Coronal–labial–dorsal

Figure 6.15 *A three-way place distinction.*

prediction here, but refer the reader to the ample literature on the special status of the coronal (see for example the papers collected in Paradis & Prunet 1991). It is not clear, however, to what extent the cross-linguistic findings tally with the acquisitional ones.

As we can see, however, the apparent markedness hierarchy, inherent in the model, reflects the relative strength hierarchy proposed by Rose (2000) and shown in (2.27) of Chapter 2, for Amahl and Trevor acquiring English (6.5).

(6.5) dorsal > labial > coronal

A further enhancement of the initial stage (place only) is the addition of the SV node. This will, if the default option is taken, provide an oral–nasal contrast. Jakobson predicts that this contrast will occur before any place distinction has been made. Notice, however, that the other branch of the SV node is approximant, one of which may occur relatively early. The prediction made by this theory, then, is that the oral–nasal contrast will generally precede that of between obstruent and approximant.

If we look at Amahl's inventory at Stage 1, as developed by Rice (1996), we find that he has established the contrasts in the form of features (Figure 6.16).

As we can see in Figure 6.16, Rice treats the two approximants as merely manifestations of continuant. We saw in the data in Chapter 2 relating to fricative avoidance that, as well as target /w/ itself, from Stage 1, for some time, Amahl replaces target /f/, in syllable initial position, with [w]. Although this is not shown there, since there are

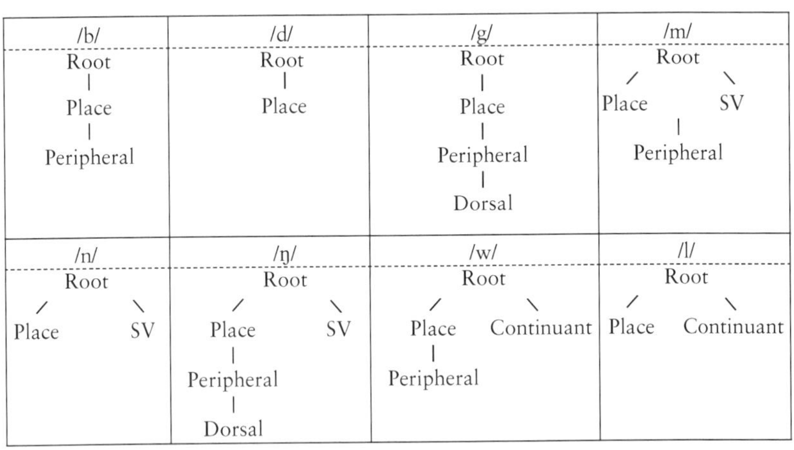

Figure 6.16 Amahl's inventory at Stage 1.

no tokens from the early stage to illustrate it, the same applies to target /v/ although this appears to be variable throughout the data, even to the later stages. For example, at Stage 29, we encounter [wʌlʔtsə] for *vulture.*

(6.6) Amahl

[wɔk]	*fork*
[wæwæ]	*flower*
[wɒwu]	*follow*
[wɒt]	*watch*
[wɒt]	*wash*

For some time, up until a firm contrast is established between /f/ and /w/ (6.6) at Stage 16, and in order for such a contrast to be established, Rice suggests that that feature SV which is what must account for the difference between continuant /f/ and /w/ has been fixed. In the interim, there are various fluctuations in the manifestation of /f/-initial words.

(6.7) Amahl before Stage 16

[ʋaɪ/vaɪ/laɪ/waɪ/vlaɪ/ʋlaɪ/y̥lai]	*fly* (Stage 9)
[flɒg/wɒg/wlɒg/βʳɒg]	*frog* (Stage 11)
[wɔk/fɔk]	*fork* (Stage 15)
[fʊt/ɸʊt]	*foot* (Stage 15)

As we saw above, at Stage 1, Amahl has not acquired any voicing distinctions which begin to emerge in initial position around Stage 12, although they do start to appear in intervocalic position at Stage 7, and were almost adult-like by Stage 13/14.

In an evaluation of the Rice and Avery model, relative to distinctive feature hypothesis (Ingram 1992), Ingram (1996) shows the features present in the systems of four children – two with very limited inventories and two with more complex ones.

The first of these children labelled Kevin, has a consonant inventory of [d] and [t]. The former substitutes for /b d g ð/ and the latter for /p t k/. In other words, the only contrast present in his system is that of [±voice]. In terms of the theory we are discussing, these can be shown as in Figure 6.17. Ingram has merely one extension of the laryngeal node as [voice].

The other child with a limited contrast is labelled Mike. His substitutions are [n] for /n w/ and [d] for /d s ð/ (Figure 6.18).

A better test of the model is to see if it can capture the systems of Matthew (6.8) (Maxwell & Weismer 1982) and Hildegard (Leopold

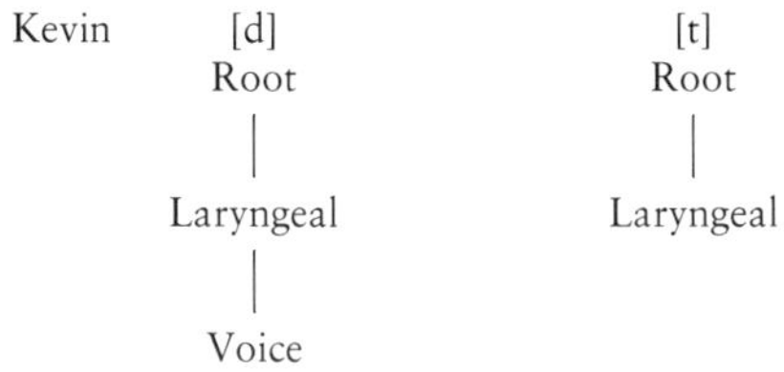

Figure 6.17 *Kevin's contrasts.*

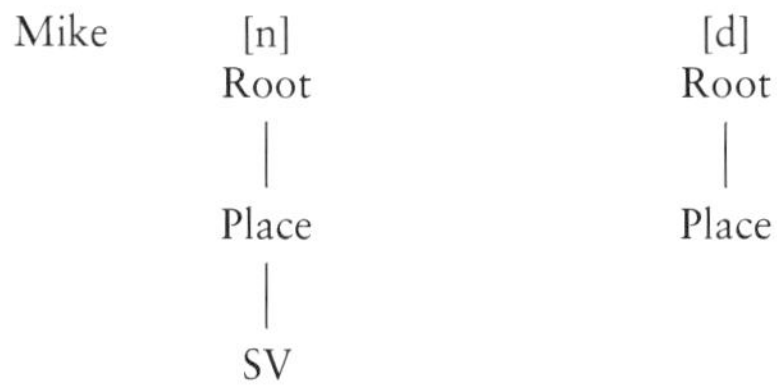

Figure 6.18 *Mike's contrasts.*

1947), both of whom have the same surface inventories but differ in the substitutions.

(6.8)	Matthew	[m] /m/	[n] /n/
		[b] /b p f v/	[d] /t k d g ʤ ʧ ʃ s θ z/
		[w] /w/	[j] /j/
	Hildegard	[m] /m/	[n] /n/
		[b] /b p/	[d] /d ʧ t k g/
		[w] /w r f/	[j] /l/

If we take a look at the substitutions in the productions of these children, therefore, we find that their systems are different. The diagrams in Figure 6.19 show their manner features.

Both children clearly have an established place contrast of labial and coronal in each of these pairings. For Matthew, the branching under the SV node allows for the established pairs of sonorants – plain SV with the default 'nasal' setting and an SV node with a further addition of 'oral' allows for the two approximants in Matthew's system. The basic contrast for Hildegard lies under the Air flow node where we find a continuant contrast. Notice that, for Hildegard, similar to Amahl, these approximants are an expression of continuance, since /f/ is one of the targets for which [w] is a substitute.

Let us see the extent to which the data from Stoel-Gammon and Cooper (1984) can be accommodated by this model. The main thrust of that paper, as we have seen, was to accentuate the differences in the

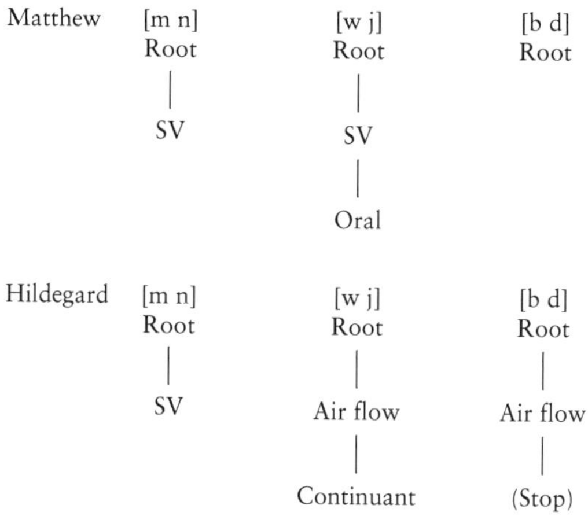

Figure 6.19 *Matthew and Hildegard's manner features.*

acquisition patterns exhibited by the three children. The claim had to be that all children develop their own individual learning paths and, while there are some universals, which are biologically determined, the child plays an active role in the learning path. Goad and Ingram (1987) re-examine their data, considering the patterns that emerge at the thirty-five word stage.

Goad and Ingram identify three types of individual variation: performance variation, environmental variation and linguistic variation. What they are claiming is that reported differences are largely the result of the first two of these types of variation but that it is only the last of the three which helps us to understand the language acquisition device. Let us consider the possible effect of the other types of variation. Performance variation is the result of genetically determined differences between children. For example, the rate of acquisition of the first may be slower or faster, varying from child to child. Some children exhibit preferences for certain sounds. Goad and Ingram mention a labial preference shown by some children, which can be confirmed by the tendencies we observed in Chapter 2. Environment variation can also explain some differences in children's acquisition. For example, they note, Joan (Velten 1943), showed an early preference for /z/ which, it was suggested, could be attributed to the influence of French and French-influenced English in her input.

When these types of variation have been factored out, Goad and Ingram maintain, the remaining linguistic variation becomes a good deal more restricted. With these considerations in mind, then, they proceed to examine the data from Daniel, Sarah and Will at the thirty-five word stage. A number of the differences identified by Stoel-Gammon and Cooper can be attributed to either environmental or performance variation. There is a difference shown by the children in rate and accuracy of acquisition. For example, Daniel's lexical acquisition is more rapid than that of Sarah with an inverse correlation in terms of accuracy, these two factors are considered to be the result of performance variation. Environmental and performance can influence frequency – a certain sound can be frequent, either because the child prefers it or because the parents encourage it, but they may occur because they are frequent in the child's input (see the discussion in Chapter 5 regarding frequency and input).

This leaves the analysis on linguistic variation. Goad and Ingram excluded sounds that occurred very infrequently in the data, as well as the result of harmony, and discovered that, contrary to the initial observation, that at all stages the children's systems are apparently different from one another, closer scrutiny of the oppositions being acquired shows a sequence of development. In syllable initial position they found the following: consonant vs vowel; labial vs coronal; continuant vs stop; nasal vs oral; voiced vs voiceless; coronal vs dorsal and then either liquid vs non-liquid or labial vs dorsal. In syllable final position Daniel and Will have acquired the consonant–vowel opposition by the end of the study, whereas Sarah only produces open syllables. Readers are referred to Goad and Ingram's (1987) paper for further elaboration on these findings, but the overall claim being made is that with a different methodology from Stoel-Gammon and Cooper (1984), the degree of linguistic variability is considerably reduced.

If we consider these findings from the perspective of the feature theory we have been discussing, we can see that they are all predictable within that theory.

The stages in Figure 6.20 have been shown as representing the newly acquired contrast and can be assumed to be incremental.

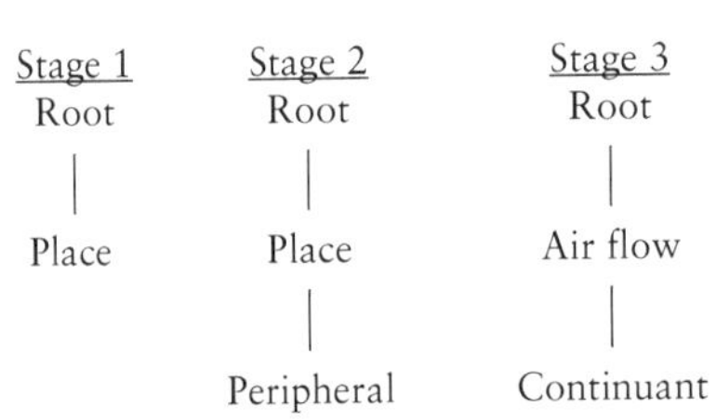

Figure 6.20 *The newly acquired contrast.*

6.6 The syllable

A question that we need to ask now is how is it possible for pre-verbal infants to learn their language-specific phonotactics without access to the full set of phonological feature specification at the initial state of the grammar? We saw earlier that the development that takes place during the first year of life is considerable and that linguistic input is indeed an obligatory element in the process of acquisition. With an introduction to how phonological features can be underspecified, or unspecified rather, we can now stipulate that when very young infants show the ability to discriminate speech sounds in experiments, it is not because they are equipped with a full specification of all phonological features coupled with markedness guidelines by UG informing them of what is simple and complex.

Accordingly, we can suppose that segmental discrimination during the earliest stages is based much more on phonetics and acoustics than phonology. If we define phonetics as the categorisation of raw acoustics, phonetics is not specific to humans. However, since phonological development takes place only in the human species, we have phonetics on one hand and a language-specific sound system (the final state of acquisition) on the other. When speech originates from a speaker's mouth and reaches the listener's ear, the transmission of sounds is taking place in the phonetic component, where each sound is given a phonetic representation. This is the component where animals 'perceive' human speech, parrots 'speak', and humans imitate speech sounds. For comprehension, the phonetic representation is then transformed into a phonological representation, which is under the control of a language-specific grammar, and then mapped on to the semantic component. Phonology is a mental operation and the force responsible for transforming the phonetic representation into a representation which is language-specific. Thus, phonology is the ability to phonologise or internalise the phonetic representation.

In human speech signals, after anything that is related to sound frequency is eliminated from the input, what is left in terms of linguistics is rhythm. Since linguistic rhythm is essentially durational pattern, it is impossible to postulate rhythm without reference to a linguistic unit that bears it. Although there are no clear phonetic or acoustic correlates of intensity due to its different manifestations, for example duration, stress, tone, pitch, and so on, we can assume that the rhythm-bearing unit is a grouping of sonority values into syllables. In view of the fact that infants as young as newborn are able to discriminate rhythmic classes (for example Mehler et al. 1988) and any event must be evaluated against something in order to be perceived, it is feasible to assume that there is a default setting of the rhythm which could be either the trochaic rhythm in (6.9a) or the iambic rhythm in (6.9b):

(6.9) a. (**X** X) (**X** X) (**X** X) (**X** X) (**X** X)
b. (X **X**) (X **X**) (X **X**) (X **X**) (X **X**)

The unmarked status of the trochaic rhythm has been suggested before, but there seems to be no clear evidence for this default setting. Production studies do not provide much support for the trochaic bias. While it is most likely that the child's experience has exerted sufficient influence on the grammar to have changed the initial setting of the rhythmic pattern by the time first words appear, most production studies are on the acquisition of trochaic languages (for example Allen & Hawkins 1980; Fikkert 1994). Perceptual studies that have been reported to date do not fare much better, since they are very few in number and the target languages tend again to be trochaic. For instance, English-acquiring infants were not found to show a preference for the trochaic stress pattern until the second half of their first year (Jusczyk et al. 1993a; Morgan 1996; Turk et al. 1995). Perceptual preference for the trochaic pattern was also found in German infants as young as six months, but not four months, of age by Weissenborn et al. (2002). In fact, Weissenborn et al. (2002) found a clear preference for the trochaic pattern by 4-month-old infants when they were familiarised with the trochaic pattern before testing. Interestingly, when Vihman (2004) investigated English-acquiring infants' perceptual preference for stress patterns, she found that infants have no preference for trochaic over iambic disyllables at either six, nine, or twelve months of age, contrary to Jusczyk et al. (1993a). Perhaps there is no default rhythm setting.

In fact, the traditional classification of languages according to linguistic rhythm is problematic, since not all languages fit in somewhere along a straight line where there are complex syllables with vowel reduction dominating the language on one end and simple syllables without vowel reduction on the other end. For example, Polish has complex syllables without vowel reduction. The difficulty in categorising languages in terms of rhythm stems from the fact that there are asymmetries in how the components, which constitute rhythm, are organised by each language, as shown by Hayes (1995) in his extensive typological survey of stress rules. Although researchers have suggested different ways of classifying languages in terms of rhythm (for example Bird 2002; Ramus et al. 1999), there is still no consensus on this matter. Nevertheless, the significant role played by the syllable is beyond doubt. If there is no default rhythm setting, the only way that infants can distinguish more than two different linguistic rhythm classes is if their linguistic ability is encoded with a 'basic' syllable.

The psychological reality of the syllable has been shown in a study of phonological representations of Catalan and Spanish speakers by Pallier (2000) who found that since the adult perceptual system is sensitive to the syllabic position of phonemes, even when not required by experimental tasks, the brain elaborates a syllabically structured underlying representation. Blevins (1995) provides comprehensive arguments for the importance of recognising the syllable as a phonological constituent and how the syllable serves to organise segments in terms of sonority. Also, there is ample evidence that some kind of syllable structure is present in newborns. Bijcljac-Babic et al. (1993) tested eighty-six 4-day-old infants using a non-nutritive sucking task, to see whether they could discriminate polysyllabic utterances. Their results indicated that the infants noticed a difference between disyllabic and trisyllabic sequences and that the discrimination was not merely on the basis of overall duration. Furthermore, when sixty-six newborns were tested using the same procedure, but this time investigating whether infants use prosodic cues to identify words in speech, it was shown that they could discriminate the accented patterns of both disyllabic and trisyllabic words (Sansavini et al. 1997).

The syllable, denoted by the symbol, σ, is defined by the existence of a nucleus, a position that is basically occupied by a vowel. A flat structure, as in Figure 6.21a accommodates the fact that consonants can appear either before or after the nucleus. However, since asymmetry is found in all languages between the onset and the coda, the structure of the syllable is believed to be hierarchical, as in Figure 6.21b.

The syllable in the initial state can probably not be clearly defined

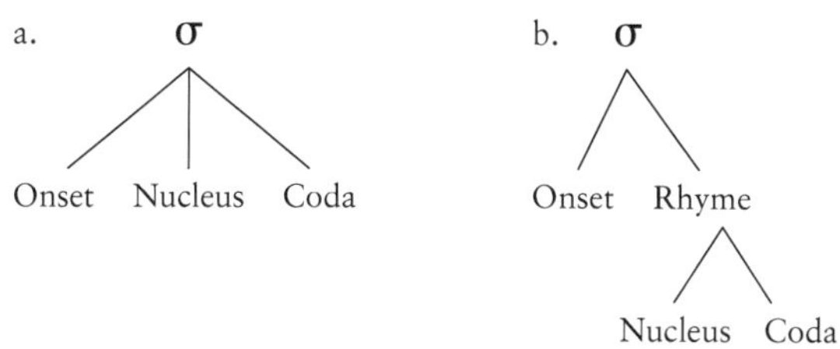

Figure 6.21 *Syllable structure.*

as in Figure 6.21b or not even in terms of consonants and vowels in a phonetic way. Therefore, we can only assume that linguistic rhythm is perceived by infants in terms of syllables, which contain sonority peaks and troughs, roughly corresponding to what we define as vowels (V) and consonants (C), respectively. While each sonority peak defines a unique syllable in the same way as in adults, the sonority values are probably not as clear as in adults, evidenced by the fact that in the very early stages, the infant does not seem to be able to define syllable boundaries precisely (Jusczyk 1997). Nevertheless, infants are particularly sensitive to vowels, due to their salience in terms of sonority. A high sensitivity to vowels implies that infants can distinguish between vowels and non-vowels. Thus, the knowledge that the infant has of the syllable is that the peaks have higher sonority values than those of the surrounding troughs. The question is: What is the shape of the basic syllable?

The CV-syllable is enshrined as the basic syllable in both phonological theory and almost all child production studies. The status of CV as the basic syllable is based largely on typological studies and transcriptions of infant productions. Jakobson's typological observation that there are no languages that disallow syllables with initial consonants or open syllables lies at the heart of the unchallenged assumption of the basic CV syllable, which takes many forms, such as a rule (for example the CV-rule in Îto 1986), a template (for example the coda condition in Îto 1986), a principle (for example the Minimal Onset Satisfaction Principle in Roca & Johnson 1999), or a constraint (for example ONSET and NOCODA in OT; Prince & Smolensky 2004[1993]).

However, the status of CV as the basic syllable is not exactly unquestionable, since onsetless syllables and complex nuclei are most often allowed in CV-languages (Blevins 2006) and it is extremely difficult to find a language that has no other syllable shapes than CV. Many follow Blevins (1995) in citing Hua, a Papuan language of New Guinea, as an example of a pure CV-language (probably the only example), as opposed to the very small group of predominantly CV languages, such as Cayuvava and a number of Polynesian languages, such as Maori and Hawaiian, that also allow V syllables as well as Japanese that allow nasals and the first consonant of geminates to appear in the coda position. However, according to the original source of the Hua data, which visibly contain other syllable types than CV (Haiman 1998), vowel-only syllables are not exactly rare (John Haiman, personal communication).

Although the basis of assuming CV as the basic syllable is not as clear as we would like it to be (see Reimers 2008, for discussions contesting the basic CV-syllable), we still need to postulate the syllable as a phonological constituent, whatever its basic shape is, in order to explain acquisition within a phonological theory, since phonological acquisition does not occur in the order of acquiring segments, syllables, words, phrases, and sentences. The shape of utterances perceived and produced by children cannot be accounted for by just phonological features and syllables, since we need to refer to a larger unit, namely prosody, where development also takes place.

As we mentioned briefly in Chapter 4, some languages (for example French) are defined as 'syllable-timed', in that all syllables are of roughly equal weight and lack unstressed vowels, while others are defined as 'stress timed' because of an alternation of stressed and unstressed syllables as shown in (6.9) above. Another property that divides languages is that of 'quantity sensitivity'. A quantity sensitive language is characterised by the fact that what are known as 'heavy syllables', those with either a long vowel or a vowel and consonant in the rhyme, attract stress, overriding to some extent the rhythmic pairing of syllables demonstrated in (6.9). Such syllables are referred to as bimoraic. That is that they contain two moras. The mora, denoted by the μ symbol, is a unit of timing of rhyme segments. Therefore a V or CV syllable will be **monomoraic** and CVV or CVC **bimoraic**. This definition will be important in the account of studies on children's early word forms in the next section.

6.7 Prosodic development

Given that children's early word productions are drastically truncated relative to adult targets, we might want to ask the question: What is it that controls the shape of the utterance? Based on data from Fikkert (1994), Demuth (1995) presents an account of constraints on word shape. Her findings are contested by data from Salidis and Johnson (1997).

Languages tend to adhere to a minimal word constraint which may either be disyllabic or bimoraic. Both these types of minimal word would consist of a binary foot, either a syllabic foot or a moraic foot, as we show in Figure 6.22.

Fikkert (1994) and Demuth (1995) claim that children pass through various stages in the acquisition of the minimal word. They further suppose that, initially children do not possess a long–short

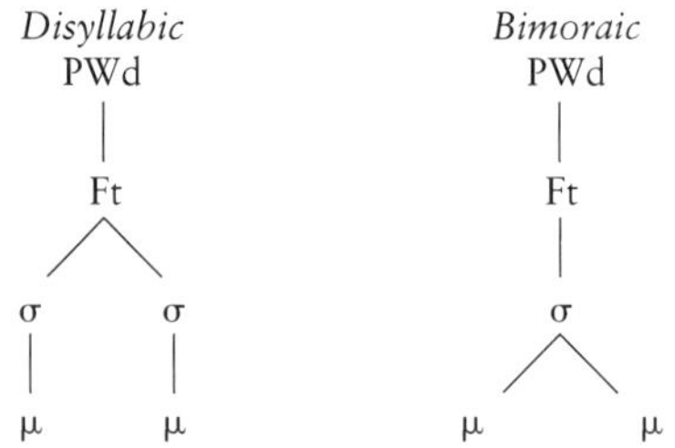

Figure 6.22 *Disyllabic or bimoraic foot.*

vowel contrast, meaning that CV and CVː are equivalent prior to the acquisition to such a contrast. The earliest word-forms are, therefore, sub-minimal CV(V). In all cases, the initial onset will be shown as optional, but we have left out this detail. Also, no gloss is provided for these words from Dutch.

(6.10) Stage I

[kaː], [kɑ]	/klaːr/	*klaar*
[daː], [dɑ]	/daːr/	*daar*
[tiː], [tɪ]	/dit/	*dit*

The second stage (6.11) sees the introduction of the disyllabic form suggesting that, at this stage a constraint on word size (which Demuth terms ALIGN$_{\text{PRWD}}$ although Pater uses WORDSIZE), is undominated. This constraint differs from one that might be suggested for adult productions, say MINWD, in that it provides a template for, not only minimal word, but also the maximal one. The CVCV template causes some vowel insertion, although Demuth's ranking omits mention of this, as well as deletion.

(6.11) Stage IIa

[ˈaːpə]	/aːp/	*aap*
[ˈboːtɔ]	/boːt/	*boot*
[ˈnɛnɛ]	/koːnɛin/	*konijn*
[ˈtɛnə]	/trɛin/	*trein*
[ˈʊɑfɑ]	/ʃiːˈraf/	*giraf*

The ranking Demuth suggests is: NOCODA, ALIGN >> MAX (the constraint MAX is termed PARSE-SEGMENT by Demuth) – the absence of the DEP (FILL for Demuth) can be explained by the fact that she demonstrates ranking and re-ranking on the various productions of *olifant* /oːliːfɑnt/ where no epenthesis occurs. At this stage, the child produces [hoːtɑ] for *olifant*.

By the next stage (Stage IIb), the coda has been added, leading to the re-definition of the minimal word as bimoraic. The child is now variably producing [hoːtɑ] and [fɑut] for *olifant*, suggesting a ranking of ALIGN >> MAX >> NOCODA. Demuth claims that this ranking will yield either variant as optimal (implying that the child might use either form). However, if we look at the constraints operative here, we can see that this is not the case – in spite of the fact that NOCODA has been demoted, it must still be the constraint that decides between the two forms and causes [hoːtɑ] still to emerge optimal (Tableau 6.5).

Tableau 6.5

/oːliːfɑnt/	ALIGN	MAX	NOCODA
fɑ	*!	*****	
☞hoːtɑ		***	
fɑut		***	*
oːlɑfɑn	*!	*	*
oːliːfɑnt	*!		*

Notice that, although [hoːtɑ] and [fɑut] incur the same number of MAX violations, the additional NOCODA violation makes [fɑut] less harmonious.

At the next stage when the word template has expanded, the form [oːlɑfɑn] clearly emerges optimal since it incurs only one violation of MAX. Clearly the final candidate (faithful to the adult form) would incur no violations whatsoever, but is prevented from emerging because of a higher ranked *COMPLEX constraint.

The final stage sees the demotion of *COMPLEX and the promotion of MAX, ensuring that any candidate that involves a deletion will fail and the maximally faithful [oːlifɑnt] will be victorious.

Salidis and Johnson (1997) claim that, while this order of acquisition of word forms may work for Dutch, it does not apply to English. Their data show that Kyle produced sub-minimal, minimal and supraminimal forms at all the stages studies from 12–19 months (only at the very earliest stage – eleven months did he not produce forms of more than two moras). They, therefore, contest Fikkert's findings. However, their thesis is that Kyle (6.12) adheres to a bimoraic minimal – which is hard to maintain when he produced sub-minimal forms (6.13–6.19) throughout the period of the study.

(6.12) Kyle (Salidis & Johnson 1997)

Age (months)	No. of targets	Examples	
11	3	[bʊk], [bʌ], [ʃu], [su]	*book*, *shoe*
12	2	[baw], [ba], [ʃu], [su]	*ball*, *shoe*
13	4	[dɛs], [dæs], [dəs], [da]	*dance*, *done*
14	9	[bɛʌ], [bʌ], [mɪlk], [mʌk]	*bear*, *milk*
15	15	[dag], [ga], [gin], [gi]	*dog*, *green*
16	12	[ɛ], [gɛ], [hɛp], [hæp]	*ear*, *help*
17	13	[waɪs], [baɪs], [sawt], [sas]	*rice*, *salt*
18	81	[tiz], [ʧiz], [ko], [kaʊw]	*cheese*, *cow*
19	71	[bud], [bɠrd], [ʧɪp], [tɪp], [tip]	*bird*, *chip*

(6.13) Kyle: Sub-minimal productions

Age	Target		Age	Target	
11	*bread*	[bɛ]	15	*mirror*	[mə]
11	*hair*	[hɛ]	15	*bike*	[bɛ]
12	*fish*	[fɪ]	17	*carry*	[kɛ]
13	*belt*	[bə]	18	*stroller*	[də]
14	*pear*	[pə]	18	*way*	[wɛ]
14	*carry*	[kə]	18	floor	[fʊ]

(6.14) Kyle: Minimal productions

Age	Target		Age	Target	
11	*ball*	[ba]	13	*coop*	[kup]
11	*block*	[gak]	11	*dog*	[da]
11	*walk*	[wak]	18	*dog*	[dæk]
11	*hat*	[hæt]	15	*truck*	[tʌk]
11	*cup*	[kʌp]	16	*shapes*	[sɛps]
11	*shoe*	[su]	18	*giant*	[gi]
12	*picture*	[pəʃɛ]	18	*green*	[gri]

(6.15) Kyle: Reduced forms

Age	Target		Age	Target	
11	*bubble*	[bo]	13	*turkey*	[ki]
11	*daddy*	[di]	14	*pepper*	[pɛp]
12	*cuddle*	[ka]	14	*bunny*	[bi]
12	*tofu*	[fu]	14	*flowers*	[fɪs]
13	*starfish*	[dæs]	15	*puzzle*	[pʌz]
13	*outside*	[saɪd]	16	*berries*	[bɛz]

(6.16) Kyle: Supra-minimal productions

Age	Target		Age	Target	
12	*oatmeal*	[maʔmaʔ]	17	*mailbox*	[mɛbaks]
12	*banana*	[mənamə]	18	*starfish*	[dafɪs]
13	*ceiling*	[sii] (2 sylls)	18	*muffins*	[mʌfɪnz]
14	*noodle*	[nunu]	18	*crackers*	[kækəs]
14	*backpack*	[bækpæk]	18	*music*	[mʌzɪk]
15	*oatmeal*	[miə]	18	*waffle*	[wafəl]
16	*elbow*	[ebo]	19	*glasses*	[gæsəz]

(6.17) Kyle

Age	Disyllabic minimal words	Examples	
11/12	0		
13	2	*bear*	[bɛʌ]
14	3	*pen*	[pɛnə]
15	9	*zebra*	[bəzə]
16	9	*caterpillar*	[kæpə]
		alligator	[ægʌ]
17	9	*polar bear*	[bəbə]
		banana	[mɛnə]
18	16	*water*	[watə]
		byebye	[bæbæ]
19	15	*oink oink*	[wɪ wɪ]

(6.18) Kyle: (C)VV productions

Age	Target		Age	Target	
11	*done*	[da]	16	*water*	[wa]
12	*fire*	[fa]	16	*three*	[fwi]
13	*hi*	[haɪ]	17	*cereal*	[so]
14	*banana*	[bi]	17	*chair*	[ʧu]
15	*tree*	[ti]	19	*seaweed*	[si]

(6.19) Kyle: (C)VC and (C)VVC productions

Age	Target		Age	Target	
11	*shoes*	[suz]	15	*Steve*	[duf]
11	*soup*	[sʌp]	16	*brown*	[baʊm]
13	*dance*	[dæs]	16	*blanket*	[bʌk]
13	*box*	[baks]	17	*red*	[wɛd]
14	*glove*	[gʌvf]	19	*seven*	[sev]

So if the minimal word cannot be relied upon to predict children's early word forms, what is it that determines how they will deal with polysyllabic targets? The forms taken recognise the foot structure of the language. Demuth (1996) suggests that children's word forms reflect either the foot structure or the minimal word. Thus, English learners will tend to home in on the main stress of the word together with the final syllable – so *elephant* will surface as [ɛfʌn] and *eraser* as [reɪzə]. Dutch children employ roughly the same strategy except that σ́σσ can emerge with either of the two unstressed syllables deleted – *andere* [ɑnre] or [ɑndə]. In Sesotho, which has no stress but penultimate vowel lengthening, child productions are disyllabic, and take the form of a trochaic foot, much like English and Dutch. In the language K'iche' Maya, which exhibits iambic word-final stress, early words are monosyllabic, taking the final (stressed) syllable of the target language.

Pater (1997) and Pater and Paradis (1996) list the form of truncations of polysyllabic words. One observation that can be made from the data presented, is that English-acquiring children do indeed reduce words to the stressed syllable plus the final syllable. The following patterns (6.20) are observable in the data.

(6.20) The 'elephant' data from Pater and Paradis 1996 (produced by Julia 22–26 months, Derek 24–34 months and Trevor 17–23 months)

abacus	[ækʊs]
Allison	[aijə] [æːsʌn]
animal(s)	[æmʌ] [æmʊ] [æmu]
	[æml̩s]
	[ɑːmo]
	[amos] [æmos] [æməs]
broccoli	[baki]
buffalo	[bʌfo]
camera	[kæmə]
chocolate	[tɔkət]
	[ʧɔʧɛt] [ʧɔːkɪt]
Christopher	[krisfə]
cinnamon	[sɪmɛn]
elephant(s)	[ɛfɪnt]
	[ɛwfən]
	[apɛn] [aʊfənts]
favourite	[fɛvɪt]
furniture	[fɚʧɚ]
Margaret	[margɛt] [margɪt]
medicine	[mɛsɪn]

popsicle	[paku] [pɑki]
sesame	[sɛmə] [sɛmi]
spatula	[bæʧʌ]
tricycle	[twaɪkl]

The following schema (6.21) shows the patterns of reduction of three different target word shapes.

(6.21) Word shape: $\acute{\sigma}_1\sigma_2\sigma_3 \rightarrow \sigma_1\sigma_3$ Examples: *elephant* [ɛfɪnt], *animal* [æmʊ]

Word shape: $\sigma_1\acute{\sigma}_2\sigma_3 \rightarrow \sigma_2\sigma_3$ Examples: *banana* [nænə], *pyjamas* [daməs]

Word shape: $\sigma_1\acute{\sigma}_2 \rightarrow \sigma_2$ Examples: *again* [gɛn], *enough* [nʌf]

Where the non-initial stressed syllable is sonorant-initial (in particular a liquid or glide), then there is a tendency for an obstruent from the initial unstressed syllable to replace it. For example, Gitanjali's *koala* [fi-kala], *balloon* [fi-bun], Julia's *delicious* [dɪʃəs], Trevor's *gorilla* [gʌːwa].

The suggestion about the word shape is that children's outputs are bimoraic. That is to say that when they produce monosyllables, these have to be heavy and otherwise they produce disyllabic words to attain this minimality. All the examples cited above will conform to the constraint WORDSIZE. The placement of trochaic stress on the leftmost syllable can be assured by a constraint ALIGN-L (the head syllable is aligned with the left edge of the word). We also know, however, that the final syllable is produced in all the word shapes shown above. Pater (1997) and Pater and Paradis (1996) propose a constraint ANCHOR-RIGHT (any element on the right edge in the input has a correspondent on the right edge in the output). To ensure that the target stressed syllable is indeed the output stressed syllable, a constraint STRESS-FAITH is proposed (Tableau 6.6). The optimal output will, of necessity, violate $\text{MAX}_{\text{I-O}}$ in that deletions occur.

Tableau 6.6 From Pater & Paradis 1996: 546

$\acute{e}_1.le_2.phant_3$	STRESS-FAITH	ANCHOR-RIGHT
$[(\acute{e}_1.le_2)]$		*
$[l\acute{e}_2phan_3)]$	*	
F$[(\acute{e}_1phan_3)]$		

Notice that the optimal candidate violates neither of the constraints.

Kehoe (2000) found that, although children around twenty-two months tended to produce disyllabic (one stress-foot) words and some of the oldest children in her study produced two stress feet, word edges were more important in accounting for size and shape of word forms. The inclusion of unstressed syllables is not necessarily accounted for by the single effect of footedness. In general, Kehoe's analysis, although proposing different constraints could also be appropriate to the findings encapsulated in Pater 1997 and Pater and Paradis 1996.

Studies on Japanese (Ota 1998) and Hebrew (Adam 2002) have also found that although all children appear to go through a sub-minimal stage, the minimal word as defined above applies to early child language.

Ota (1998) looked at data from a child acquiring Japanese. Although the children went through a sub-minimal stage where they produced full versions of monomoraic lexical words which do exist in Japanese, they showed variability in their production of longer words, which might result either in truncated forms or in full forms at the same period of acquisition. Only the truncated variants are of interest to us here. These seem to have much in common with the findings of Pater and Paradis, in that they are no less than bimoraic. By and large, heavy, bimoraic, syllables appear to be retained as well as ends of words (6.22).

(6.22) Aki (2;1–2;4)

[pai]	/ippai/	'lots'
[takkɯ]	/toɾakkɯ/	'truck'
[poŋki]	/poŋkiki/	name of TV show
[koːki]	/çikoːki/	'aeroplane'
[doːʃa]	/ʤiːdoːʃa/	'car'

Adam (2002) considered data from a number of studies of children acquiring Hebrew and found that, for the initial stage the subjects produced sub-minimal monosyllabic words, either the stressed syllable or the final syllable, by and large but then progressed to disyllabic forms (6.23).

(6.23) Hebrew child data from Adam 2002

[sé.fer]	/sé.fer/	'book'
[ʤá.ma]	/pi.ʤá.ma/	'pyjamas'

[é.tet]	/ʃar.ʃé.ret/	'necklace'
[dé.det]	/la.ré.det/	'to get down'
[ká.xat]	/la.ká.xat/	'to take'
[té.fon]	/té.le.fon	'telephone'
[tí.na]	/kle.man.tí.na/	'tangerine'

Thus far, although with certain caveats, there seems to be a pattern emerging with regard to the patterns of emergent prosodic structure, children produce minimal words, either in terms of the disyllabic or the bimoraic word, by and large, sub-minimal truncations are disfavoured. Even in Japanese the sub-minimal productions are circumscribed and occur during the same period as the minimally bimoraic truncations. However, an analysis of a longitudinal diary study of Suzanne, a child acquiring Parisian French by Demuth and Johnson (2003) casts a certain amount of doubt on this claim.

Unlike English and Dutch, but in common with Japanese, adult French has a great number of sub-minimal lexical words and we list a selection in (6.24).

(6.24)	[ra]	*rat*	'rat'
	[bɔ̃]	*bon*	'good'
	[ba]	*bas*	'low'
	[pɛ̃]	*pain*	'bread'
	[do]	*dos*	'back'

It appears that Suzanne (6.25) went through the same stages as those of the Dutch and English children. However, what is interesting about her productions is that, unlike the Japanese children, she reduced both monosyllabic bimoraic and disyllabic targets to monomoraic forms.

(6.25) Suzanne

a.	[pɛ]	/peɲ/	*peigne*	'comb'
	[bɔ]	/bʁɔs/	*brosse*	'brush'
	[pɔ]	/pɔm/	*pomme*	'apple'
	[ta]	/sabl/	*sable*	'sand'
	[ta]	/taʁ/	*tard*	'late'
	[tɛ]	/fʁɛz/	*fraise*	'strawberry'
	[vɛ]	/vɛʁ/	*verre*	'glass'
b.	[tɔ̃]	/ʃosɔ̃/	*chausson*	'slipper'
	[ba]	/balɛ/	*balai*	'broom'
	[po]	/ʒypɔ̃/	*jupon*	'petticoat'
	[ba]	/basɛ̃/	*bassin*	'basin'

[da]	/madam/	*madame*	'Mrs'
[ma]	/fʁɔmaʒ/	*fromage*	'cheese'
[bi]	/buʒi/	*bougie*	'candle'
[da]	/salad/	*salade*	'salad'

It is noticeable that the majority of her disyllabic targets are reduced to their second syllable. This might be explained by the fact that, in general, French stresses the word or phrase final syllable.

Trisyllabic targets are reduced to disyllables and Demuth and Johnson suggest that the disyllabic foot represents her maximal preference (6.26).

(6.26) Suzanne

[ɔjɔ/bɔjo]	/dɔmino/	*domino*	'domino'
[byby]	/ɔmnibys/	*omnibus*	'bus'
[mɛne]	/pɔʔtmɔmɛ/	*porte-monnaie*	'purse'
[dade]	/ʁəgaʁde/	*regardez*	'look!'

We can contrast these productions with those of English acquiring Gitanjali, shown in Chapter 3, who inserted filler syllables in place of the unstressed initial syllables of truncated forms (for example [figiDo] for *mosquito* and [fikala] for *koala*). The same phenomenon can be found in Amahl's data where the dummy filler syllable is [ri] which was one of the examples in (1.15) of Chapter 1.

Another difference that singles Suzanne out from the children in the other studies we have considered, is that her sub-minimal, CV, period was considerably longer that that of the others. We might, therefore, want to consider the possibility that the minimal word as suggested above might be subject to language-specific constraints and that the fact that Suzanne's input contained a reasonable number of monomoraic words might explain why she continued to produce them for a longer period.

We saw in Chapter 4 in the study by Whalen et al. (1991) that the ambient language appears to have an influence of intonational pattern on babbling productions and it might appear also that it has some influence on the shape of early words.

Vihman et al. (2006) studied the disyllabic productions of American English, French and Welsh children at the four and twenty-five-word points. At these early stages, the infants studied produced both monosyllables and disyllables and Vihman and colleagues were interested in the influence of the ambient language on the rhythmic pattern of the disyllables and on the segment duration of the intervocalic consonant. Since the favoured type of intervocalic consonant in all three languages is a stop (the second in English is nasal and in French and Welsh is fricative), they investigated only intervocalic stop consonants. The three languages differ rhythmically. That is to say, that English is fundamentally a trochaic language where stress is marked by greater intensity, higher pitch, longer duration and a qualitative difference in full vs reduced vowels (although the patterns are more complex than that). French is generally described as a syllable timed language where stress is marked by longer duration on the phrase final syllable, thus rendering disyllabic utterances as iambic. Welsh falls between the two, having a trochaic pattern, but with the stressed vowels short and length marked on the following consonant. The initial syllable is marked by greater intensity but with pitch prominence on the final. Interestingly, at the four-word stage, all three groups of children produced final syllable lengthening. Overall, only one child from each language group produced all three elements of the test within a ±10 per cent range of adult values. By the 25-word stage, children's vocalisations in all three groups more closely approximated that of the adults. Overall, the forms produced by children, however, could not readily be assigned to the appropriate language group at four words (the French children being the most homogeneous of the three at this stage). By the twenty-five-word stage, they have all made progress towards the adult norm, producing greater similarity within language groups and greater differences between languages. In spite of the general picture of moving towards the adult model, there were inter-group differences in the extent of their matching to adult patterns. French and Welsh were generally closer and intra-group variability less. The English children remained more variable.

From what we have shown in this chapter, we could say that, by and large, there seems to be a pattern emerging in production that points to the possibility that UG might dictate direction of prosodic acquisition, although we cannot deny the influence of the ambient language. In the next chapter, we return to segmental acquisition to see to what extent we can show that there are features common to all children, no matter what the target language.

7

PATTERNS WITHIN PATTERNS

In this chapter, we look again at the patterns encountered in the first two chapters and consider why these patterns should occur and what they tell us about the learner's capacity in acquisition and also give a phonological analysis of these phenomena.

It has generally been recognised that, at a certain stage in their development, usually set at around the time that they have acquired their first fifty words, children begin to develop their phonological grammars. Just as in their acquisition of morphology (see Brown 1973 and Chapter 5), where apparently correct irregular past tense forms such as *went* are later replaced with *goed*, in some cases, it would appear that children's phonology regresses. Amy, who at an early stage of her development, with a vocabulary of far fewer than fifty words, was able to pronounce *juice* accurately, however, when her vocabulary increased, *juice* became [dus]. As we commented in Chapter 5, the best known instance of this type of regression is documented by Leopold (1947) whose daughter, Hildegard, between the ages of 0;10 and 1;9 pronounced the word *pretty* reasonably accurately, at least with a consonant cluster (either [pɹ] or [pw]) but who from then on proceeded to pronounce the word as [bɪdi].

We shall be considering the patterns which become evident from this fifty-word stage and, to some extent, the development of children's phonology thereafter. In particular, in Chapter 1, we identified a number of tendencies from child language that can also be found in adult forms in various languages. We will, briefly, outline the patterns so far looked at.

7.1 Patterns revisited

Reduplication was discussed at some length in Chapter 1 and it was shown that this tendency is present in the adult forms of many of the world's languages to indicate plurality, intensity, etc. One of the questions we have to ask about reduplication in child language is whether children exhibit such a pattern because they are presented with reduplicated forms of truncated words, such as French [dodo] from dormir [dɔʁmiʁ] 'sleep' which are produced by the child because that is the form in which they are addressed by the caretaker or whether the motherese form was initially an imitation of the child's own production. It is clear that types of reduplication are also prevalent in so-called 'baby talk' and extend to nicknames. Such names as 'Jojo' for Joanna frequently persist long after all other types of reduplicative form have disappeared. It might be suggested that reduplication plays a role in achieving the minimal word (discussed in Chapter 6).

Observing that, while all children do appear to exhibit some reduplication, there are those termed 'reduplicators' who use the device extensively and others, 'non-reduplicators', who use it rarely, Schwartz and colleagues (1980) looked at the productions of two groups of children of ages ranging from 1;3 to 2;0, half reduplicators and half non-reduplicators, over a period of some six weeks. Their criteria for reduplication were perhaps less stringent than those which we applied in Chapter 1, since their example tokens required merely a repeated consonant, and while most of their examples do also exhibit identical vowels, some such as [kɪkə] *chicken* do not. The purpose of the study was, first, to investigate the ability of each of the two groups to produce multisyllabic words (it was suggested that monosyllables are less likely to be reduplicated) and, second, to produce final consonants, since reduplications tend to avoid final consonants. The findings were supportive of the hypothesis in that the mean ratio of produced forms to total attempted forms for non-reduplicated multisyllables and final consonants were 0.11 and 0.20, respectively for the reduplicators and 0.67 and 0.44, respectively for the non-reduplicators. Schwartz et al. (1980) suggest that the use of reduplication was a conspiracy in the sense of Kisseberth (1970) to constrain the production of multisyllabic words and final consonants. In terms of an optimality theoretic (OT) account, we could suggest that a constraint that requires faithfulness to the input in terms of syllables is outranked by one that instructs the speaker to repeat the first syllable (or consonant). Yip (1995), discussing reduplication in adult languages, suggests a constraint REPEAT, which she suggests outranks *REPEAT. However, it seems to us that this is too crude a device when it comes to child data. Let us see how we might use this constraint, along, of course, with NOCODA, in the system of a reduplicator. Because the data provided by Schwartz et al. are limited and provide few similar tokens from the two groups of children, we are producing hypothetical examples gleaned from the data available in the literature (Tableau 7.1). Notice that we have not included the absolutely faithful candidate, since we assume that the child would not produce complex onsets at this stage.

Tableau 7.1

/blæŋkɪt/	REPEAT	NOCODA	FAITHσ	FAITH/$_{\text{CONS}}$
bæki	*			*
☞baba			*	*
bækɪt		*		

Clearly, for the child who could produce [bækɪt], the two constraints REPEAT and NOCODA would have to be demoted below the two faithfulness ones, whereas for the child for whom the output was [bæki], REPEAT would be demoted to below FAITHσ but NOCODA would still remain highly ranked.

In Chapter 1, we also listed a number of phenomena under the heading 'avoidances'. These include the loss of entire syllables, usually indicating that the child avoids unstressed syllables in favour of stressed ones. These patterns were discussed in Chapter 6 under the heading of 'Prosodic development'. However, in addition, segments can be avoided for a number of reasons. One reason is the child's apparent inability to produce a certain sound or type of sound. This might, from the phonologist's point of view, be explained through the non-specification of a certain contrast (see Chapter 6). Often, as we shall see below, the sound in question is substituted by another that the child is able to produce. Sometimes, however, the offending segment is omitted altogether. In (2.8c) in Chapter 2, we saw that one of Amahl's strategies to avoid fricatives, in the early stages, was to omit the offending sounds altogether (see again in 7.1):

(7.1)	[it]	*seat*	[ɑp]	*sharp*
	[up]	*soup*	[aʊt]	*house*
	[nu]	*nose*	[b̥i]	*please*

This strategy is also apparent in some early utterances from German-acquiring children Naomi and Annalena (Grijzenhout & Joppen 1998):

(7.2)	[abɐ]	/zaʊbɐ/	*sauber*	'clean'
	[at^{h}]	/zat/	*satt*	'satisfied'

We shall consider other strategies for fricative avoidance later. More commonly, however, avoidances are the result of cluster simplification which will be discussed in more detail below.

We also looked at additions, that is to say that we found that some children add consonants at the beginning of words or insert dummy syllables in place of the unstressed ones they have avoided. This could be construed as a requirement in the child's grammar to satisfy the constraint ONSET (syllables must have onsets). There are languages that require all syllables, even initial ones, to have onsets, although there appear to be no languages that only allow CV syllables. A further form of addition is the epenthesis of a vowel to break up consonant clusters.

Also in Chapter 1 we listed examples of consonant harmony, which were further expanded in Chapter 2. Notice that, although consonant harmony for primary place of articulation is unattested in adult language, it is very widespread in child language. We saw many examples of place harmonisation from English, French, Dutch, Arabic, Spanish and Portuguese. Although it has been suggested that the coronal place is the most likely target for harmonisation, we found that labial and dorsal may also be targeted in some languages (including English to a lesser extent). Harmonisation appears more likely to be regressive but there are also cases of progressive harmony to be found in the literature. The preference for regressive harmony, of course, reflects the anticipatory nature of speech, also shown in cases of assimilation of adjacent consonants in adult languages. In addition to harmony for place of articulation, we also encounter harmony to the nasal feature, for example Amy's [mʌmi] for *tummy*, as well as *mummy*, and [nɪnə] for *dinner* – and for the lateral feature, where other approximants harmonise with a lateral in the same word. In the case of the data from Amahl lateral harmony works in both directions – [lɒli] for *lorry* but [lɛlo] for *yellow*. In this chapter we shall look at further twists on these harmony patterns.

7.2 Canonical onset clusters

Clusters, as we saw in Chapter 2, can be initial, final or medial, where the two adjacent segments cross syllable boundaries in words. According to McLeod and co-workers (2001), based on calculations made by Locke (1983) on a study of 104 languages, taken from Greenberg's (1978) work on language typology, 39 per cent had word-initial onset clusters only; 13 per cent had solely final clusters and the remaining 48 per cent had both. Clearly, only languages that exhibited clusters were represented in the sample.

Within these groups, different challenges are presented to the learner. In the initial set, first there are what we described in Chapter 2 as canonical clusters, consisting of an obstruent followed by an approximant. In such cases, sonority rises from the initial element to the second one by a reasonable distance. Second, there are clusters consisting of /s/ (or in the case of German /ʃ/) followed by a stop consonant and /s/ followed by a nasal. Some languages, such as Arabic, present the learner with onset clusters of equal sonority and even anti-sonority clusters. As we shall see in this chapter, some languages also have clusters of greater complexity than this, including both anti-sonority clusters and those with more than two segments, which are not confined to the /s, ʃ/-initial.

7.2.1 Accounting for canonical onset clusters

In Chapter 3, we briefly introduced an optimality theoretic account of cluster simplification. The suggestion made was that there is a markedness constraint *Complex, which causes learners to avoid complex clusters, but which also applies in those languages that prohibit such clusters. We investigated a number of the patterns and considered how an OT analysis could account for the patterns discovered. At that point, we attempted to simplify the account mainly in terms of an interaction between this *Complex constraint and a faithfulness constraint, either Max (no deletion) or No-Coal (no coalescence), while the choice of the deleted member of the cluster was determined through relative sonority. You will recall that the universally preferred onset (Clements 1990) is that of lowest sonority based on the condensed scale in (7.3).

(7.3) *Relative sonority scale*
*Vowel >> *Approximant >> *Nasal >> *Fricative >> *Stop

Thus, when the child encounters a canonical Obstruent + Approximant cluster such as /br/, then the obstruent /b/ would be retained and the approximant /r/ would be lost. We were also able to show that, for the most part this ranking was also applicable to /s/-clusters. Notice, in the case of /s/ + stop clusters such as /sp/ the second, rather than the first member of the cluster, is retained because the fricative is of higher sonority than the stop that follows it. When it came to /s/ plus sonorant clusters (/sl/, /sw/ or /s/ + nasal), then two possible patterns could emerge. There are those children, such as Amahl (Smith 1973), who routinely lose the /s/ and retain the approximant or nasal and those, such as Gitanjali (Gnanadesikan 2004), who maintain the sonority pattern and retain the /s/ or some substitute for it. We were able to account for the difference between these two patterns, despite the fact that the sonority scale must be a fixed feature of language, based as it is on a phonetically measurable reality, by suggesting that the children who lose /s/ do so because fricatives are not yet part of their inventory (see Tableau 3.4, in Chapter 3). We will pursue these themes further later in this chapter.

You will have noticed in Chapter 2 that, while deletion of one or other of the segments involved seems to be the more common strategy to deal with the cluster simplification problem, some children also resort to epenthesis. See, for example, the data sets from European Portuguese and from Jordanian Arabic, (7.4) and (7.5), repeated from Chapter 2.

(7.4)	European Portuguese				
	Luis	[kɨɾɐ̃dɨ]	/gɾɐ̃dɨ/	*grande*	'big'
		[mõʃtɨɾu]	/mõʃtɾu/	*monstro*	'monster'
		[pɛdɨɾɐ]	/pɛdɾɐ/	*pedra*	'rock'
		[fɨɾawdɐ]	/fɾaɫdɐ/	*fralda*	'nappy'
		[fɨlojʃ]	/floɾɨʃ/	*flores*	'flowers'

(7.5)	Jordanian Arabic			
	Ameera	[bawaat]	/bwaat/	'boots'
	Khaleel	[kitaab]	/ktaab/	'book'
		[kalaab]	/klaab/	'dogs'
	Maya	[tileen]	/treen/	'train'
		[muʔallem]	/mʔallem/	'teacher' (masc.)

Further examples can be found in two Libyan Arabic-acquiring children (7.6) (Altubuly 2009):

(7.6)	Modi	Nodi	Adult target	
	[ʔaluːf]	[xaruːf]	/xruːf/	'sheep'
	[zabal]	[ʒabal]	/ʒbal/	'mountain'
	[zadiːd]	[ʒidiːd]	/ʒdiːd/	'new'
		[ziman]	/zmaːn/	'time ago'
		[siħaː]	/Sħaː/	'woke up'
	[batal]	[bakar]	/bgaːr/	'cows'

Any grammar we write for such children will need to show a different faithfulness constraint. The relevant constraint, which was alluded to briefly in Chapter 3 is one which also relates the input to the output but in a different way. Notice that all input material is retained and something else is added in the output. The name of the constraint is DEP (short for dependency). This constraint requires any material in the output to be dependent on equivalent material in the input. Clearly, in (7.4), (7.5) and (7.6) there is nothing to break up consonant clusters, which remain. So what is relevant here is the interplay between DEP and *COMPLEX (Tableau 7.2).

Tableau 7.2

/pɛdrɐ/	*COMPLEX	MAX	DEP
pɛdrɐ	*		
pɛdɐ		*	
☞pɛdɨrɐ			*

Notice that we have also included the constraint MAX in the reckoning because it could have been a legitimate strategy for the child to have deleted the /ɾ/. Indeed the European Portuguese acquiring child Inês in Chapter 2 (2.4) solves the cluster problem in just that way, as you can see in (7.7).

(7.7) Inês

[kɛ]	/kɾɛmɨ/	*creme*	'cream'
[abi]	/abɾɨ/	*abre*	'open' (imperative)
[pajɐ]	/pɾajɐ/	*praia*	'beach'
[tikiko]	/tɾisiklu/	*triciclo*	'bicycle'

7.2.2 The acquisition of canonical onset clusters

The best known and most comprehensive longitudinal study of the acquisition of phonology is Smith's (1973) account of Amahl's progress over some two years. During this time, Amahl acquired all types of onset cluster but it can be seen that his /s/ + obstruent clusters were the last. We have ignored putative Cj onset clusters as in *music*, which were not acquired during this period, because there can reasonably be said to be a doubt about whether Cj can form an onset or whether the /j/ is actually part of a diphthong /ju/ in English. This appears to be acquired somewhat later by children, its lack persisting well into the school years in many cases.

It will be recalled from section 2.1.2, that Amahl was a child who was later producing fricatives. We listed some of the strategies he employed to overcome this deficiency in (2.8) of that chapter. It turns out that the sound that gave him the most trouble and which he acquired later was /s/, so we shall leave the acquisition of this sound and the various clusters in which it is contained until the next section.

Canonical clusters begin to appear at Stage 9 – the period of a week from two years and 189 days (roughly 2;6) until two years and 196 days, although the output is somewhat variable at this stage. Although the odd fricative does appear in the data below, the clusters' targets are all stop + approximant, and fricative targets are attempted slightly later:

(7.8) Amahl at Stage 9

blue	[buː] [bluː]
clock	[klɒk] [glɒk] [ɣlɒl]
clean	[kliːn] [kʷiːn] [tliːn]
pretty	[bɪdi] [bʷɪdi]
please	[pliː] [bliː]

At Stage 9 also, Amahl does employ epenthesis – for example for *bread* he variably produces [bərɛd] and [bəɣɛd].

The period in which these forms were recorded was, of course, very short, as were all the separate periods in Smith's data. We can, nevertheless, get a flavour of the variability that is typical of acquisition at this stage. Ignoring substitutions, we can propose the child's grammar. Because OT is able to incorporate variable rankings, this pattern can be shown in Tableau 7.3.

Tableau 7.3

/bluː/	*Complex	Max
☞buː		*
☞bluː	*	

The dotted line between the two constraints indicates that they may be ranked in either order, *Complex >> Max yielding [buː] or, alternatively Max >> *Complex yielding [bluː]. We would show this variable ranking with a comma between the constraints rather than the double arrows: *Complex, Max.

By Stages 11–12 (2;207–2;227 days) Amahl appears almost to have mastered the stop + approximant cluster. There is one lapse in the data at this stage and this is [daɪv] for *drive* at Stage 12, and also, *bread* was variably [bɛd] [brɛd] and [blɛd] at the intervening Stage 10 and did not settle to be target faithful until Stage 13 (2;233–2;242 days).

(7.9) Amahl at Stages 11–12

		Stage
[blæk]	black	11
[blækɪt]	blanket	11
[blæŋkɪt]	blanket	12
[blɐd]	blood	11
[blu]	blue	11
[blɛd] [brɛd]	bread	12
[klɒk]	clock	12
[klaɪmd]	climbed	11
[glɒt] [grɒt] [krɒt]	cross	12
[pliː]	please	11

We can now propose that MAX outranks *COMPLEX in Amahl's grammar. He is still having some problems with target fricatives, however. We saw that he produced a fricative in place of a stop for one of the variants of /k/ in *clock* at Stage 9. At Stage 11 we see the beginnings of the labiodental /f/ with /v/ following shortly afterwards. Although we find [flɒg] for *frog* at this stage, he also produces [w] ([wɒg]) as he did at earlier stages – see for example his [wæwæ] for *flower* in (2.8) in Chapter 2 – along with [wlɒg] and [βʳɒg]. At Stage 11 he still produces [blɒm] for *from*. His *frog* is actually target faithful by Stage 15 and he has target /v/ at Stage 12.

7.3 NON-CANONICAL ONSET CLUSTERS

7.3.1 /s/-clusters

The /s/-cluster, which may also be a /ʃ/-cluster as in German, is a prevalent feature of Germanic languages from which we have most data. As we commented above, /s/-clusters come in three different forms. The first type is /s/ + stop which we found is treated by the majority of learners in much the same way as a canonical cluster. That is to say that /s/, being of higher sonority, is lost and the stop is retained. There are two types of /s/ + sonorant cluster, the canonical /s/ + approximant and the rather less common /s/ + nasal.

All the children reported in Chapter 2, initially reduced /s/ + stop to the stop, a situation which persisted for some time. In the case of

Amahl, as we have seen, this could partially be because he did not acquire /s/ until around Stage 22 (3;22–3;28 days) and the first /s/ starts to appear in clusters with approximants, although not necessarily target faithful shortly thereafter. We do not encounter an /s/ + stop until Stage 26 (3;113–3;158 days).

(7.10) Amahl at Stage 26

[strɔːbri] [strɔːbəri]	*strawberry*
[stɑːt]	*start*

We know, however, that Gitanjali and Julia could both produce /s/ where it was less sonorous than the other member of the cluster. We have insufficient data to be able to trace their development of /s/ + stop clusters, so it is not clear whether they followed the same course as those of Amahl. Gnanadesikan does comment, however, that /s/ + stop clusters are later acquired by Gitanjali also.

Although we suggested that /s/ + approximant and /s/ + nasal are, to some extent, different problems, which perhaps they are, they appear to be dealt with in much the same way in the early stages. We presented a comparison of the /s/ + sonorant targets of two children, who exhibit the two different strategies. These two children appear to be typical of many other children, who fall into one or other camp in this respect.

(7.11)

Amahl		Gitanjali	
[no]	*snow*	[so]	*snow*
[mɔ]	*small*	[sʊki]	*snookie*
[laɪt]	*slide*	[sip]	*sleep*
[wip]	*sleep*	[fok]	*smoke*
[ŋeɪk]	*snake*	[fɛrə]	*sweater*
[mɛu]	*smell*	[fɛw]	*smell*

Amahl, the child with no fricatives, retains the sonorant from the target, whereas Gitanjali consistently produces fricatives because of their lower sonority, which makes them 'better' onsets based on the scale shown in (7.3) above. We show a ranking for the no fricative child, repeated from Chapter 3 (Tableau 3.4), in Tableau 7.4.

Tableau 7.4

/sno/	*FRIC	*ONSET/SON	*ONSET/FRIC
so	*		*
☞no		*	

The two different patterns manifested by Amahl and Gitanjali are also found in German and Dutch (Goad & Rose 2004) (the sound represented by the symbol [ʋ] is a labiodental approximant which for some speakers is used to replace [ɹ] in English).

(7.12)	Annalena (German)			Robin (Dutch)		
	[lɑfə]	[ʃl]afen	'sleep'	[faːpə]	[sl]apen	'sleep'
	[misən]	[ʃm]eißen	'throw'	[suːpː]	[sn]oepje	'sweet'
	[nɛl]	[ʃn]ell	'quick'	[fajə]	[zʋ]aaien	'sway'

Julia and Trevor (Pater & Barlow 2003) incorporate an element of the sonority pattern exhibited by Gitanjali, in that they produce the /s/ in /s/ + liquid and /s/ + glide targets, but deviate from her pattern in the direction of Amahl when it comes to /s/ + nasal clusters, where they retain the nasal in preference to the /s/.

(7.13)	Julia	[nis]	*sneeze*
		[nek]	*snake*
		[mɛʊ]	*smell*
	Trevor	[mæp]	*snap*
		[nomæn]	*snowman*
		[niːz]	*sneeze*

For these two children, therefore, we will need to retain the *FRICATIVE constraint but to rank it between *ONSET/LIQUID and *ONSET/GLIDE, thus making a nasal initial word preferable to one with an approximant. Again, the phonetically attested sonority ranking remains intact, but we are able to interpolate the constraint dispreferring fricatives at the strategic point in the ranking. The tableau we showed for Julia's system in (3.9) of Chapter 3, has the constraint *ONSET/SON but clearly this needs to be broken down into the different levels of sonorant in order to be able to distinguish between her treatment of target /s/ + approximant clusters and her target /s/ + nasal. The new ranking for Julia must be:

(7.14) $\text{FAITH}_{[\text{LAB}]}$ >> *ONSET/GLIDE >> *ONSET/LIQUID >>
*FRICATIVES >> *ONSET/FRICATIVE >> *ONSET/STOP

Gitanjali's productions are somewhat more interesting in that, while retaining the preferred fricative onset, she also exhibits coalescence. So, while Amahl appears to delete segments from the target, she retains all the input information and amalgamates it (7.15).

(7.15) $s_1\, m_2\, o_3\, k_4 \rightarrow f_{1\,2}\, o_3\, k_4$

As we can see, the manner of articulation (fricative) of the /s/ has been retained and the place of articulation (labial) of the /m/ has been appropriated. Thus, in some sense, no deletion has occurred. Let us see how this might be represented in an OT tableau (Tableau 7.5). We have used the constraint UNIFORMITY rather than NO-COAL (no coalescence) favoured by Gnanadesikan in her account of Gitanjali's strategies.

Tableau 7.5

/smok/	*COMPLEX	*ONSET/SON	*ONSET/FRIC	MAX	UNIFORMITY
smok	*	*	*		
mok		*		*	
sok			*	*	
☞fok			*		*

Notice that the high ranking of *COMPLEX rules out the faithful candidate. The candidate [mok] is ruled out relative to [sok] because of the universal ranking of *ONSET/SON >> *ONSET/FRIC since both violate MAX. The optimal candidate [fok] triumphs because it does not violate MAX which, itself, outranks UNIFORMITY. The two onset constraints are only really critically ranked relative to each other while *COMPLEX is in contention with MAX in particular, and MAX has to outrank UNIFORMITY. The rankings as shown seem to indicate that the onset constraints in some way outrank MAX, but they should not be read as such. These rankings are schematised in (7.16).

(7.16) *COMPLEX >> MAX >> UNIFORMITY
*ONSET/SON >> *ONSET/FRIC

Although we cannot necessarily establish a ranking directly between *COMPLEX and UNIFORMITY, they are linked via transitivity through their relationship with MAX.

It might be possible to establish a better ranking if we were to employ the comparative tableau model (Prince 2002). Under this model, the constraint violations for the optimal candidate are compared with those for the various suboptimal candidates. Instead of asterisks for violations, as shown above, a 'W' denotes the violations which favour the winner and 'L' those which favour the loser. If both candidates (or neither candidate) violate a certain constraint, then there is no winner or loser mark. Let us work through Tableau 7.5 to see whether any further ranking can now be established. In Tableau 7.6 we show a demonstration of one of the failed candidates in relation to the winner. We shall then go on to demonstrate how to establish the overall ranking by means of a cancelling out process.

Tableau 7.6

	*COMPLEX	*ONS/SON	*ONS/FRIC	MAX	UNIFORMITY
fok~smok	W_1	W_1	1		L_1

The next stage is to repeat this exercise for all the losers and then show how a sole winner mark in any column ensures that the candidate bearing it is immediately ruled out and its entire row of violation marks is discounted. We show this as a staged operation in Tableau 7.7a and Tableau 7.7b. Notice the '1' in a particular cell shows that there is a violation of that constraint by the candidate but that it favours neither of the pair.

Tableau 7.7a

/smok/ ☞fok	*COMPLEX	*ONS/SON	*ONS/FRIC 1	MAX	UNIFORMITY 1
~smok	W_1	W_1	1		
~mok		W_1	L	W_1	L
~sok				W_1	L

Tableau 7.7b

/smok/	*COMPLEX	*ONS/SON	*ONS/FRIC	MAX	UNIFORMITY
☞fok			1		1
~smok	~~W_1~~	~~W_1~~	~~1~~		
~mok		~~W_1~~	~~L~~	~~W_1~~	~~L~~
~sok				~~W_1~~	~~L~~

The first stage of the operation is to locate a column with a single 'W' – which turns out to be the constraint *COMPLEX. We highlight this cell and thus establish the ranking of this constraint as highest.

We then cross out the entire row for [smok]. The cancellation of the [smok] row leaves a single 'W' in the [mok] row. When we delete this one we can establish the next highest ranked constraint: *ONS/SON. Having eliminated the candidate [mok], we can see that there remains a single 'W' in the MAX column, so we repeat the operation, leaving us with the ranking below:

(7.17) *COMPLEX >> *ONS/SON >> MAX >> *ONS/FRIC, UNIFORMITY

It remains impossible to rank the two final constraints, since both are violated by the winning candidate.

The solution proposed for Gitanjali might seem not to apply to her renderings of words such as *snow* and *sleep*, where we might suggest that a MAX violation occurs, since the /s/ is retained and the following sonorant appears to be deleted. If we bear in mind, however, that the place features of /n/ and /l/ are, in fact, coronal [+anterior], as are those for /s/, then coalescence would yield the same result as deletion.

For Amahl, the constraint *FRICATIVE persists somewhat longer, as we saw, thus as Stage 11 *sleep* still occurs as [lip]. Nevertheless, by around Stage 15 (2;261–2;271 days) his /s/ + approximant targets, like those of Lucy, were produced with coalescence, as we saw from the examples in (2.9) of Chapter 2, repeated here as (7.18).

(7.18)	Lucy (unpublished data)		Amahl	
	[fımın]	*swimming*	[fımın]	*swimming*
	[fɒn]	*swan*	[fıŋ]	*swing*
	[ɬaıd]	*slide*	[ɬip]	*sleep*
	[ɬipın]	*sleeping*	[ɬʌg]	*slug*

At this point, the constraint *FRICATIVE must have been demoted but there must still remain a constraint *[s] which outranks *ONSET/FRIC, thus permitting the candidate [fıŋ] to emerge as optimal (Tableau 7.8).

Tableau 7.8

/swıŋ/	*COMPLEX	*ONS/SON	*[s]	*ONS/FRIC	MAX	UNIFORMITY
swıŋ	*	*	*	*		
wıŋ		*			*	
sıŋ			*	*	*	
☞fıŋ				*		*

Notice that we cannot establish a ranking between *ONS/SON and *[s], since neither is violated by the winning candidate. However, the ranking established through the exercise in Tableau 7.7 might be informative.

A little later we have evidence of some kind of coalescence affecting /s/ + nasal clusters which are produced as voiceless nasals – *smell* is produced as [m̥ɛl].

7.3.2 Other types of onset cluster

Most of the data sets we have access to when considering consonant clusters, are from Indo-European languages, indeed, in this chapter, we have mostly considered English. It will be noticeable that all these languages exhibit the same types of cluster. Languages such as Japanese do not permit tautosyllabic clusters, so need not concern us at this juncture, although, of course, Japanese does allow heterosyllabic clusters, either containing geminates or nasal followed by homorganic consonant. However, there are languages, even within the broader Indo-European family, which permit more complex clusters; for example, Slavic languages exhibit some extremely complex clusters which apparently result from the historic deletion of a short vowel.

Łukaszewicz (2007) studied the syllable onsets in a child, Ola, acquiring the Slavic language, Polish, between the ages of 4;0 and 4;4. Polish allows a wider range of two place onset clusters than the languages we have been considering so far. Apart from canonical obstruent + approximant clusters where the sonority distance between the consonants is at least two points on the reduced sonority scale we presented in Chapter 2, which we show inverted in (7.19):

(7.19)	*Sonority scale:*	1.	Stops	[p, t, k, b, d, g, . . .]
		2.	Fricatives	[f, s, f, v, . . .]
		3.	Nasals	[m, n, . . .]
		4.	Liquids	[l, r, . . .]
		5.	Glides/high vowels	[j/i, w/u, . . .]
		6.	Non-high vowels	[ɑ, æ, ɛ, o, . . .]

In terms of transcription, we follow Łukaszewicz in using the apostrophe for palatalised consonants. We find nasal + approximant (*mleko* [mlɛkɔ] 'milk') as well as nasals in second position (*znowu* [znɔvu] 'again'); stop + fricative (*kwiatki* [kf'jatk'i] 'flower (nom.

pl)') and Fricative + Stop (*wpadł* [fpatw] '(he) burst into'), along with onsets containing a sonority plateau such as nasal + nasal (*mnie* [mɲɛ] 'me'); fricative + fricative (*swojgo* [sfɔjɛgɔ] 'his (gen.sg.)' and stop + stop (*ptaszek* [ptaʃɛk] 'bird').

At this stage in her development, Ola reduces all onset clusters to singletons, but let us look at the strategy she employs (7.20).

(7.20) Ola: Targets with glides as C_2

[sɔntsɛ]	/swɔɲtsɛ/	*słońce*	'sun (nom.sg.)
[suxa]	/swuxa/	*słocha*	'listen (3 sg.pres.)'
[gɔva]	/gwɔva/	*głowa*	'head (nom.sg.)'
[pɛs]	/p'jɛs/	*pies*	'dog (nom.sg.)'
[vɛs]	/v'jɛʃ/	*wiesz*	'you know'

Ola: Targets with liquids as C_2

[da]	/dla/	*dla*	'for'
[mekɔ]	/mlɛkɔ/	*mleko*	'milk'
[bata]	/brata/	*brata*	'brother (gen.sg.)'
[pɔsɛ]	/prɔʃɛ/	*proszę*	'please'
[kuja]	/krula/	*króla*	'king'

As we can see, Ola consistently loses the approximant retaining the 'better' onset. In such cases, we can suggest that she incurs a Max violation in order to avoid a violation of *Complex. When confronted with a fricative + nasal target, a fricative + stop or a stop + fricative target, she follows the pattern we encountered with Gitanjali, the segment of lower sonority survives:

(7.21) Ola

[zajɔmɛ]	/znajɔmɛj/	*znajomej*	'acquaintance'
[suf]	/snuf/	*snów*	'dream (gen.pl.)'
[bɛja]	/zb'jɛra/	*zbiera*	'collect (3 sg.pres.)'
[pat]	/fpatw/	*wpadł*	'(he) burst into'
[katk'i]	/kf'jatk'i/	*kwiatki*	'flower (nom.pl)'
[pɛʦɨtaj]	/pʃɛʦɨtaj/	*przeczytaj*	'read (imper.)'

Deletion is not the only strategy employed by Ola, she also incurs a violation of Uniformity in that she coalesces coronal stop + fricative or fricative + stop clusters as affricates. Polish makes a distinction between stop + fricative sequences of the type [tʃ] as in *trzy* [tʃi] 'three' and affricates [ʃ] as in *czy* [ʧi]. Ola's strategy in such cases is to combine the [+continuant] and [–continuant] features of the cluster into a single affricate (7.22).

(7.22) Ola

[ʦɛba]	/tʃɛba/	*trzeba*	'one must'
[ʦuw]	/stuw/	*stół*	'table'
[ʥɛntsa]	/zdɛɲtɕa/	*zdjęcia*	'photograph (nom.pl.)'
[ʥɛvɔ]	/dʒɛvɔ/	*drzewo*	'tree (nom.sg.)'

An example that is not listed as coalescence by Łukaszewicz is target /znɔvu/ (*znowu* 'again'), for which the child produces [dɔvu]. Here, the conditions mentioned above do not pertain, although the target cluster contains coronal consonants. This interesting example shows that the feature [–sonorant] from /z/ combines with [–continuant] of /n/ to produce [d], which, of course, retains the place and voice features of the original cluster. The ranking proposed to explain the examples in (7.22), is shown in Tableau 7.9. (Notice, however, that this ranking does not account for *znowu* which we shall discuss below.)

Tableau 7.9

stół /s_1t_2	*COMP$_{ONS}$	IDENT$_{[-CONT]}$	IDENT$_{[STRID]}$	MAX	IDENT$_{[+CONT]}$	UNIFORMITY
☞[$ts_{1\,2}$]					*	*
[s_1t_2]	*!					
[s_1]				*!		
[t_2]				*!		
[t_{12}]			*!		*	*
[s_{12}]		*!				*

This particular ranking requires the output form to retain both the [–continuant] and [+strident] features of the input, so the suboptimal candidates which coalesce as either [t_{12}] (no stridency) or [s_{12}] (retaining continuance) both fail. The coalescence in *znowu* could perhaps be accounted for if we were to suggest that the universally ordered constraints *ONS/NAS > *ONS/FRIC > *ONS/STOP are included in the ranking, we would be able to account for this output. The issue here is how these constraints might be ranked with regard to IDENT$_{[STRID]}$, since the input contains a strident which does not survive.

One question that needs to be addressed here, however, is why should it be that in the case of non-coronal clusters a segment is deleted, thereby incurring a violation of the higher ranked MAX? In Chapter 3, we showed that Gitanjali's favoured solution to cluster simplification was coalescence (see also Tableau 7.5 above). The motivation for the coalescence exhibited by Gitanjali was her preference for labial sounds. However, in cases such as *clean* [kin], where there is no labial to preserve, it appears that a MAX violation occurs rather than a UNIFORMITY violation. Gnanadesikan (2004) suggests that, in fact, the optimal candidate here still violates UNIFORMITY with a combination of Dorsal + Coronal:

(7.23)		Input		Output
clean	$k_1 l_2 i_3 n_4$	→	$k_{12} i_3 n_4$

On the face of it, this could imply that the retention of the dorsal outranks the retention of the coronal, thus producing a ranking:

(7.24) IDENT/LAB > IDENT/DOR > IDENT/COR

The only type of anti-sonority onset cluster occurring in English is the /s/ + stop type. In Polish examples we have seen, anti-sonority clusters appear also to be restricted to fricative + stop and the fricatives are strident. In many dialects of Arabic, however, other more complex clusters do occur. These, like the Polish examples, may involve flat sonority but may also involve anti-sonority patterns. We shall now look at the type of simplification patterns that occur in such languages.

The cluster reduction displayed by Loli between 1;6 and 2;0 (Altubuly 2009) acquiring Libyan Arabic appears to make use of a hierarchy of place of articulation. Dialects of Arabic, as we have seen, exhibit non-canonical complex onset clusters including those with falling sonority as well as flat sonority. Consider the data in (7.25):

(7.25) Loli (Altubuly 2009)

Target	*Child form*	*Gloss*
Target Coronal + Dorsal (or vice versa) → coronal		
/ɣsal/	[lal]	'wash'
/ʕsal/	[lal]	'honey'
/ʕṣiːḍaː/	[tida]	Libyan dish
/tʕaːli/	[tali]	'come'
Target Labial + Coronal (or vice versa) → labial		
/dwaː/	[waː]	'medicine'
/ʃwaj.ja/	[waj.ja]	'little bit'
/sbuːl/	[buːl]	'corn'
/smuːni/	[muːni]	'fat'

/ʃmaːl/	[maltu]	'nappy'
/zmaːlTuː/	[maltu]	'nail colour'
/ʒbal/	[bal]	'mountain'
Target Labial + Dorsal (or vice versa) → labial		
/kbuːt/	[buːt]	'coat'
/gmar/	[mal]	'moon'

Many of the deletions might be considered to be influenced by Loli's dislike of fricatives, which we shall discuss in the next section, but this cannot explain all of them. One observation that can be made is that dorsals never survive and that labials always survive. For example, where the target contains two fricatives, as in /ʕṣiːḍaː/ → [tida] Loli replaces the coronal fricative with the equivalent stop, or where the target form is /dwaː/ and *[da] would be the preferred output according to sonority, in fact the child retains the preferred labial place in preference to the coronal. This strategy is, of course, somewhat similar to Julia's (see Tableau 3.5 in Chapter 3). We can, therefore, establish a hierarchy, this time, reminiscent of that we found in the harmony processes of Clara acquiring French in (2.28) of Chapter 2.

(7.26) labial > coronal > dorsal

Interestingly, as we shall see in the next section, Loli does not exhibit place harmony, although we can find other types of harmony.

One of the problems with trying to chart the progress made by children in the acquisition of some feature is that, even with very detailed longitudinal studies such as that presented by Smith (1973), the child will not necessarily utter the words we want it to utter at regular intervals. In addition, such studies are very time-consuming and take years to yield results. One way of speeding up the process is to employ an apparent time method as has been popular in sociolinguistic research. This apparent time method tries to simulate the passing of time in language change by recording speakers from different age groups and comparing how they deal with some feature that the researcher wishes to study. Daana (2009) used a similar method to attempt to discover the type of progress made by her subjects in the acquisition of various types of onset cluster. While this methodology cannot be said to be ideal, since different subjects were studied, it does allow us to gain an insight into the order in which the various types of cluster are mastered. The method is, nevertheless, perhaps more appropriate to the study of acquisition than to the study of language change, since acquisition is a building process, whereas language change must suppose that language changes from one generation to the next ignoring the fact that the older subjects in the study will not retain all the features of their youth and their language will also change, even though perhaps to a lesser extent than the younger generation.

Daana's method was to record five groups of six children ranging in age from two to seven years old. Clearly within these groups there was considerable variability but, nevertheless, she was able to discern various trends and, in the absence of any further collaboration from Jordanian or any other Arabic dialect, we shall report those trends.

It has to be pointed out that the method used to elicit relevant tokens was to show the children pictures which meant that the children in all the age groups were attempting the same words. This method enabled the researcher to track the acquisition of clusters easily; although her other aim was to chart the development of the Arabic plural. This does not concern us here, but we must be wary about claiming mastery, since we have no spontaneous tokens.

There are few restrictions on onset consonant clusters; they may rise in sonority, be of flat sonority or, indeed, fall. The target forms of the tokens elicited are shown in (7.27).

(7.27)	[**mr**aaje]	'mirror'	rise
	[**tr**een]	'train'	rise
	[**kl**aab]	'dogs'	rise
	[**bw**aab]	'doors'	rise
	[**ʒm**aal]	'camels'	rise
	[**kf**uuf]	'gloves'	rise
	[**kt**aab]	'book'	flat
	[**ħS**aan]	'horse'	flat
	[**mʕ**allem]	'teacher'	fall
	[**rf**uuf]	'shelves'	fall
	[**mʔ**aSS]	'scissors'	fall

It will be noticed that some of the clusters of rising sonority have a respectable distance between the sonority of the two consonants, whereas others have a smaller one. Clusters /tr/, /kl/ and /bw/ all have the canonical obstruent + approximant form, while /mr/, /ʒm/, and /kf/ have much closer distances between the sonority values of the two members. If these children were to follow the same course as Amahl, we would expect them to master the canonical 'good' clusters first.

Most of the clusters were reduced to singletons by the 2-year-old children, as might have been anticipated from what we have discovered so far. However, some children at this age can manage to produce clusters. The interesting thing about such productions is that it is not the canonical clusters which predominate in the output – the two favoured are /mr/ where the rise in sonority between the nasal and the approximate is very slight and /ħS/ with a sonority plateau. One significant feature of these clusters, which may account for the ability of the young child to produce them, is that they employ different areas of the vocal tract in their articulation. Thus, it might be suggested that this is a purely biologically controlled ability. When the children reach three, they are beginning to acquire clusters which display rising sonority such as [treen] *train* and [klaab] *dogs*. The last clusters to be mastered are those with falling sonority, which are not adult-like until at least the age of seven.

7.3.3 Extrasyllabic consonants

As we have commented, the only type of onset permitted in English with more than two segments is one where the initial sound in /s/ followed by a canonical cluster and a similar story can be told about German where /ʃ/ replaces /s/ in such clusters. Indeed, this is a typical feature of Germanic languages in particular. It has been suggested (see Barlow 2001; Gierut 1999) that the /s/ does not actually belong in the syllable but should be treated as an adjunct attached to the syllable node rather than forming part of the onset as shown in Figure 7.1a. Goad and Rose (2004), on the other hand suggest that the appendix is attached to the prosodic word as shown in Figure 7.1b.

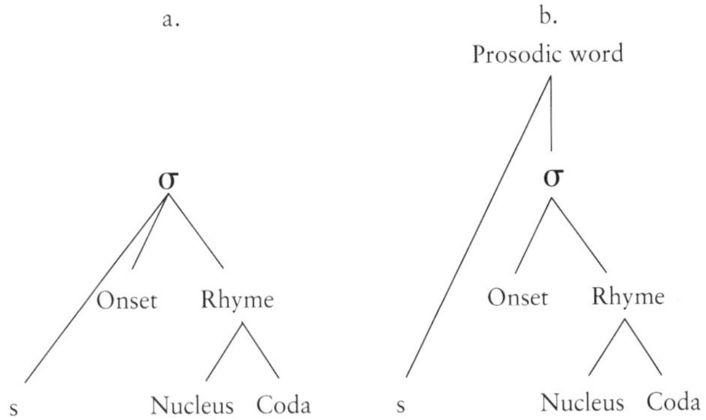

Figure 7.1 *Extrasyllabic consonants.*

This analysis, according to its proponents, explains the different stages at which canonical and /s/-initial clusters are acquired.

A similar proposal is made about apparently anti-sonority consonant clusters in Polish. Łukaszewicz (2006) discusses the acquisition of what she describes as extrasyllabic segments. These are segments that fail to comply with the sonority sequencing generalisation (7.28), which of course is also defied by /s, ʃ/.

(7.28) *Sonority sequencing generalisation (SSG)*
The sonority profile of a syllable must rise until it peaks and then fall.

This means that our canonical onset cluster is absolutely fine, because it complies with the generalisation since the initial obstruent is less sonorous than the approximant that clusters with it and the vowel will be more sonorous than the approximant, forming the peak. Sonority will then fall away.

In Polish, however, sonority may rise again in the coda without forming a new syllable as it would, for example, in English in a disyllabic word such as *bottle* [bɒtl]. The Polish word /vjatr/ 'wind' is monosyllabic but with a non-compliant coda. Łukaszewicz tells us that, word internally, syllabification complies with the SSG and ignores onset maximisation in words such as /kɔn.tɔ/ 'bank account', these aberrant clusters occur on word edges.

You will recall that Polish permits two obstruents to form a cluster with fricatives and stops occurring in either order. These, according to the analysis presented in Łukaszewicz 2006, do not constitute violations of the SSG, however, sonorants of the type shown above, do clearly violate SSG. We will not pursue the complexities of the argument for the extrasyllabicity of these segments, and its interaction with other processes of the language, and refer the reader to Łukaszewicz's paper.

The study contained in this paper concerns the acquisition of these extrasyllabic segments by a child Ania between the ages 3;8 and 5;1, with a certain amount of corroborative evidence from other Polish acquiring children.

Development is in four stages. At Stage 1, in spite of the apparent mastery of other clusters, Ania deletes the extrasyllabic element. The omitted elements from the orthographic forms are shown emboldened as in the original. These truncated forms are compared with other forms of the same stem, where the offending sound is syllabifiable.

(7.29)

Ania	Target word		Compared with	
[srɛbnɨ]	*srebrny*	'silver' (Adj.)	[srɛbrɔ]	'silver' (N.)
[vjat]	*wiatr*	'wind' (nom.sg.)	[vjatru]	'wind' (gen.sg.)
[bup]	*bóbr*	'beaver' (nom.sg.)	[bubra]	'beaver' (gen.sg.)
[zjat]	*zjadł*	'ate' (masc.sg)	[zjadwa]	'ate' (fem.sg)

Notice that in the last two examples (7.29), the child has acquired final devoicing which is a prominent feature of Polish.

At Stage 2 (3;11), Ania has introduced another strategy to deal with the offending consonants. What is described as a 'fleeting' /ɛ/ is epenthesised in order to incorporate the extrasyllabic consonant into the structure (7.30).

(7.30) Ania

[vjatɛr]	*wiatr*	'wind'
[mɔtɔtsik'ɛl]	*motocykl*	'motorcycle'
[bɔbɛr]	*bóbr*	'beaver'

Epenthesis does not occur across the board, however, leading Łukaszewicz to speculate that the child has formed a hypothesis that some of these words have an underlying /ɛ/ in line with other forms in Polish which exhibit /ɛ/ ~ zero alternations.

At Stage 3 (4;0), Ania's productions are adult-like but, interestingly, there is a further twist to the story because at Stage 4 (4;11), in a selected set of items, devoicing of the pre-extrasyllabic consonant is suspended and assimilation to this sonorant appears. The comparison of the two stages is shown in (7.31).

(7.31) Ania

		Stage 3	Stage 4
wiatr	'wind' (nom.sg.)	[vjatr]	[vjadr]
niósi	'(he) carried'	[ɲusw]	[ɲuzw]
wyrósł	'(he) grew'	[vɨrusw]	[vɨruzw]

7.4 Consonant clusters in other positions

7.4.1 The acquisition of codas

McLeod et al. (2001) suggest that word-final coda clusters are acquired, in general, rather sooner than word-initial clusters. Certainly, we saw in (2.19) of Chapter 2 that Amahl had mastered a certain number of coda clusters by Stage 6, although, as we saw in (7.8) and (7.9) above, canonical onset clusters were beginning to appear at Stage 9, but did not become established (not always exactly target-faithful) until Stages 11 and 12.

The types of coda we find at Stage 6, or sooner, fall into two categories. The first that we commented on in Chapter 2, are the /nd/ clusters which were target faithful by Stages 6 and 7. We have included only monomorphemic clusters, as past tense markers (/t d/) and plural markers were only just beginning to appear. We find, for example, [kʌmd] for *came* at Stage 8 and [klaɪmd] at Stage 11. We list some of the monomorphemic clusters in (7.32) with the stage at which they appear in parentheses.

(7.32)	Amahl		Stage (6)
	[waɪnd]	*find*	
	[wɪnd]	*wind*	(7)
	[aɪnd]	*behind*	(7)
	[b̥ɛnd]	*bend*	(5)
	[wɛnd]	*friend*	(5)
	[d̥ænd]	*stand*	(5)

The target *friend* next occurs at Stage 16, this time with a consonant cluster in initial position ([y̥rɛnd]).

The other category of coda cluster that appears relatively early is the stop + stop cluster. By and large, the targets for these clusters would be fricative + stop, but they occur at the stage before Amahl has truly acquired fricatives.

(7.33)	Amahl		Stage (3)
	[wɔpt]	*soft*	
	[wɛpt]	*flex*	(4)
	[wɪpt]	*lift*	(6)
	[wapt/waft]	*draught*	(3)
	[b̥ɒkt]	*box*	(9)

We do not find any /l/ + stop clusters in these early stages, perhaps because post-vocalic /l/ would generally be vocalised, as we commented in Chapter 2. Kirk (2008), in an elicited study of the acquisition of clusters by children in Rhode Island USA deliberately omitted any examples of liquids as the first element of a coda cluster, because the dialect in question, like that being acquired by Amahl, is non-rhotic and most post-vocalic /l/s are vocalised. (See Chapters 2 and 3 for discussion of vocalisation.)

7.4.2 Medial clusters

As we saw above, Amahl did not start acquiring onset clusters until Stage 9 and they were not established until Stages 11 and 12. Even then, /s/-clusters lagged behind. There is some evidence of coda clusters from Stage 3 (see (7.32) and (7.33) above). We know that at Stage 1, he has no medial clusters either, however, by Stage 2 heterosyllabic medial clusters do start to appear. These are generally homorganic nasal + stop clusters as we show in (7.34).

(7.34)

Amahl		*Stage (2)*
[æŋgi]	*angry*	
[wɪŋgə]	*finger*	(2)
[mæŋgo]	*mango*	(2)
[nʌmbə]	*number*	(2)
[ɪndaɪt]	*inside*	(2)
[æŋgu]	*handle*	(2)
[wɛndi]	*friendly*	(4)
[b̥ændɪt/bæŋgɪt]	*bandage*	(4)

Barlow (2003) reports on three children acquiring Spanish. We discuss two of them here.

In common with the children reported on so far, BL4 (2;8) reduces tautosyllabic clusters to the less sonorous of the pair, both in initial and medial position, as we can see from the sample in (7.35).

(7.35) BL4 (Barlow 2003)

[pato]	/plato/	'plate'
[patanos]	/platanos/	'bananas'
[kumpanos]	/kumpleaɲos/	'birthday'
[libo]	/liβro/	'book'
[ten]	/tren/	'train'
[etela]	/estreja/	'star'
[tike]	/tiɣre/	'tiger'

As we explained in Chapter 2, this pattern reflects the universal preference for low sonority onsets (see Clements 1990). You will notice, however, that BL4 does produce a medial heterosyllabic cluster, just as we found for Amahl. We show some examples in (7.36).

(7.36) BL4 (Barlow 2003)

[elefante]	/elefante/	'elephant'
[elfin]	/delfin/	'dolphin'
[manzana]	/mansana/	'apple'

[sombelo]	/sombrero/	'hat'
[dulses]	/dulses/	'sweets'
[albol]	/arβol/	'tree'
[tampa]	/estampa/	'stamp'
[falta]	/falda/	'skirt'
[leŋga]	/leŋgua/	'tongue'

Notice that although Spanish does not permit tautosyllabic /s/ + consonant clusters, BL4 does not produce such clusters heterosyllabically either. The overall pattern exhibited, similarly to Amahl, is sonorant + obstruent. This reflects the universal preference encapsulated in the Syllable Contact Law (Murray & Vennemann 1983), which states that the sonority of a coda must not be lower than the onset that follows it. Thus, a new syllable will begin in a sonority trough. We may wish to make a note that there are exceptions to this 'law', for example the English word *atlas* which has a sonority trough as a coda. This is because English, in common with many other languages, does not permit /tl/ as an onset, because of the OCP. It might be more exact, therefore, to describe this as a tendency.

The other child reported on by Barlow, SD1 (3;4) has, unusually, acquired tautosyllabic clusters but not heterosyllabic ones. She does, however, conform to the favoured pattern when reducing medial sonorant + obstruent clusters, in that it is always the less sonorous obstruent that is retained (7.37).

(7.37) SD1 (Barlow 2003)

[brika]	/briŋka/	'(she) jumps'
[blaka]	/blaŋka/	'white'
[exetes]	/xente/	'people'
[duθes]	/dulses/	'sweets'
[ʧaklas]	/ʧaŋklas/	'sandals'
[legua]	/leŋgua/	'tongue'

Like BL4, Ola (Łukaszewicz 2007), respects the syllable contact law and, as we saw in (7.20) and (7.21) above, avoids tautosyllabic clusters. Where the target contains a cluster, whether tautosyllabic or heterosyllabic, Ola converts it to a heterosyllabic one that adheres to this law. Her strategy for target stop+sonorant clusters is particularly interesting. In the data in (7.38) we show some examples of this strategy. One point should be made in the context of these data; Ola replaces both liquids /l/ and /r/ with /j/ in isolation but consistently avoids them in clusters (as we also showed above). However, in the context of medial clusters, she replaces all approximants with nasals. Some of the targets in (7.38) contain stop+nasal tautosyllabic clusters and others contain stop+approximant clusters. In either of these cases, Ola employs the strategy of metathesis and reverses the order of the stop and sonorant in order to achieve a smoother contact between syllables. (We have inserted full-stop marks between the syllables in the transcription of Ola in 7.38).

(7.38)	Ola			
	[jun.do]	/nudno/	*nudno*	'boring'
	[vɨm.baw]	/vɨbraw/	*wybrał*	'choose' (3 sg.masc.past)
	[dɔm.ba]	/dɔbra/	*dobra*	'good' (fem.)
	[wu.pan.da]	/upadwa/	*upadła*	'fall' (3 sg.fem.past)
	[pɔ.mɔŋ.ga]	/pɔmɔgwa/	*pomogła*	'help' (3 sg.fem.past)
	[ɔŋ.gɔ.ʥɛ]	/ɔgrɔʥɛ/	*ogrodzie*	'garden' (loc.sg.)

Metathesis, the process of zchanging the order either of segments as in such commonly encountered forms as [wɔps] for *wasp* or reversing the order of onset segments in longer words such as Leah's (unpublished data) [pæŋkutə] for *computer*, is often characterised as speech errors (see Fromkin 1973 for a large catalogue of such errors among which are many which involve metathesis).

7.5 Substitution patterns

Within the patterns of cluster simplification, we can find evidence of other processes at work. Some of these are avoidance strategies, as we suggest in the case of Loli in (7.25) above. Others are somewhat coincidental as we saw when looking at the data from Amahl in Chapter 2 and included in (7.11) above. As we saw there, Amahl, retained sonorants from /s/ + sonorant clusters, but the result was not transparent, as we can see from the two examples repeated here (7.39):

(7.39)	Amahl	[wip]	*sleep*
		[ŋeɪk]	*snake*

We went on to show that the reason for these outputs had to do with the consonant harmony that was prevalent in Amahl's productions at this stage. The point here is that even with the omission of /s/, these words are coronal-initial and are, therefore, targets for the harmonising effect triggered by the following labial and dorsal consonants. Where the final consonant is, itself, a coronal, as in *slide*, then the initial /l/ is produced as [d]. Meanwhile, let us tentatively propose a constraint limiting the occurrence of coronals in the presence of either labials or dorsals. We shall refine this constraint in due course. We can label this constraint *COR/LABIAL,DORSAL (7.40).

(7.40) *COR/LABIAL,DORSAL
Coronals harmonise regressively with the place of articulation of a following labial or dorsal.

The order in which the place labels are placed should ensure only regressive harmony. We know that Amahl, like Trevor (Chapter 2, in 2.23), also exhibits, to a lesser extent, progressive harmony but only involving dorsals. Clearly this constraint does not cover that type of harmony. This new constraint can be incorporated into our Tableau 7.4 above. As we have there, we are omitting the faithful candidate and the inviolable (at this point) constraint *COMPLEX which rules it out.

In Tableau 7.10 we see that although the candidates [lip] and [wip] both violate the constraint against sonorant onsets, [lip] also incurs a further violation which rules it out.

Tableau 7.10

/slip/	*FRICATIVES	*ONS/SON	*ONS/FRIC	*COR/LAB,DORS
sip	*		*	
lip		*		*
☞wip		*		

7.5.1 Fricative avoidance

According to Jakobson, it must be predicted that children will acquire fricatives after stops (see (3.5j) and (3.5k), in Chapter 3). This prediction is made on the basis of observed order of acquisition and also on the basis of language typology. Although some of Jakobson's predictions do not seem to be borne out in real language data and some children do acquire some fricatives alongside stops, it is clear that, in general, stops come first. We might explain this from the ease of articulation point of view. Stops require a less subtle positioning of the articulators than do fricatives. As we saw above and in Chapter 2, one device employed in the avoidance of fricatives is simply to delete them. Ingram (1975) analysed data from a number of studies looking at the progress in the acquisition of fricatives and affricates in word initial position and concluded that they go through a number of stages in the direction of acquiring adult-like forms. Ingram makes the observation that some of the children avoided words with initial target fricatives and affricates in the early stages, but when they found they needed them, the order that emerges from the data analysed can be seen in (7.41).

(7.41) Deletion > Tighter closure (fricatives replaced by stops or affricates, for example ð → d) > Looser closure (glides or liquids, for example f → w) > Acoustically similar fricative but with loss of stridency or place of articulation (for with example θ → f) > Target faithful

We can find examples of all these type of substitution in the data from Amahl, although not necessarily in that strict order. It is clear, however, that the examples of initial fricative deletion occur at Stage 1. We repeat the illustrative data from (7.1) above along with data from Daniel (Menn 1971) who seems only to avoid initial fricatives.

(7.42)	Amahl	[it]	*seat*	[ɑp]	*sharp*
		[up]	*soap*	[aʊt]	*house*
		[nu]	*nose*	[b̥i]	*please*
	Daniel	[it]	*seat*	[iz/is]	*cheese*
		[ɨʃ]	*fish*	[ufs]	*juice*

Although Ingram is discussing initial fricatives, two of our examples from Amahl are taken from target fricatives in final position. We have included one example of /h/ loss – this occurs in all target /h/-initial words at this stage and persists for some time. It could constitute a case of fricative avoidance or, as is common in many dialects of English, simply be an example of /h/-dropping. The other fricatives avoided here are /s/ and /ʃ/ in initial position. From the first stage for some time, labial target /f/ invariably becomes labial [w] in initial position, although it becomes /p/ in final or pre-consonantal position, as we can see in the data set in (7.43).

(7.43) Amahl

[wɪt]	*fish*	[wæː]	*fire*
[wæwæ]	*flower*	[wʊt]	*foot*
[wɪŋə]	*finger*	[wit]	*feet*
[wɑpt]	*laughed*	[maɪp]	*knife*
[wɛpt]	*left*	[wɪpt]	*lift*

Simultaneously, with deleting the target coronal fricative, Amahl resorts to stopping as we can see in the data in (7.44).

(7.44) Amahl

[d̥ʌt]	*shut*	[d̥aɪ]	*shy*
[g̊ɪŋɪŋ]	*singing*	[d̥id̥in]	*sitting*
[d̥ɪdə]	*scissors*	[d̥i]	*see*
[g̊ɛg̊u]	*thank you*	[d̥ɛ]	*there*
[d̥u]	*shoe*	[d̥aɪt]	*light*
[wip]	*sheep*	[g̊ɪk]	*think*
[wibə]	*zebra*	[d̥u]	*zoo*

We can also see, in some of the data in (7.43) and (7.44) that a following labial or dorsal sound will cause a coronal to harmonise. (We shall return to patterns of harmony in later.) From the point of view of the underspecification theory discussed in Chapter 6, however, these substitutions are interesting. You will recall that the coronal is deemed to be the unmarked, or default, place or articulation. This could well account for the consistency with which /f/ is replaced by [w]. Ingram (1975) provides examples of substitutions for fricatives made by a number of children, one of whom is Amahl, and it appears that [w] is the most likely segment to substitute for /f/, if any such substitution has taken place. On the other hand, coronals /s, ʃ, θ, z, ð/ either gain a place of articulation from another consonant in the word (*singing, thank you, sheep, think, zebra*) or are replaced by the corresponding stop.

Notice that we could account for the initial [d̥] of *shut* by the presence of the final [t]. However, no such explanation can be offered for the [d] of *see*. The other examples are clear enough, if the place node is enhanced, then the unspecified place will search for one with the features specified. Thus in *sheep* it will find the labial place and in *think* it will find the dorsal place.

Two other types of harmony discussed in Chapter 2 were lateral and nasal harmony. Let us first consider lateral harmony. This is a situation where the presence of a lateral approximant in a word will cause another approximant in the same word to harmonise for the feature [+lateral], even although in one case shown below (*real*), the coronal target of the lateral is missed. In (7.45), we repeat some of the data from Chapter 2, which illustrate this.

(7.45) Amahl

[lɒli]	*lorry*
[liu/lil]	*real*

[lili]	*really*
[lolin]	*rolling*
[luli]	*usually*
[lɛlo]	*yellow*
[lɛlɪn]	*yelling*
[læli]	*Larry*

In fact, it is only target /j/ and /r/ which are affected by this harmony; /w/ is produced faithfully. The Rice and Avery (1995) feature theory can also help to explain these facts. We know that /w/ is specified for the place labial and for continuance. The other approximants, being coronal, are not specified for place, therefore, the lateral default under the oral branch of sonorant voicing. Where no place is offered, lateral spreads. If the labial place is available, then that will spread into the placeless approximants.

(7.46) Amahl

[wæbɪt]	*rabbit*
[wum]	*room*
[wɛpt]	*left*
[wɪpt]	*lift*

This lateral harmony may also allow for the substitution of a target fricative if no other specified feature is available, as we saw from Amahl in (2.42) of Chapter 2. Here we see, again, that the target has a coronal fricative (7.47). There is one apparent exception in this list, that is *trolley* (as well as *troddler* which is not in the list below). We commented in Chapter 2 that this substitution would appear to provide evidence that Amahl perceives /tɹ/ as [ʧɹ] – indeed it is very likely that this would be the actual pronunciation.

(7.47) Amahl

[lilin]	*ceiling*
[wɪdo lɪl]	*window sill*
[lɒli]	*trolley*
[lɪlɪŋ]	*shilling*
[lælo]	*shallow*

The same solution is adopted by Loli acquiring Libyan Arabic (7.48).

(7.48) Loli

[lal]	/ɣsal/	'wash'
[lal]	/ʕsal/	'honey'
[lali]	/SAli/	'pray'

Like Amahl's, Loli's featureless target fricatives will assume the manner feature [stop] if there is a stop in the word (7.49).

(7.49) Loli

[dit]	/ʒɪt/	'she came'
[daddi]	/ʒaddi/	'grand father'
[dida]	/saʕiːda/	proper name
[tida]	/ʕSiːḍaː/	Libyan dish
[daːd]	/suʕaːd/	proper name
[kuku]	/kux/	'bungalow'

Like Daniel (Menn 1971), but unlike Amahl, Loli also exhibits nasal harmony which can be used for fricative substitution (7.50).

(7.50) Loli

[nuni]	/ʕjuːni/	'my eyes'
[nini]	/ʃini/	'what'

Since, in common with many other Arabic-acquiring children, Loli produces target /r/ as [l], we can see from (7.51) that the nasal can also substitute /l/ for Loli.

(7.51) Loli

[nuna]	/nuːra/	proper name
[naʔma]	/laħma/	'piece of meat'

We can summarise the patterns exhibited by Loli in terms of a relative strength hierarchy as shown in (7.52):

(7.52) stops, nasals > laterals > fricatives

This hierarchy predicts that the empty fricative will search for the strongest feature to harmonise with. If there is a stop or a nasal available, then that is where the empty node will find its feature, however, in their absence, it will make do with the lateral. Because the nasal is stronger than the lateral, nasal harmony involving the lateral will occur. We have no data from Loli to show whether laterals are ever replaced by stops or whether stops are ever subject to nasal harmony. We did see, in Chapter 2, however, that for Daniel and Amy, the nasal appears at some point to have outranked the stops in terms of strength.

Some of the harmony processes we have encountered, however, involve place of articulation which we shall consider in the next section.

7.5.2 Place of articulation harmony

The underspecified feature model proposed by Rice and Avery (1995), based on Avery and Rice (1989), which we have been using as a tool to describe the manner of articulation harmony in the previous sub-section, must predict the place strength hierarchy as shown in (7.53).

(7.53) Dorsal > labial > coronal

Indeed, this is precisely the hierarchy that emerges for the majority of English-acquiring children as we saw in Chapter 2 (see Rose 2000). It was not necessarily the hierarchy reflected in the harmony processes from other languages, to which we will return later.

Pater and Werle (2001, 2003) present an OT account of this type of harmony based on data from Trevor up to the age of 2;4. Trevor, as we saw in Chapter 2, exhibits both regressive harmony and progressive. The coronal is targeted both by the dorsal and the labial and the labial is targeted by the dorsal. The dorsal can only act as a trigger and never a target. In (7.54) we give a list of forms produced between the ages of 1;3.4 and 1;9.2 of examples of all the possibilities. (The key to the codes shown in (7.54): T = coronal, K = dorsal, P = labial, and V = vowel.)

(7.54) Trevor

[gɔg]	*dog*	regressive coronal → dorsal	(TVK)
[kok]	*coat*	progressive coronal → dorsal	(KVT)
[kæːg]	*cat*	progressive coronal → dorsal	(KVT)
[gɪːguː]	*tickle*	regressive coronal → dorsal	(TVK)
[gʌg]	*bug*	regressive labial → dorsal	(PVK)
[kʌk]	*cup*	progressive labial → dorsal	(KVP)
[gɪgʊ]	*pickle*	regressive labial → dorsal	(PVK)
[bɛːp]	*bed*	progressive coronal → labial	(PVT)
[bʌbə]	*butter*	progressive coronal → labial	(PVT)
[pap]	*top*	regressive coronal → labial	(TVP)

The two issues addressed here are: the direction of the harmony and the nature of the trigger. Pater and Werle (2003) point out that the variability shown in (7.54), that is bidirectionality and two triggers, are only apparent at the earliest stages and by the time Trevor has reached the age of 1;11 only regressive and dorsal triggered harmony remain, that is TVK and PVK.

Another way of describing consonant harmony is 'non-adjacent assimilation'. We know that such assimilation is not found in adult languages, but adjacent assimilation is extremely common. For example it is very unusual for a nasal not to share a place of articulation with an adjacent stop. Similarly, there is a strong tendency for two adjacent obstruents to agree in voicing. Such behaviour can be explained in terms of ease of articulation. Crucially, although progressive assimilation can be found in languages, for example the English plural morpheme assimilates to the voicing setting of the stem final consonant (thus *kæts* but *dɒgz*), assimilation tends to be overwhelmingly regressive. The explanation, given briefly in Chapter 2, is that we tend to anticipate the sound we are about to make, since speech is not made up of a string of isolated segments but rather an overlapping series of gestures.

Pater and Werle present Tableaux showing Trevor's changing grammar through three stages of his development. The constraints they propose are shown in (7.55 to 7.57).

(7.55) FAITH[DOR], FAITH[LAB], FAITH[COR]:
Retain the input place of articulation for dorsal, labial or coronal.

(7.56) AGREE:
Consonants agree in place of articulation (thus leading to assimilation or harmony).

(7.57) AGREE-L-[DOR]:
A consonant preceding a dorsal must be homorganic with it.

Notice that the constraint in (7.57) gives a special status to the dorsal consonant. Trevor passes through three stages. These are listed below (Pater & Werle 2003: 395). Following the description of each stage, we shall present the tableau that gives the relevant ranking at that stage.

(7.58) *Stage 1*
Consistent regressive dorsal harmony to labial and coronal targets
Variable progressive dorsal harmony to coronal targets
Variable regressive and progressive labial harmony to coronal targets

At this stage AGREE and FAITH[COR] will not be ordered, since this ranking will account for the variability in progressive harmony. They illustrate this with the example of an input /kot/ *coat* which may variably surface as [kok] (where AGREE outranks FAITH[COR]) and

[kot], which would result from the reverse ranking. Since progressive harmony does not occur in words such as *cup* both FAITH[LAB] and FAITH[DOR] have to outrank AGREE. However, as we saw, dorsal attacks labial regressively, so we can now sort out the relative ranking between FAITH[DOR], FAITH[LAB], and factor in AGREE-L-[DOR]. All this is shown in Tableau 7.11.

Tableau 7.11 *Stage 1* (Pater & Werle 2003: 397)

Input	Output	F[DOR]	AGR-L-[DOR]	F[LAB]	AGREE	F[COR]
TVK	TVK		*!		*	
	☞KVK					*
PVK	PVK		*!		*	
	☞KVK			*		
KVT	☞KVT				*	
	☞KVK					*
KVP	☞KVP				*	
	KVK			*!		
TVP	☞TVP				*	
	PVP					*
PVT	☞PVT				*	
	☞PVP					*

Notice that the emboldened inputs may be subject to change or variation. The one input that is not subject to either, KVP, is not emboldened, this indicates that labial will never target dorsal. Where there appear to be two optimal outputs, this is because harmony is bidirectional at this stage.

At Stage 2, progressive harmony has disappeared which means that, although the ranking appears to be more or less the same as at stage 1, an important difference has emerged, the variable ranking has shifted. Now a firm ranking has been established between F[COR] and AGREE, indicating that only regressive harmony persists. The only variable at this level is whether the dorsal targets the labial or not. By this stage, we can see, other outputs are target faithful. We show Stage 2 in Tableau 7.12.

By Stage 3, as Trevor approaches two years old, only regressive dorsal harmony targeting coronals remains. Tableau 7.13 shows that both dorsal and labial place remains faithful and only coronal is vulnerable.

Tableau 7.12 *Stage 2* (Pater & Werle 2003: 398)

Input	Output	F[DOR]	AGR-L-[DOR]	F[LAB]	F[COR]	AGREE
TVK	TVK		*!			*
	☞KVK				*	
PVK	☞PVK		*			
	☞KVK			*		
KVT	☞KVT					*
	KVK				*!	
KVP	☞KVP					*
	KVK			*!		
TVP	☞TVP					*
	PVP				*!	
PVT	☞PVT					*
	PVP				*!	

Tableau 7.13 *Stage 3* (Pater & Werle 2003: 398)

Input	Output	F[DOR]	F[LAB]	AGR-L- [DOR]	F[COR]	AGREE
TVK	TVK			*!		*
	☞KVK				*	
PVK	☞PVK					
	KVK		*!	*		
KVT	☞KVT					*
	KVK				*!	
KVP	☞KVP					*
	KVK		*!			
TVP	☞TVP					*
	PVP				*!	
PVT	☞PVT					*
	PVP				*!	

The other claim made by Pater and Werle is perhaps a bit more contentious. They want to show that the dorsal place is universally stronger than either labial or coronal. This would, of course, be the prediction made by the Rice and Avery feature system discussed in Chapter 6 and expounded in the previous subsection in respect to manner harmony. Pater and Werle provide evidence of the failure of dorsals to assimilate to the place of articulation in Korean, while other places are susceptible to adjacent assimilation. The data from Korean that they provide, shown in (7.59), demonstrate the relative strength of the three places, that is dorsal is never targeted but can target either coronal or labial, labial can only target coronal; neither is the subject of assimilation by coronals.

(7.59)	/əp+ko/	→	[əkko]	'bear on the back+conj'	(labial ← dorsal)
	/kamki/	→	[kaŋki]	'a cold/influenza'	(labial ← dorsal)
	/pat+ko/	→	[pakko]	'receive and'	(coronal ← dorsal)
	/han+kaŋ/	→	[haŋkaŋ]	'the Han river'	(coronal ← dorsal)
	/kot+palo/	→	[koppolo]	'straight'	(coronal ← labial)
	/han+bən/	→	[hambən]	'once'	(coronal ← labial)
	/paŋ+to/	→	[paŋto]	'room as well'	(dorsal/coronal)
	/kuk+pap/	→	[kukpap]	'rice in soup'	(dorsal/labial)

The data shown appear to be collaboration for the claim that the place strength ranking we showed in (7.53) has some universal validity. However, we showed in Chapter 2 that not all languages seem to exhibit the same preferences.

As we saw in Chapter 2, while the patterns discussed by Pater and Werle are very common in English acquiring children, other patterns of harmony can be found in the literature. They suggest that the reason that Dutch, for example, appears to have a preference for labial harmony, including targeting dorsals, can be attributed to the prevalence of vowel-to-consonant assimilation in Dutch discussed by Levelt (1994), where labiality spreads. A number of the examples can be attributed to this spreading, but it is hard to make this claim for all of the examples. The same appears to be true of the German cases shown in the same chapter, where target /gɛlp/ is manifested as [bɛlp]. We also found labials targeting dorsals in Jordanian Arabic as well as one case from English.

Pater and Werle comment on the case of Clara acquiring Canadian-French who appears to exhibit coronal targeting dorsal. According to their hypothesis, this should not happen since the coronal place is deemed to be the weakest position and, therefore, more vulnerable. Such harmony is always regressive and only occurs in CVCV words. Their suggestion is that, because stress in French is final, the trigger consonant is initial in a stressed syllable, and the pattern exhibited is the result of positional faithfulness (Beckman 1997), that is that the weaker onset is influenced by the place of the stronger, stressed, one.

It is not clear how all the counterexamples to their proposed universal hierarchy can be explained. It would appear that, by and large, coronal is the most vulnerable to attack, but there might be no real strength ranking between dorsal and labial.

7.6 Conclusion

In this chapter, we have concentrated on the most common types of pattern found in child language. We have attempted to consider in depth a number of the phenomena listed in Chapters 1 and 2 but have not covered some that might possibly deserve further investigation. The sorts of substitutions we have discussed have involved consonants as it is apparent in the literature that, although children do sometimes substitute vowels, for example, as we observed in Chapter 2, Joan (Velten 1943) had a tendency to produce [u] in place of other vowels, by and large, vowels seem to be more target true than consonants. We noted, for example, in Chapter 2 and also in our account of Pater and Werle's discussion of harmony found in Dutch, that vowels tend to influence preceding consonant place of articulation, rather than the consonant influencing the vowel. This might be attributed to the anticipation of a following vowel. Thus, a rounded vowel might well induce a preceding labial consonant and a front vowel might well cause a dorsal consonant to be manifested as a coronal.

We have discussed deletions, insertions and coalescence only in the context of segmental phonology, although syllable deletion is obviously very prevalent. This was covered in depth in Chapter 6. Segments, on the other hand are deleted or inserted in order to avoid consonant clusters.

In the concluding chapter, we shall provide an overview of our investigation and look at various aspects that are interesting but that space did not allow us to include in these chapters.

8

CONCLUDING REMARKS

As suggested by the title of this book, a variety of child phonology patterns from different languages were presented. In order to gain a sound understanding of phonological acquisition, we investigated to what extent various theories of acquisition are capable of providing an account for child data and discussed some important issues. In this final chapter, we sum up all the major points of our investigation in the hope of presenting a clear overview of all our discussions. The knowledge of the reader acquired throughout the book will now be put into perspective by the presentation and further discussion of current issues in phonological acquisition.

We set out into the area of phonological acquisition with illustrative sets of data that were presented in **Chapter 1**, and which called for the active participation by the reader in phonological analysis. There was no in-depth discussion nor was there any reference to theory in this chapter and data sources were also omitted, since the aim was to familiarise the reader with common patterns of child speech and to promote objective phonological analysis of child data. Also, by presenting data from adult languages of the world, we showed that the processes observed in young language acquirers are not arbitrary nor specific to children. **Chapter 2** continued to present more patterns observed in child data and revisited some of the patterns from the first chapter, adding explanatory discussion and making reference to theoretical concepts. Here, the sources of the data were provided along with the names of the children concerned in order to allow the reader to discover the intra- and inter-child variability, in other words the various strategies employed by learners.

One pertinent question that was not pursued in the first two chapters concerned the reduplicative patterns commonly observed in children at the onset of speech production and presented as a linguistic process employed by both adults and children in the first chapter. It is only natural to suppose that reduplicative babbling is a precursor of first words and linked with reduplication in early production.

While Jakobson suggested that there is no link between babbling and first words and some studies have found very little influence from the native language on vocal development during the babbling stage, other studies have observed reduplication patterns from babbling in first words. It is extremely likely that onomatopoetically reduplicated words in the input may influence the child's babbling and reduplication, since there are observations that young children eagerly reproduce extra-grammatical adult onomatopoetic reduplications. However, it is not clear what the underlying mechanisms are and to what extent it is a universal phenomenon.

An alternative perspective to the linguistic view is that of motor stereotypy, according to which babbling is a rhythmic motor activity, not different from stereotyped movements that are common in infants during the first year of life, such as repeated movements of the limbs under developing control. It could be that babbling starts out as biomechanical behaviour which develops into linguistic behaviour – phonetic exercise turning into phonological play activity – thus filling the gap between play and communication. If we view consonant harmony along these lines, as a phonetically motivated phonological phenomenon, then reduplication could be considered a phonological phenomenon motivated by motor stereotypy. However, we must bear in mind that not all children babble before they speak or, as we saw in Chapter 7, use reduplication as a productive strategy, although most children do babble and many reduplicate in varying degrees. Nonetheless, the link between gesture and speech, or phonetics and phonology, is an interesting topic that is worthy of future research.

The universality of child patterns in the first two chapters led us to explore the notion of Universal Grammar (UG) in **Chapter 3**, where we examined whether phonological theories can provide adequate explanations. First, we investigated markedness, a principle that is claimed to be innate, which guides the learner in acquisition. We saw how the inconsistent usage of the term in different domains makes it difficult to come to a consensus about its exact meaning because of the different manifestations of markedness in language data. Hence, we looked at concrete claims of markedness originating in linguistic analysis itself. While the Jakobsonean markedness theory had difficulties with variability in child language and the Stampean markedness theory had problems in accounting for phenomena which have no phonetic basis, optimality theory (OT) appeared to offer more than just a remedy to the difficulties of previous theories through the flexibility provided by its architecture. We pointed out some of the problems created by this flexibility and the explanatory efficiency of the theory.

One of the consequences of the flexibility found in OT is the extreme difficulty in distinguishing grammatical and extra-grammatical factors in the data, as physiological development in child production cannot be attributed to grammar. As for the explanatory efficiency of OT, with evaluation of the structure (markedness) being separated from repair (constraint ranking), variability in child language is explained as individuality, which seems to counteract the clear connection established within the theory between acquisition and typology through markedness constraints. A consequence of the flexibility found within OT that was not discussed is the development of the theory in recent years. Modifications towards explicit modelling of phonological acquisition have been proposed, resulting in advances taking the form of not only new constraints and sophisticated learning algorithms, but also OT models under various names, such as functional OT, stratal OT, stochastic OT, and so on. We can take this to suppose that there is still more work to be undertaken before OT can be applicable as a complete theory of phonological acquisition.

For our purposes, however, the main problem we found in OT was its basic assumption that the onset of speech production is equated with the initial state of the grammar and the child's underlying representations are fully specified. There are data indicating that the child's underlying representation at the onset of speech production may not contain the full set of phonological features, to which markedness refers, and it is now accepted as a fact that since perception precedes production, the child's phonological grammar has already turned in the direction of language specificity at the onset of production. These shortcomings are not specific to OT, but an inherent consequence of most models of first language phonological acquisition being production-based and thus neglecting perceptual aspects of acquisition. Nevertheless, the standard assumption of the initial state of the grammar cannot be valid for the stage at which first words appear in children. Thus, before taking these as invalidating phonological theory, which otherwise has the explanatory adequacy of cross-linguistic observations in child and adult languages, we turned to perceptual studies in search for what the child brings to the task of language learning.

Our investigation into the beginning of phonological acquisition took us to the pre-production stage of acquisition in **Chapter 4.**

Infant perceptual studies show that human infants have a bias for speech and that even neonates can discriminate speech contrasts in any human language. In the early days of infant perceptual studies, researchers tended to interpret the incredible abilities exhibited by infants as a biological predisposition to distinguish the universal set of phonetic contrasts. However, with an analogical demonstration of how phonetic units differ from phonemic categories, we could see that the discriminative capacity of the youngest infants is based on acoustic and phonetic discrimination abilities. When we looked at perceptual development, we found that at around six months, the infant starts to organise the vast amount of phonetic information according to categories that are specific to the ambient language. This is the beginning of phonology, when the universal learner starts to attune to the linguistic environment and development moves towards acquiring mental representations for the storage of speech sounds.

We found that by the time infants utter their first words, the process of becoming perceptually attuned is more or less complete, but the question of whether speech perception is a human-specific attribute remained unanswered. Hence, we sought comparative studies of human versus non-human speech perception, only to find that they do not show any difference between humans and non-humans. Since this does not imply that the same cognitive mechanisms are used for human language across species, and since a left hemispheric cerebral dominance for language has been claimed to be specific to our species, we looked at structural and functional brain asymmetries in human infants and adults and in non-humans. Although evidence is far from pointing clearly and unequivocally to language being unique to humans, nor is it the case that there is no neurological difference between humans and non-humans either. Therefore, with no clear answers about the initial state of the grammar and being, rather, directed away from the idea that language is specific to humans, we were led to pursue our investigation of the ongoing 'nature-or-nurture' debate into the area of non-linguistic explanations of child patterns.

The current trend in phonological acquisition research is for theorists to take account of behavioural studies on perception that employ experimental procedures, rather than relying solely on child production data that have been collected in various ways, ranging from longitudinal diary studies of one child to non-longitudinal cross-linguistic data with a large number of children, and for behavioural studies to seek further support for their findings in brain studies, which is becoming increasingly facilitated due to recent advances in brain-imaging techniques. A welcome aspect of this is the inclination of various theories of language acquisition to take a more scientific approach. However, caution must be taken when consulting perceptual studies.

First of all, experimental procedures with children are notoriously difficult. Second, although perceptual discrimination performance in infants and young children is above chance, it is not the case that they perceive in the same way as adults, since their performance is far below that shown by adult native listeners. Third, as infants acquire meaning at around ten months of age and seem to not distinguish minimal pairs of meaningful words until approximately six months after the appearance of first words, there must be a difference between contrasts distinguished using nonsense words as opposed to real words. Furthermore, it seems to be difficult to obtain the same results in replications of behavioural studies when different procedures (high-amplitude sucking, heart rate measures, visual habituation and dis-habituation, head turn testing, and so on) are employed. Also, since researchers have not yet been able to reach a consensus as to what exactly is a perceptual unit, it is possible that studies of human speech perception by human infants and non-humans use a measure that is different from what is actually being used. As for linguistic rhythm, an important aspect of language, but a topic that has received far less attention than segments, we must remember the fact that only humans can move their bodies to rhythm, which in turn is supported by the ability of people with hearing impairment to sing, dance, and even use rhythm linguistically in the form of poetry. Despite all this, we cannot place enough emphasis on the fact that perceptual studies do provide a conspicuous insight into language acquisition, where future research can be expected to reveal more, for example in studies of bilinguals, which has only just started.

In **Chapter 5** we introduced some studies that lie outside mainstream linguistic theory to explore the view that language is acquired on the basis of computation or statistical learning. Here, we asked the question of how large a role is played by language experience in phonological development and experienced a vivid illustration of the important role played by the input and the sensitivity of pre-verbal infants to statistically tractable distribution of language elements. We saw how a connectionist model of production, which assumes perceptual errors and production errors based on physiological and motor constraints being part of child production patterns, can plausibly explain child data, but faces difficulties in accounting for why some consonant harmony patterns are more prevalent than others. Clearly, the physiological development of the child cannot be language-specific nor have any influence from input, but it affects speech production. Thus, we discussed how physiological factors influence production patterns.

To further investigate the validity of input-based approach to child production, we considered a study examining the ambient language influence on the order of acquisition of English codas and saw that predictions made by high probability and frequency for early coda production does not hold for all children. Since input-based models acknowledge that there are other factors influencing acquisition than distributional properties in the adult language, we looked at infant-directed speech (IDS) and visual cues as potential influences on child patterns. While the purpose of IDS seems not only to aid perception, but it also allows the infant to access features of the language to aid their production, visual cues also appear to play an important part in aiding the child to recognise and reproduce sounds.

However, as was the case with linguistic theories, we found that there is no single input-based theory that can account for all the phenomena seen in child language. While we must acknowledge that infants seem to be incredibly sensitive to quantitative information in the input language, which undoubtedly influences them in a way that such experience contributes to changes in the linguistic system, the main problem with non-linguistic accounts of acquisition is that they are all based on occurrence frequency of various linguistic units and patterns in the input. Some of the implications are the difficulties in explaining the U-shaped curved of learning and observations of cross-linguistic tendencies in children and of different production strategies used by children acquiring the same language. It is also difficult to define exactly what type of linguistic input is analysed by the learner as well as how often various linguistic elements occur within a language, which is not limited to the adult target language, as mentioned before. Thus, we can suppose that not enough is known about the factors in the linguistic environment that contribute to the language learning in order to justify acquisition based purely on language experience.

Another implication of acquisition being based purely on occurrence frequency is the assumption that phonetic units are acquired before phonemes. Since the relationship between phonetic units and phonemic categories is not uni-dimensional or as simplistic as our demonstration using a hypothetical example of paper and paper products that we presented in Chapter 4, the first problem encountered is in explaining how phonetic units develop into phonemes in the child. Speech sounds within any language, whether it is in a child or an adult, cannot be compared without any reference to their function in the language. An account relying solely on quantitative measures would predict a strict order of acquisition, despite children exhibiting different production strategies, and the assumption of phonetic acquisition as a prerequisite would furthermore predict some languages to be more complex than others, which contradicts the view that no language is easier or more difficult to acquire than another. Thus, it is reasonable to suppose that there are other factors than those we have looked at in this chapter. In fact, there are input-based studies suggesting that once infants have started attuning to the phonetic categories of the ambient language at around ten months of age, mere exposure to distributional properties of the ambient language is not enough and that social interaction plays an important part too. However, since it is not the case that autism, which has a negative effect on social interaction, prevents children from acquiring a native language, it would be interesting to see whether future research investigating linguistic development in autistic children would show how much language learning is influenced by factors related to social interaction.

When we consider how earlier linguistic accounts of child production studies neglected the influence of the ambient language and assumed that either each child has its own individual learning style or innate predisposition is underlying child patterns both within and across all languages, in which case a set of unmotivated derivational rules in the spirit of SPE was offered as explanation, the inclination of language acquisition research to commit to language experience without assuming any innate abilities is quite understandable. On the other hand, since frequency-based approaches do not have the tools for explaining the use of various strategies by children acquiring the same language or exploring the possibility that phonetic acquisition may not be a prerequisite of phonological acquisition, it is likely that that there is another crucial factor influencing acquisition.

The fact that the observed cross-linguistic developmental similarities are too extensive to be ignored and any normally developing child is capable of mastering any one of the thousands of languages of the world equally well is exactly that which gives us the reason to believe that there must be some unifying concept underlying them, *ceteris paribus*. While experience-based models of phonological acquisition deny that anything is innate in the child learner, approaches that assume markedness to play a role, however small that may be, do not deny the influence of the ambient language on child patterns, as it is thought that the input triggers the default settings to be set, re-set, or develop further. The dilemma for linguistic theories of acquisition is that it is markedness cannot be examined directly, since it is so often the case that it coincides with what is considered to be simple and/ or occurs most frequently in the languages of the world and various child production data are heavily influenced by the ambient languages. However, since this line of thought fits in with observations of various strategies used by children, it was considered appropriate to return to linguistic models of acquisition in the next chapter, but this time to examine linguistic models that take perception and ambient language influence into consideration.

Given that ambient language influence plays a much larger part than has hitherto been assumed, the theme of **Chapter 6** was early phonological production where we considered explanations of how the child might build up a phonological structure of segments, syllables and prosody. We looked at how the input to the child is related to the child output and found that there is sufficient evidence to allow us to assume that the adult surface forms serve as the input to the child, except in cases of misperception that occur in children. We then saw how linguistic models sought to overcome the dilemma caused by the developmental gap between perception and production and we contemplated what could be the underlying representation used by the child in both production and comprehension.

A straightforward single grammar model within the framework of OT runs into problems with misperceptions, since all contrasts are assumed to be accurately encoded in the underlying forms, as well as with production since it does not allow earliest child production to contain any marked forms, even if such forms are of high occurrence frequency or of high phonotactic probability. We saw an improvement in an alternative OT model with constraints operating in two domains, perception and production. However, since the grammar in this model also assumes only one set of underlying representations and does not differentiate surface forms from lexical forms, an obstacle is created by the child who produces unmarked surface forms and, at the same time, marked output forms that are not coupled with meaning. As it is not unusual for children to learn new words by repeating them, the main problem with any single grammar model, since there is only one set of underlying representations, is that it cannot account for novel words that enter the lexicon through phonology without elaborating a mechanism that not only distinguishes between real words and non-words, but also connects these two types of word in terms of development.

Subsequently, we turned to a two-lexicon approach based on autosegmental phonology that assumes two sets of underlying representations by incorporating the concept of underspecification. We showed that while it overcomes previous problems, it is not really a model with two separate grammars, since it is merely underspecification contained in the theoretical framework that necessitates adult forms in the input to be de-specified for the purpose of production where they become respecified. Consequently, it must assume phonological accuracy in the child's perception of the adult form, which further presupposes full specification of phonological features at the underlying level. The assumption of underlying representations in the child being fully specified implies that all features are given innately and development does not take place in this area of phonology. Since the child's comprehension of an adult form only implies an accurate mapping of it to the meaning and there are studies revealing that full specification cannot be assumed for earliest lexical representations, thus suggesting that the complexity in featural composition is something that develops in the child, we moved on to investigate the phonological theory of underspecification.

We illustrated how the fundamental premise of underspecification theory, the child initially having only a minimal structure beyond the simple consonant–vowel contrast and building structure one step at a time, provides a unified account of what we have encountered so far. However, since segmental acquisition is only one side of the coin and underspecification theory cannot answer the question of how preverbal infants learn their language-specific phonotactics without access to the full set of phonological feature specifications, we looked at prosodic development in children. First, we investigated the psychological reality of the syllable as a linguistic unit and saw that although we do not find adequate evidence to justify the assumptions of the basic CV syllable or trochaic bias in infants, the syllable is utilised by infants in linguistic analyses of the input, since they are capable of distinguishing different linguistic rhythm from birth. Yet, since prosodic development refers to a larger unit than phonological features and syllables, we were led to examine the shape of utterances perceived and produced by children. Here we saw that children's word forms reflect either the foot structure or the minimal word and although we could observe some patterns of emergent prosodic structure, prosodic development seems to be subject to language-specific constraints.

Thus, having seen that what the child brings to the task of language learning is possibly only underspecified phonological features and the syllable and that the influence of the ambient language is undeniably immense, the current trend in phonological acquisition studies, both within and outside linguistic theory, looking towards the concept of bootstrapping seems to be a natural consequence. Bootstrapping is based on the idea of using what you know to acquire new abilities: Prenatal auditory experience feeds into neonatal perception; when the acoustic and phonetic knowledge of the input language is linked to meaning or concepts, phonological representation of word forms is bootstrapped from the perceptual system; and syntactic structures are bootstrapped from phonological knowledge. Also, this mechanism is thought to reorganise the initial biases observed in infants, such as language discrimination based on rhythmical properties, discrimination of phonetic contrasts that seem to be categorical, preference for speech over non-speech, and discrimination of lexical versus grammatical words. Of these biases, the first two have been found in non-humans, as mentioned in Chapter 4, but although future research could find the other two in non-humans as well, the underlying mechanism behind infants extracting information from the input before and/or after birth may still be specific to humans, since what is extracted at the initial state may not be specific to spoken language. This is supported by the fact that grammar is also found in sign languages and the non-hearing population can also sense rhythm. If bootstrapping starts inside the womb where speech sounds are not heard clearly and there are no innate rhythm-bearing units to guide the infant, we might wonder how newborns, who are not yet exposed to distributional properties of the ambient language, would know what to look for in the linguistic input.

In **Chapter 7** we returned to the theme of child patterns produced by children from around their fifty-word stage and revisited some of the data from the first two chapters. More data were introduced and this time we also looked at the influence of the building process on the segmental output. The two main foci of the chapter were consonant cluster patterns, since they are most typical object of simplification processes, which do not occur randomly, and substitutions made by children both in such areas as fricative avoidance, which could include an element of harmony, and harmonisation of place of articulation. By looking at cross-linguistic differences in child patterns, variability within a language group and variation within a language, we reconfirmed that the influence of the ambient language cannot be underestimated and that different strategies are available for children to use, even among those acquiring the same language. We also found, however, that even across very disparate language groups, there are patterns that can be detected in the strategies observed and that there are similarities to be found in the progress of acquisition. We also showed how some of the theoretical tools introduced in earlier chapters could be employed to model the patterns exhibited.

It may be worth mentioning that the data presented in this book are different from data presented in normative studies frequently used in clinical assessments, as we have drawn these from linguistic analyses of child production. While normative data are important in the clinical assessment of child phonology, they seem to be in short supply and most of them are on consonants. In addition to the fact that phonological acquisition is obviously more than just mastering the pronunciation of consonants, caution is called for when referring to 'older' resources, since such studies tend to differ in the criteria used with a further consequence of differing in the age of consonantal acquisition. Also, when looking at large sample studies, it may be a good idea to bear in mind that since individual variation cannot be maintained in such studies, phonemic acquisition may be lost in phonetic acquisition. While linguistic analyses view various child data as phonological systems, normative data studies tend to refer to child production that differs from that of the adult as error patterns.

Although data were presented from as many languages as possible, we could not help but to concentrate heavily on European and, specifically, English data because of their richness and the availability of cross-linguistic data being far from adequate for our investigation into what may underlie phonological patterns exhibited by children. However, CHILDES, the central database for child languages that was established to promote child language research is continuously expanding, which means that child data are becoming increasingly more accessible than ever before. Nevertheless, we must face the fact that more than half of the world's languages are tone languages, on which hardly any comparative data are available. Thus, we could hope for more research in child tone languages, which will no doubt lead to new insights into the process of acquisition, by virtue of phonological contrasts being manifested through prosodic elements, rather than segmental features.

Throughout the book, we have contemplated non-disordered child data. However, data from children with delayed acquisition present useful confirmation of some of the patterns we have discussed, since they mirror paths followed by normally acquiring children and data from disordered speech have the potential to reveal mechanisms underlying phonological acquisition. An interesting future direction is the investigation of whether there is a connection between speech errors and child patterns, and if so, to what extent such connection can tell us about language.

Finally, our overall conclusion is that phonological patterns in children exhibit both language-specificity and general trends that go across child and adult languages. Since investigations of 'new' child languages that have not been reported before, of which there are very many, would reveal more phonological patterns in children, the patterns presented here are by no means comprehensive. However, although the child's phonological system lacks complexity compared to adult language, there is good reason to suppose that children have phonological systems that are abstract in more or less the same ways as adults. When the focus is on the acquisition of language-specific phonology, emphasis tends to be on the differences between languages, and when it is on cross-linguistic similarities, the influence of language-specific phonological properties tend to be neglected. Perhaps this lies at the base of why we were not able to find a single theory that was compatible with all the observed child patterns. Without espousing any particular theory, we have attempted to be as objective as possible in our analyses and discussions as well as to point to pitfalls that could possibly be found in coming closer to the truth. While experimental studies on child language abilities could benefit from considering cross-linguistic tendencies and aiming to demonstrate the child's more basic grammatical competence, theoretical work on developmental phonology should reconsider innateness assumptions, since the role played by UG appears to be much smaller than has hitherto been claimed, and make better provision for the influence of the language that the child is exposed to. However, caution is called for when contemplating cross-linguistic tendencies, since cross-linguistic occurrence frequency should not equated with markedness. Although the domain of cross-linguistic observations is where manifestations of markedness are clearly observable, it can only serve as a diagnostic base of markedness. We are hopeful that future research would bring together researchers from various disciplines where they would converge on being faithful to what is uttered through the mouth of each child; data without any biases of theory or belief, since developmental phonology is predicated on patterns found in child phonology.

Appendix 1

DATA SOURCE LIST FOR CHAPTER 1

(In alphabetical order of the target words or glosses)
(Target words or glosses listed alphabetically)

Target word or gloss	*Language*	*Child output form*	*Source*
abacus	English	[ækʊs]	Pater & Paradis 1996 (Trevor)
adviser	English	[fi-vajzə]	Gnanadesikan 1996/2004
alligator	English	[hɛgɜdə]	Johnson (unpublished) (Unnamed 1;10)
Allison	English	[æ:sʌn]	Pater & Paradis 1996 (Trevor)
Amsterdam	English	[hæmstədæm]	Ken: Reimers (unpublished)
Anpanman	Japanese	[manman]	Girl 1;1–1;4: Baboo database*
away	English	[weɪ]	Smith 1973
baby	English	[bebɪ]	Ingram 1989
	English	[bebe]	Ingram 1974
bad	English	[bæt]	Bowen 1998
ball	French	[babab]	Ingram 1974
	Dutch	[ˈbálə]	Demuth 1996
Bambi	Portuguese	[ɑˈbiˈbi]	Freitas 1996
banana	Maltese	[baba] [nana]	Helen Grech (personal communication)
	English	[bɑnə]	Smith 1973
		[nɑnə]	Johnson (unpublished) (Unnamed 1;10)
bat	English	[dæt]	Bowen 1998
bead	English	[bit]	Smith 1973
beans	English	[minz]	Menn 1971
bear	German	[bebe]	Dressler et al. 2005

beer	Catalan	[βεβεʒzə]	Lleó 1990
belly	German	[baʊbaʊ]	Dressler et al. 2005
belong	English	[bɒŋ]	Smith 1973
big	English	[bɪk]	Smith 1973
		[gɪg]	Menn 1971
bike	English	[baɪ]	Ingram 1989
blanket	English	[baba]	Ingram 1974
blocks	Dutch	[kɔkoː]	Fikkert 1994
Bob	English	[bɒp]	Ken Reimers (unpublished)
book	English	[bʊ]	Ingram 1989
		[gʊk]	Menn 1971
boot	Dutch	[tɔt]	Fikkert 1994
boy	Portuguese	[ˈmunu]	Freitas 1996
bread	Portuguese	[ɑˈpɑ]	Freitas 1996
	English	[bɛd]	Berko Gleason 1989
broccoli	English	[baki]	Pater & Paradis 1996 (Julia)
buffalo	English	[bʌfo]	Pater & Paradis 1996 (Julia)
bugle	Japanese	[dappa]	Ueda 1996
cake	French	[toto]	Vihman 1996 (Charles)
car	English	[ga]	Bowen 1998
	French	[toto]	Leroy & Morgenstern 2005
cat	Japanese	[neto]	Ueda 1996
cheese	English	[ʧi]	Ingram 1989
child	French	[fãfã]	Scullen 1997
chimpanzee	English	[ziː]	Johnson (unpublished) (Unnamed 1;10)
Christina	English	[fi-dinə]	Gnanadesikan 1996/2004
cicada	Japanese	[temi]	Ueda 1996
cinnamon	English	[sɪmɛn]	Pater & Paradis 1996 (Julia)
clothes	Chinese	[jiji]	Shuming Chen (personal communication)
comb	Spanish	[popa]	Macken 1992
conductor	English	[ridʌktə]	Smith 1973
container	English	[fi-tenə]	Gnanadesikan 1996/2004
cup	English	[gɐp]	Bowen 1998
daddy	English	[dada]	Ingram 1974
disturb	English	[ristɜb]	Smith 1973

dog	Zuni	[wewe]	Kroeber 1916
	English	[dagda]	Klein 2005
	English	[gɒ́gɒ]	Lucy: Johnson (unpublished)
	English	[gɔg]	Menn 1971
doggie	Japanese	[wawa]	Vihman 1996 (Emi)
door	J. Arabic	[baba]	Daana 2009
down	Greek	[káko]	Kappa 2001
dress	Dutch	[ˈjoeRək]	Demuth 1996
drip	Russian	[kap-kap]	Dressler et al. 2005
duck	English	[gʌk]	Menn 1971
dummy	Maltese	[gaga]	Helen Grech (personal communication)
elephant	English	[ɛʔvɛn]	Johnson (unpublished) (Unnamed 1;10)
escape	English	[geɪp]	Smith 1973
exhaust	English	[rirɔst]	Smith 1973
father	Zuni	[tata]	Kroeber 1916
favourite	English	[fɛvɪt]	Pater & Paradis 1996 (Julia)
fish	Japanese	[takana]	Ueda 1996
flag	English	[flæk]	Bowen 1998
flower	English	[wæwæ]	Smith 1973
fly	Greek	[pepái]	Kappa 2001
get up	Greek	[kíko]	Kappa 2001
giraffe	English	[waf]	Johnson (unpublished) (Unnamed 1;10)
give	French	[nene]	Dressler et al. 2005
grandmother	French	[meme]	Scullen 1997
guitar	Japanese	[ʤunʤun]	Boy 3;1–3;6: Baboo database*
hammer	Russian	[tuk-tuk]	Dressler et al. 2005
hat	French	[bobo]	Vihman 1996 (Laurent)
	Chinese	[maʊ maʊ]	Shuming Chen (personal communication)
hello	French	[hailo]	Vihman 1996 (Laurent)
hen	French	[gogo]	Vihman 1996 (Laurent)
here	French	[lala]	Vihman 1996 (Laurent)
horse	Dutch	[paːp]	Fikkert 1994
house	Spanish	[kaka]	Macken 1992
injection	Russian	[kɔl-kɔl]	Dressler et al. 2005

Jane	English	[deɪn]	Bowen 1998
juice	Japanese	[ʤuʤu]	Kaz: Reimers (unpublished)
jump	Russian	[pɨk-pɨk]	Dressler et al. 2005
	English	[dʌmp]	Bowen 1998
kangaroo	English	[wu:]	Johnson (unpublished) (Unnamed 1;10)
Kappa (surname)	Greek	[pápa]	Kappa 2001
kiss	English	[gɪk]	Smith 1973
kitty	English	[kaka]	Vihman 1996 (Leslie)
lady	French	[dadap]	Ingram 1974
ladybird	Japanese	[tenten]	Kaz: Reimers (unpublished)
lorry	English	[lɒli]	Smith 1973
meat	Zuni	[titi]	Kroeber 1916
milk	Dutch	[ˈmɛlək]	Demuth 1996
monkey	Japanese	[sadu]	Ueda 1996
mosquito	English	[fi-giro]	Gnanadesikan 1996/2004
mother	Zuni	[mama]	Kroeber 1916
mummy	Portuguese	[ɑmɑˈmɑ̃]	Freitas 1996
	English	[mama]	Ingram 1974
neck	English	[nɛt]	Bowen 1998
nose	German	[nana]	Dressler et al. 2005
	French	[nene]	Ingram 1974
orange	Catalan	[ʒɔʒɔ́nta]	Lleó 1990
pear	English	[bɛə]	Bowen 1998
peek-a-boo	Swedish	[dæd:æ]	Vihman 1996 (Hanna)
peg	English	[bək]	Smith 1973
pen	English	[pɛm]	Cruttenden 1978
pig	English	[bɪg]	Bowen 1998
play	French	[tutu]	Ingram 1974
pot	French	[pɔpɔ]	Ingram 1974
potato	English	[beɪdu]	Smith 1973
pussycat	French	[mimi]	Johnson (unpublished)
quack-quack	English	[gaga]	Vihman 1996 (Leslie)
rabbit	French	[papa]	Dressler et al. 2005
Rebecca	English	[fi-bɛkə]	Gnanadesikan 1996/2004
rewind	English	[fi-wajn]	Gnanadesikan 1996/2004
rice cracker	Japanese	[me:me:]	Ota 2001
running	Russian	[gɔm-gɔm]	Dressler et al. 2005

see	English	[di]	Smith 1973
shoe	English	[u]	Menn 1971
	Portuguese	[ˈpatu]	Freitas 1996
shoes	Catalan	[papátəs]	Lleó 1990
	J. Arabic	[bobo]	Daana 2009
show	English	[do]	Smith 1973
shrimp	Japanese	[hebi]	Ken: Reimers (unpublished)
shy	English	[daɪ]	Smith 1973
sleep	French	[dodo]	Scullen 1997
slide	English	[ladla]	Klein 2005
slipper	Dutch	[pɔf]	Levelt 1994
sock	English	[tɔk]	Smith 1973
soup	French	[tutup]	Ingram 1974
	Spanish	[popa]	Macken 1992
spaghetti	English	[fi-geɾi]	Gnanadesikan 1996/2004
spatula	English	[bæʃʌ]	Pater & Paradis 1996 (Trevor)
spoon	English	[bum]	Cruttenden 1978
sting	Russian	[kɔl-kɔl]	Dressler et al. 2005
stone	English	[non]	Menn 1971
sweet/candy	Chinese	[tʰaŋ tʰaŋ]	Shuming Chen (personal communication)
taco	English	[kako]	Ingram 1974
take	English	[kek]	Ingram 1974
tape	English	[dɛbdɛ]	Klein 2005
telephone	English	[tɛfo]	Johnson (unpublished) (Unnamed 1;10)
thank you	Swedish	[dada]	Vihman 1996 (Hanna)
	English	[ga:ga:]	Vihman 1996 (Stig)
tomato	English	[mɑdu]	Smith 1973
top	English	[bɒp]	Smith 1973
tram	Dutch	[ten]	Levelt 1994
tricycle	English	[twaikl]	Pater & Paradis 1996 (Derek)
truck	Spanish	[koka]	Macken 1992
tub	English	[bʌb]	Menn 1971
two	English	[du]	Klein 2005
type	Greek	[pípo]	Kappa 2001
umbrella	English	[fi-bejə]	Gnanadesikan 1996/2004
urinate	French	[pipi]	Scullen 1997
water	J. Arabic	[mama]	Daana 2009

yellow	English	[lɛlo]	Smith 1973
zoo	English	[du]	Smith 1973

*Baboo is a Japanese parenting website with a database of children's production forms compiled by individual parents (http://www.baboojapan.com).

Appendix 2

SOME DEFINITIONS

MAJOR CATEGORIES OF SOUND

Consonant – a sound involving an interruption to the airflow in the mouth.

Vowel – a sound involving no such interruption.

Obstruent – a sound in which there is a build up of air pressure behind an obstruction (stops, fricatives and affricates).

Sonorant – a sound where there is no such build up since the air is able to escape through a secondary channel (nasals, approximants, vowels).

Approximant – a sound where the constriction in the mouth is less close than that of a fricative (liquids and glides).

PLACE OF ARTICULATION BY ACTIVE ARTICULATOR

Labial – sounds made with the lips, the lower lip being the active articulator (/p/ /b/ /f/ /v/ /m/ /w/. This definition can also be applied to vowels involving lip rounding.

Coronal (sometimes referred to as alveolar or dental) – sounds made with the blade or tip of the tongue as active articulator (/t/ /d/ /s/ /z/ /θ/ /ð/ /ʃ/ /ʒ/ /ʃ/ /ʒ/ /n/ /l/ /ɹ/ /j/. This definition is also applied to front vowels.

Dorsal (also frequently referred to as velar) – sounds made with the body of the tongue as active articulator (/k/ /g/ /x/ /ɣ/). This definition is also applied to back vowels.

Manner of articulation

Stop – a sound involving a complete closure between two articulators (/p/ /b/ /t/ /k/ /g/). This term is used for the glottal stop [ʔ] which involves the closure of the vocal folds in the glottis.

Fricative – a sound involving a less than total, but still very narrow obstruction to the air flow, so that as the air particles pass through the opening turbulence is created (/f/ /v/ /θ/ /ð/ /s/ /z/ /ʃ/ /ʒ/ /ç/ /ʑ/ /x/ /ɣ/).

Affricate – a sound combining a stop articulation and a fricative one in the same place of articulation. Instead of the air being released cleanly from the stop closure air turbulence follows release (/ʧ/ /ʤ/ /ʦ/ /ʣ/).

Nasal – strictly speaking not a manner of articulation, rather a secondary cavity through which air may pass. A nasal consonant will typically consist of an oral stop articulation where the velum is lowered to allow air also to pass into the nasal cavity (/m/ /n/ /ɳ/ /ŋ/). In the case of nasal vowels, air passes simultaneously through the nose and the mouth.

Lateral – a sound with a central constriction of the air, but where air can pass down the lowered sides of the tongue (/l/). This lateral has two manifestations in some languages such as English, the more consonantal clear /l/ [l] with a primary constriction at the alveolar ridge and the more vocalic dark /l/ [ɫ] where the back of the tongue is raised towards the velum in advance of the coronal gesture. The lateral fricative /ɬ/ is a similar articulation except that the sides of the tongue are close enough to the back teeth for turbulence to result.

Rhotic – any sound which is recognised as <r>. This is a disparate set of sounds which ranges from the English approximate, through the tap and trill to fricatives such as those produced in, for example, French and German. Rhotic, or central, approximants differ from laterals by virtue of the fact that the air passes over the middle of the tongue rather than down the sides.

Strident – a feature connected with fricatives and affricates involving a large amount of energy at high frequencies making the sound of higher intensity. The term sibilant is used to describe strident coronal sounds /s/ /z/ /ʃ/ /ʒ/ /ʧ/ /ʤ/. Other coronal fricatives /θ/ and /ð/ do not have the same intensity.

GLOTTAL (OR LARYNGEAL) FEATURES

Voiced – sounds involving a configuration of the vocal cords closely approximating, which allows for their vibration as the air from the lungs passes through. This may also be described as 'slack vocal cords'.

Voiceless – principally, in the context of this book, sounds which do not involve vocal fold vibration. The vocal folds are further apart and fairly stiff.

Fortis – a sound with high overall muscular tension.

Lenis – a sound with low overall muscular tension.

Constricted glottis – represents glottal stops, the total closure of the vocal cords.

Spread glottis – the configuration of the glottis that allows for aspiration to occur.

SYLLABLES

Syllable – a grouping of sounds such that a high sonority nucleus is surrounded by margins of lower sonority.

Nucleus – this will typically be a vowel but may also contain sonorant segments such as nasals and laterals.

Margins – onset and coda.

Onset – consonants preceding the nucleus within the syllable.

Coda – consonants following the nucleus within the syllable.

Rhyme – the part of the syllable consisting of the nucleus and coda. These have frequently been found to act as a unit independent from the onset.

Mora – a unit of phonological weight involving only rhyme units. Vowels are considered to be inherently moraic, whereas consonants only gain moraic status by virtue of their position following a vowel and preceding another consonant.

Heavy syllables – those with a branching rhyme (two moras).

Sonority – the relative intensity (or loudness) of a sound all other factors being equal. Low vowels such as /ɑ/ are highest on the sonority scale and voiceless stops the lowest.

Phonotactic constraints (or phonotactics) – these refer to the possible sequences of consonants or vowels that may occur, principally within a syllable. The phonotactic constraints of an onset, for example, govern the number and order of consonants that are acceptable within the syllable onset.

Stress

Stress is the prominence of a syllable relative to its neighbours. It may be manifested by increased intensity (loudness), pitch or length.

Foot – in languages that display relative stress, syllables are paired into stressed and unstressed, or strong and weak.

Trochaic feet – the pattern of stressed and unstressed (sw).

Iambic feet – the pattern of unstressed and stressed (ws).

Quantity sensitive languages – those which accentuate heavy syllables.

Stress timed languages – those which exhibit the sort of binary pairing of syllables discussed above and in which weak syllables will tend to be reduced.

Syllable timed languages – those whose syllables are of more or the less the same weight.

REFERENCES

Adam, G. (2002), From variable to optimal grammar: evidence from language acquisition and language change. PhD dissertation, University of Tel-Aviv.

Albright, R. and J. Albright (1956), The phonology of a two-year-old. *Word* 12: 382–90.

Allen, G. and S. Hawkins (1980), Phonological rhythm: definition and development. In G. Yeni-Komshian, J. Kavanagh and C. Ferguson (eds), *Child phonology*, Vol. 1. New York: Academic Press: 227–56.

Altubuly, S. (2009), Phonological development in Libyan Arabic speaker children: a case study. MA dissertation, University of Essex.

Archangeli, D. (1984), Underspecification in Yawelmani phonology and morphology. PhD dissertation, MIT. New York: Garland, 1988.

Aslin, R., D. Pisoni, B. Hennessy and A. Perey (1981), Discrimination of voice onset time by human infants: New findings and implications for the effect of early experience. *Child Development* 52: 1135–45.

Avery, P. and K. Rice (1989), Segment structure and coronal underspecification. *Phonology* 5: 198–207.

Barlow, J. (1997), A constraint-based account of syllable onsets: evidence from developing systems. PhD dissertation, Indiana University.

Barlow, J. (2001), The structure of /s/-sequences: evidence from a disordered system. *Journal of Child Language* 28: 291–324.

Barlow, J. (2003), Asymmetries in the acquisition of consonant clusters in Spanish. *Canadian Journal of Linguistics* 48: 179–210.

Bates, S., J. Watson and J. Scobbie (2002), Context-conditioned error patterns in disordered systems. In M. Ball and F. Gibbon (eds), *Vowel disorders*. Boston: Butterworth-Heinemann: 145–85.

Bear, M., B. Connors and M. Paradiso (2006), Neuroscience: exploring the brain (3rd edn). New York: Williams and Wilkins.

Beckman, J. (1997), Positional faithfulness. PhD dissertation, University of Massachusetts.

Beckman, M., K. Yoneyama and J. Edwards (2003), Language-specific and language-universal aspects of lingual obstruent productions in Japanese-acquiring children. *Journal of the Phonetic Society of Japan* 7: 18–28.

Berg, T. (1992), Phonological harmony as a processing problem. *Journal of Child Language* 19: 225–57.

Berko, J. and R. Brown (1960), Psycholinguistic research methods. In P. Mussen (ed.), *Handbook of research methods in child development*. New York: John Wiley: 517–57.

Berko-Gleason, J. (1989), *The development of language* (2nd edn). Columbus, OH: Merrill.

Bertoncini, J. and J. Mehler (1981), Syllables as units in infant speech perception. *Infant Behaviour and Development* 4: 247–60.

Best, C. (1991), Phonetic influences on the perception of nonnative speech contrasts by 6–8 and 10–12 month olds. Paper presented at the Society for Research in Child Development, Seattle.

Best, C. (1995), A direct realist view of cross-language speech perception. In W. Strange (ed.), *Speech perception and linguistic experience*. Baltimore: York Press: 171–206.

Best, C. and G. McRoberts (2003), Infant perception of nonnative consonant contrasts that adults assimilate in different ways. Language and Speech Special Issue: *Phonological Development* 46: 183–216.

Best, C., G. McRoberts and N. Sithole (1988), Examination of perceptual reorganization for non-native speech contrasts: Zulu click discrimination by English-speaking adults and infants. *Journal of Experimental Psychology: Human Perception and Performance* 14: 345–60.

Biggs, B. (1965), Direct and indirect inheritance in Rotuman. *Lingua* 14: 383–445.

Bijeljac-Babic, R., J. Bertoncini and J. Mehler (1993), How do 4-day-old infants categorize multisyllabic utterances? *Developmental Psychology* 29: 4, 711–21.

Bird, S. (2002), Rhythm without hierarchy in Athapaskan languages. In *Proceedings of the 6th Workshop on Structure and Constituency in the Languages of the Americas*. Vancouver, British Columbia: UBC Press.

Bleile, K. (1991), *Child phonology: a book of exercises for students*. San Diego: Singular Publishing Group Inc.

Blevins, J. (1995), The syllable in phonological theory. In J. Goldsmith (ed.), *The Handbook of Phonological Theory*. Oxford: Blackwell Publishing: 206–44.

Blevins, J. (2004), *Evolutionary phonology: the emergence of sound patterns*. Cambridge: CUP.

Blevins, J. (2006), Syllable typology. In K. Brown (ed.), *Encyclopaedia of Language and Linguistics* (2nd edn). Oxford: Elsevier.

Bowen, C. (1998), *Developmental phonological disorders: A practical guide for families and teachers*. Melbourne: ACER Press.

Boye, M., O. Gunturkun and J. Vauclair (2005), Right ear advantage for conspecific calls in adults and subadults, but not infants, California sea lions (Zalophus californianus): hemispheric specialization for communication? *European Journal of Neuroscience* 21: 6, 1727–32.

Braine M. (1974), On what constitutes a learnable phonology. *Language* 50: 270–300.

Brown, R. (1973), *A first language*. Harmondsworth: Penguin Books.

Bryan, A. and D. Howard (1992), Frozen phonology thawed: the analysis and remediation of a developmental disorder of real word phonology. *European Journal of Disorders of Communication* 27: 343–65.

Buckley, E. (2003), Children's unnatural phonology. In P. Nowak and C. Yoquelet (eds), *Proceedings of the Berkeley Linguistics Society* 29: 523–34.

Cairns, C. and M. Feinstein (1982), Markedness and the theory of syllable structure. *Linguistic Inquiry* 13: 2, 193–226.

Cheour-Luhtanen, M., K. Alho, T. Kujala, K. Sainio, K. Reinikainen, M. Renlund, O. Aaltonen, O. Eerola and R. Näätänen (1995), Mismatch negativity indicates vowel discrimination in newborns. *Hearing Research* 82: 53–8.

Chomsky, N. (1959), Review of B. F. Skinner's verbal behaviour. *Language* 35: 26–58.

Chomsky, N. (1965), *Aspects of the theory of syntax*. Cambridge, MA: The MIT Press.

Chomsky, N. and Halle, M. (1968), *Sound pattern of English*. New York: Harper and Row.

Clements, G. N. (1990), The role of the sonority cycle in core syllabification. In J. Kingston and M. E. Beckham (eds), Between grammar and the physics of speech. Papers in *Laboratory Phonology I*. Cambridge: CUP: 283–333.

Clements, G. N. (1985), The geometry of phonological features. *Phonology Yearbook* 2: 225–52.

Clements, G. N. and E. Sezer (1982), Vowel and consonant disharmony in Turkish. In H. van der Hulst and N. Smith (eds), *The structure of phonological representations*, Vol. 2. Dordrecht: Foris: 213–55.

Cruttenden, A. (1978), Assimilation in child language and elsewhere. *Journal of Child Language* 5: 373–8.

Daana, H. A. (2009), The development of consonant clusters, stress and plural nouns in Jordanian Arabic child language. PhD dissertation, University of Essex.

Davidson, L., P. Jusczyk and P. Smolensky (2004), Implications and explorations of richness of the base. In R. Kager, J. Pater and W. Zonneveld (eds), *Constraints on phonological acquisition*. Cambridge: CUP: 321–68.

de Boysson-Bardies, B., P. Hallé, L. Sagart and C. Durand (1989), A cross-linguistic investigation of vowel formants in babbling. *Journal of Child Language* 16: 1–17.

de Boysson-Bardies, B. and M. Vihman (1991), Adaptation to language:

evidence from babbling and first words in four languages. *Language* 67: 2, 297–319.

DeCasper, A. and W. Fifer (1980), Of human bonding: newborns prefer their mothers' voices. *Science* 208: 1174–6.

DeCasper, A. and M. Spence (1986), Prenatal maternal speech influences newborns' perception of speech sounds. *Infant Behavior and Development* 9: 133–50.

Dehaene-Lambertz, G. (2000), Cerebral specialisation for speech and non-speech stimuli in infants. *Journal of Cognitive Neuroscience* 12: 3, 449–60.

Dehaene-Lambertz, G. and S. Baillet (1998), A phonological representation in the infant brain. *NeuroReport* 9: 1885–8.

Dehaene-Lambertz, G. and S. Dehaene (1994), Speed and cerebral correlates of syllable discrimination in infants. *Nature* 370: 292–5.

Dehaene-Lambertz, G., S. Dehaene and L. Hertz-Pannier (2002), Functional neuroimaging of speech perception in infants. *Science* 298: 2013–5.

Dehaene-Lambertz, G., L. Hertz-Pannier and J. Dubois (2006), Nature and nurture in language acquisition: Anatomical and functional brain-imaging studies in infants. *Trends in Neuroscience* 29: 7, 367–73.

Dehaene-Lambertz, G., L. Hertz-Pannier, J. Dubois and S. Dehaene (2008), How does early brain organization promote language acquisition in humans? *European Review* 16: 4, 399–411.

Delattre, P. (1961), La leçon d'intonation de Simone de Beauvoir, etude d'intonation déclarative comparée. *The French Review* 35: 59–67.

Delattre, P., A. Liberman and F. Cooper (1955), Acoustical loci and transitional cues for consonants. *Journal of the Acoustical Society of America* 27: 769–73.

Demuth, K. (1995), Markedness and the development of prosodic structure. In J. Beckman (ed.), *Proceedings of the North East Linguistic Society 25*. Amherst: Graduate Student Linguistic Association: 13–26.

Demuth, K. (1996), The prosodic structure of early words. In J. Morgan and K. Demuth (eds), *Signal to syntax: bootstrapping from speech to grammar in early acquisition*. Mahwah: Lawrence Erlbaum Associates: 177–84.

Demuth, K. and M. Johnson (2003), Truncation to subminimal words. *Canadian Journal of Linguistics* 48: 211–41.

Dinnsen, D. and J. Gierut (2008), *Optimality theory, phonological acquisition and disorders*. London: Equinox.

Dinnsen, D. and L. McGarrity (2004), On the nature of alternations in phonological acquisition. *Studies in Phonetics, Phonology and Morphology* 10: 23–41.

Dooling, R., C. Best and S. Brown (1995), Discrimination of synthetic full-formant and sinewave /ra-la/ continua by budgerigars (Melopsinacus undulatus) and zebra finches (Taeniopygia guttata). *Journal of the Acoustical Society of America* 97: 1839–46.

Dressler, W. U., K. Dziubalska-Kolaczyk, N. Gagarina and M. Kilani-Schoch (2005), Reduplication in child language. In B. Hurch (ed.), *Studies on reduplication*, Berlin: Mouton de Gruyter: 455–74.

Echols, C. H. and E. L. Newport (1992), The role of stress and position in determining first words. *Language Acquistion* 2: 3, 189–220.

Edwards, M. (1970), The acquisition of liquids. Unpublished Master's thesis, Ohio State University.

Edwards, M. (1996), Word position effects in the production of fricatives. In B. Bernhardt, J. Gilbert and D. Ingram (eds), *Proceedings of the UBC International Conference on Phonological Acquisition*. Somerville: Cascadilla Press.

Ehret, G. (1987), Left hemisphere advantage in the mouse brain for recognizing ultrasonic communication calls. *Nature* 325: 249–51.

Eimas, P. (1974), Auditory and linguistic processing of cues for place of articulation by infants. *Perception and Psychophysics* 16: 513–21.

Eimas, P. (1975a), Auditory and phonetic coding of the cues for speech: Discrimination of the [r-] distinction by young infants. *Perception and Psychophysics* 18: 341–7.

Eimas, P. (1975b), Speech perception in early infancy. In L. B. Cohen and P. Salapatek (eds), *Infant perception*. New York: Academic Press.

Eimas, P. and J. Miller (1980a), Discrimination of information for manner of articulation. *Infant Behavior and Development* 3: 367–75.

Eimas, P. and J. Miller (1980b), Contextual effects in infant speech perception. *Science* 209: 1140–1.

Eimas, P. and J. Miller (1981), Organization in the perception of segmental and suprasegmental information by infants. *Infant Behavior and Development* 4: 395–9.

Eimas, P., E. Siqueland, P. Jusczyk. and J. Vigorito (1971), Speech perception in infants. *Science* 171: 303–6.

Engstrand, O., K. Williams and F. Lacerda (2003), Does babbling sound native? Listener responses to vocalisations produced by Swedish and American 12- and 18-month-olds. *Phonetica* 60: 17–44.

Fais, L., S. Kajikawa, S. Amano and J. Werker (2009), Infant discrimination of a morphologically relevant word-final contrast. *Infancy* 14: 4, 488–99.

Ferguson, C. and C. Farwell (1975), Words and sounds in early language acquisition. *Language* 51: 419–39.

Fernald, A. (1985), Four-month-old infants prefer to listen to motherese. *Infant Behavior and Development* 8: 181–95.

Fernald, A. and P. Kuhl (1987), Acoustic determinants of infant preference for motherese speech. *Infant Behavior and Development* 10: 279–93.

Féry, C. (2003), Markedness, faithfulness, vowel quality and syllable structure in French. *French Language Studies* 13: 247–80.

Fikkert, P. (1994), *On the acquisition of prosodic structure.* Holland Institute of Generative Linguistics.

Fikkert, P. (2007), Acquiring phonology. In P. de Lacy (ed.), *Handbook of phonological theory*, Cambridge, MA: Cambridge University Press: 537–54.

Fikkert, P., C. C. Levelt and J. van de Weijer (subm.), Input, intake and phonological development: the case of consonant harmony, submitted to *First Language.*

Fiser, J. and R. N. Aslin (2001), Unsupervised statistical learning of higher-order spatial structures from visual scenes. *Psychological Science* 12: 499–504.

Fitch, W. T. and M. D. Hauser (2004), Computational constraints on syntactic processing in a nonhuman primate. *Science* 303: 377–80.

Freitas, M. J. (1996), Onsets in early productions. In B. Bernhardt, J. Gilbert and D. Ingram (eds), *Proceedings of the UBC International Conference on Phonological Acquisition*, Somerville: Cascadilla Press: 76–85.

Fromkin V. (1973), The non-anomalous nature of anomalous utterances. In V. Fromkin (ed.), *Speech Errors as Linguistic Evidence.* The Hague: Mouton: 215–67.

Fudge, E. (1969), Syllables. *Journal of Linguistics* 5: 253–86.

Gess, R. (1998), Compensatory lengthening and structure preservation revisited. *Phonology* 15: 353–66.

Gess, R. (2001), On re-ranking and explanatory adequacy in a constraint-based theory of phonological change. In D. Holt (ed.), Optimality theory and language change. Dordrecht: Kluwer Academic Publishers.

Gierut, J. (1999), Syllable onsets; clusters and adjuncts in acquisition. *Journal of Speech Language and Hearing Research* 42: 708–26.

Gnanadesikan, A. (1996), Child phonology in optimality theory: ranking arguments and faithfulness constraints. In A. Stringfellow, D. Cahana-Amitay, E. Hughes and A. Zukowski (eds), *Proceedings of the 20th Annual Boston University Conference on Language Development.* Somerville: Cascadilla Press: 237–48.

Gnanadesikan, A. (2004), Markedness and faithfulness constraints in child phonology. In R. Kager, J. Pater and W. Zonneveld (eds), *Constraints in phonological acquisition.* Cambridge: CUP: 73–108.

Goad, H. (1996), Consonant harmony in child language: evidence against coronal underspecification. In B. Bernhardt, J. Gilbert and D. Ingram (eds), *Proceedings of the UBC International Conference on Phonological Acquisition.* Somerville: Cascadilla Press: 187–200.

Goad, H. and D. Ingram (1987), Individual variation in phonology. *Journal of Child Language* 14: 419–32.

Goad, H. and Y. Rose (2004), Input elaboration, head faithfulness, and evidence for representation in the acquisition of left-edge clusters, in West Germanic. In R. Kager, J. Pater and W. Zonneveld (eds), *Constraints in phonological acquisition.* Cambridge: CUP: 109–47.

Gómez, R. L. and L. A. Gerken (2000), Infant artificial language learning and language acquisition. *Trends in Cognitive Science* 4: 178–86.

Goodman, M. B., P. W. Jusczyk and A. Bauman (2000), Developmental changes in infants' sensitivity to internal syllable structure. In M. B. Broe and J. B. Pierrehumbert (eds), *Papers in laboratory phonology V: Acquisition and the lexicon.* Cambridge: CUP: 228–39.

Goodsitt, J. V., J. L. Morgan and P. K. Kuhl (1993), Perceptual strategies in prelingual speech segmentation. *Journal of Child Language* 20: 229–52.

Green, A. D. (2001), American English 'r-coloured' vowels as complex segments. In *Phonology at Potsdam.* Potsdam: Universitätsbibliothek Publikationsstelle Linguistics at Potsdam: 16: 70–8.

Greenberg, J. (ed.) (1978), Universals of human language. Stanford: University of Stanford Press.

Grégoire, A. (1937), *L'apprentissage du langage.* Bibliothèque de la Fac. de Philos. et Lettres de l'Univ. de Liège, LXXIII.

Grijzenhout, J. and S. Joppen (1998), First steps in the acquisition of German Phonology: A case study, *SFB 282 Working Paper* No.110.

Haiman, J. (1998), Hua (Papuan). In A. Spencer and A. Zwicky (eds), The handbook of morphology. Oxford: Blackwell Publishing: 539–62.

Hale, M. and C. Reiss (1998), Formal and empirical arguments concerning phonological acquisition. *Linguistic Inquiry* 29: 656–83.

Harris, J. (1994), *English sound structure*, Oxford: Blackwell Publishing.

Hauser, M. and K. Andersson (1994), Left hemisphere dominance for processing vocalizations in adult, but not infant rhesus monkeys: Field experiments. *Proceedings of the National Academy of Sciences* 91: 3946–8.

Hauser, M., N. Chomsky and W. Fitch (2002), The language faculty: What is it, who has it, and how did it evolve? *Science* 298: 1569–79.

Hauser, M., E. Newport and R. Aslin (2001), Segmentation of the speech stream in a non-human primate: statistical learning in cotton-top tamarins. *Cognition* 78: B53–B64.

Hayes, B. (1995), *Metrical stress theory: principles and case studies.* Chicago: University of Chicago Press.

Heffner, H. and R. Heffner (1986), Effect of unilateral and bilateral auditory cortex lesions on the discrimination of vocalizations by Japanese macaques. *Journal of Neurophysiology* 56: 683–701.

Hienz, R., M. Sachs and J. Sinnott (1981), Discrimination of steady-state vowels by blackbirds and pigeons. *Journal of the Acoustical Society of America* 70: 699–706.

Hillenbrand, J. (1984), Speech perception by infants: Categorization based on nasal consonant place of articulation. *Journal of Acoustic Society of America* 75: 1613–22.

Hillenbrand, J., F. Minifie and T. Edwards (1979), Tempo of spectrum change as a cue in speech-sound discrimination by infants. *Journal of Speech and Hearing Research* 22: 147–65.

Hodson, B. W. and E. P. Paden (1981), Phonological processes which characterise unintelligible and intelligible speech in early childhood. *Journal of Speech and Hearing Disorders* 46: 369–73.

Holland, S., E. Plante, A. Weber Byars, R. Strawsburg, V. Schmithorst and J. Ball (2001), Normal fMRI brain activation patterns in children performing a verb generation task. *Neuroimage* 14: 4, 837–43.

Holmberg, T., K. Morgan and P. Kuhl (1977), Speech perception in early infancy: discrimination of fricative consonants. *Journal of the Acoustical Society of America* 62 (suppl. 1): S99(A).

Hume, E. (2003), Language specific markedness: The case of place of articulation. *Studies in Phonetics, Phonology and Morphology* 9: 2, 295–310.

Ingram, D. (1989), *Child language acquisition: Method, description, and explanation*, Cambridge: Cambridge University Press.

Ingram, D. (1974), Phonological rules in young children. *Journal of Child Language* 1: 49–64.

Ingram, D. (1975), Production of word-initial fricatives and affricates. In A. Caramazza and E. Zurif (eds), *Language acquisition and language breakdown: parallels and divergences*. Baltimore: Johns Hopkins University Press.

Ingram, D. (1992), Early phonological acquisition, a cross-linguistic perspective. In C. Ferguson, L. Menn and C. Stoel-Gammon (eds), *Phonological development: models, research, implications*. Tinonium: York Press.

Ingram, D. (1996), Some observations on feature assignment. In B. Bernhardt, J. Gilbert and D. Ingram (eds), *Proceedings of the UBC International Conference on Phonological Acquisition*. Somerville: Cascadilla Press.

Inkelas, S. and Y. Rose (2007), Positional neutralisation: a case study from child language. *Language* 83: 4, 707–36.

Îto, J. (1986), Syllable theory in prosodic phonology. Doctoral dissertation, University of Massachusetts, Amherst. [Published 1988. *Outstanding Dissertations in Linguistics series*. New York: Garland.].

Jakobson, R. (1941), Kindersprache, aphasie und allgemeine lautgesetze. In A. Keiler (transl.) *Child Language, Aphasia and Phonological Universals* (1968). The Hague: Mouton.

João Freitas, M. (2003), The acquisition of onset clusters in European Portuguese. *Probus* 15: 27–46.

Johnson, W. and D. Britain (2007), L-vocalisation as a natural phenomenon: explorations in Sociophonology. *Language Sciences* 29: 2–3, 294–315.

Jun, J. (1995), Perceptual and articulatory factors in place assimilation: An optimality theoretic approach. PhD dissertation, University of California, Los Angeles.

Jusczyk, P. (1977), Perception of syllable-final stop consonants by two-month old infants, *Perception and Psychophysics* 21: 450–4.

Jusczyk, P. (1997/2000), The discovery of spoken language. Cambridge MA: The MIT Press.

Jusczyk, P. (1999), How infants begin to extract words from speech. *Trends in Cognitive Sciences* 3: 323–8.

Jusczyk, P., H. Copan and E. Thompson (1978), Perception by 2-month-old infants of glide contrasts in multisyllabic utterances. *Perception and Psychophysics* 24: 515–20.

Jusczyk, P., A. Cutler and N. Redanz (1993), Infants' preference for the predominant stress patterns of English words. *Child Development* 64: 675–87.

Jusczyk, P., A. Friederici, J. Wessels, V. Svenkerud and A. Jusczyk (1993), Infants' sensitivity to the sound patterns of native language words. *Journal of Memory and Language* 32: 402–20.

Jusczyk, P., M. Goodman and A. Bauman (1999), 'Nine-month-olds' attention to sound similarities in syllables. *Journal of Memory and Language* 40: 62–82.

Jusczyk, P., D. Houston and M. Newsome (1999), The beginnings of word segmentation in English-learning infants. *Cognitive Psychology* 39: 159–207.

Jusczyk, P., P. Luce and J. Charles-Luce (1994), Infant's sensitivity to phonotactic patterns in the native language. *Journal of Memory and Language* 33: 630–45.

Jusczyk, P. W. and E. Thompson (1978), Perception of phonetic contrast in multisyllabic utterances by 2-month-old infants. *Perception and Psychophysics* 23: 105–9.

Kappa, I. (2001), Alignment and consonant harmony: evidence from Greek. In A. Do, L. Domínguez and A. Johansen (eds), *Proceedings of the 25th Annual Boston University Conference on Language Development*. Somerville: Cascadilla Press: 401–12.

Kehoe, M. (2000), Truncation without shape constraints: the latter stages of prosodic acquisition. *Language Acquisition* 8: 1, 23–67.

Kenstowicz, M. (1994), *Phonology in generative grammar*. Oxford: Blackwell Publishing.

Kent, R. (1992), The biology of phonological development. In C. Ferguson, L. Menn and C. Stoel-Gammon (eds), *Phonological development: models, research, implications*. Timonium: York Press: 65–90.

Kent, R. and G. Miolo (1995), Phonetic abilities in the first year of life. In P. Fletcher and B. MacWhinney (eds), *The handbook of child language*. Oxford: Blackwell Publishing: 303–34.

Kim, K., N. Relkin, K. Lee and J. Hirsch (1997), Distinct cortical areas associated with native and second languages. *Nature* 388: 172–4.

Kirk, C. (2008), Substitution errors in the production of word-initial and word-final consonant clusters. *Journal of Speech, Language and Hearing Research* 51: 35–48.

Kirk, C. and K. Demuth (2003), Onset/coda asymmetries in the acquisition of clusters. In B. Beachley, A. Brown, and F. Conlin (eds), *Proceedings of the*

27th Annual Boston University Conference on Language Development. Somerville: Cascadilla Press: 437–48.

Kisseberth, C. (1970), On the functional unity of phonological rules. *Linguistic Inquiry* 1: 291–306.

Klein, H. (2005), Reduplication revisited: Functions, constraints, repairs, and clinical implications. *American Journal of Speech Language Pathology* 14: 71–83.

Kluender, K.R., R. L. Diehl and P. R. Killeen (1987), Japanese quail can learn phonetic categories. *Science* 237: 1195–7.

Kobayashi, C. (1980), Dialectal variation in child language. In P. S. Dale and D. Ingram (eds), *Child language: an international perspective*. Baltimore: University Park Press.

Kroeber, A. L. (1916), The speech of a Zuni Child. *American Anthropologist* 18: 4, 529–34.

Kuhl, P. K. (1983), Perception of auditory equivalence classes for speech in early infancy. *Infant Behavior and Development* 6: 263–85.

Kuhl, P. K. (1979a), Speech perception in early infancy: perceptual constancy for spectrally dissimilar vowel categories. *Journal of the Acoustical Society of America* 66: 1668–79.

Kuhl, P. K. (1979b), The perception of speech in early infancy. In N. J. Lass (ed.), *Speech and language: advances in basic research and practice, Vol. 1*. New York: Academic Press.

Kuhl, P. K. (1981), Discrimination of speech by non-human animals: Basic auditory sensitivities conductive to the perception of speech-sound categories. *Journal of the Acoustical Society of America* 70: 340–8.

Kuhl, P. K. (1991), Human adults and human infants show a 'perceptual magnet effect' for the prototypes of speech categories, monkeys do not. *Perception and Psychophysics* 50: 93–107.

Kuhl, P. K. (1994), Learning and representation in speech and language. *Current Opinion in Neurobiology* 4: 812–22.

Kuhl, P. K. (1998), The development of speech and language. In T. J. Carew, R. Menzel and C. J. Shatz (eds), *Mechanistic relationships between development and learning*. New York: Wiley: 53–73.

Kuhl, P. K. (2000), A new view of language acquisition. *Proceedings of the National Academy of Science* 97: 11850–7.

Kuhl, P. K. (2008), Linking infant speech perception to language acquisition: Phonetic learning predicts language growth. In P. McCardle, J. Colombo and L. Freund (eds), *Infant pathways to language: Methods, models, and research directions*. New York: Lawrence Erlbaum: 213–43.

Kuhl, P. K., J. Andruski, I. Chistovich, L. Chistovich, E. Kozhevnikova, V. Ryskina, E. Stolyarova, U. Sundberg and F. Lacerda (1997), Cross-language analysis of phonetic units in language addressed to infants. *Science* 277: 684–6.

Kuhl, P. K., B. Conboy, S. Coffey-Corina, D. Padden, M. Rivera-Gaxiola and T. Nelson (2008), Phonetic learning as a pathway to language: new data and native language magnet theory expanded (NLM-e). *Philosophical Transactions of the Royal Society* B 363: 979–1000.

Kuhl, P., B. Conboy, D. Padden, T. Nelson and J. Pruitt (2005), Early speech perception and later language development: Implications for the 'critical period'. *Language Learning and Development* 1: 237–64.

Kuhl, P. K. and A. Meltzoff (1982), The bimodal perception of speech in infancy. *Science* 218: 1138–41.

Kuhl, P. K. and J.D. Miller (1975), Speech perception by the chinchilla: voiced-voiceless distinction in alveolar plosive consonants. *Science* 100: 69–72.

Kuhl, P. K. and D. Padden (1982), Enhanced discriminability at the phonetic boundaries for the voicing feature in macaques. *Perception and Psychophysics* 32: 542–50.

Kuhl, P. K., E. Stevens, A. Hayashi, T. Deguchi, S. Kiritani and P. Iverson (2006), Infants show a facilitation effect for native language phonetic perception between 6 and 12 months. *Developmental Science* 9: F13–F21.

Kuhl, P. K., F.-M. Tsao and H.-M. Liu (2003), Foreign-language experience in infancy: Effects of short-term exposure and social interaction on phonetic learning. *Proceedings of the National Academy of Science* 100: 9096–101.

Kuhl, P. K., K. Williams, F. Lacerda, K. Stevens and B. Lindblom (1992), Linguistic experience alters phonetic perception in infants by 6 months of age. *Science* 255: 606–8.

Ladefoged, P. (2001), *A course in phonetics* (4th edn). Fort Worth: Harcourt College Publishers.

Lasky, R., A. Syrdal-Lasky and R. Klein (1975), VOT discrimination by four to six and a half month old infants from Spanish environments. *Journal of Experimental Child Psychology* 20: 215–25.

Leopold, W. (1947), *Speech development of a bilingual child, a linguist's record* (Vol. II). New York: AMS Press.

Leroy, M. and A. Morgenstern (2005), Reduplication before two years old. In B. Hurch (ed.), *Studies on Reduplication*, Berlin: Mouton de Gruyter: 478–94.

Levelt, C. (1994), *On the acquisition of place*. Holland Institute of Generative Linguistics.

Levelt, C. (1996), Consonant-vowel interactions in child language. In B. Bernhardt, J. Gilbert and D. Ingram (eds), *Proceedings of the UBC International Conference on Phonological Acquisition*. Somerville: Cascadilla Press: 229–39.

Levelt, C., N. Schiller and W. Levelt (2000), The acquisition of syllable types. *Language Acquisition* 8: 3, 237–64.

Levitt, A., P. Jusczyk, J. Murray and G. Carden (1988), Context effects in two-month-old infants' perception of labiodental/interdental fricative contrasts. *Journal of Experimental Psychology* 14: 361–8.

Liberman, A., F. Cooper, D. Shankweiler and M. Studdart-Kennedy (1967), Perception of the speech code. *Psychological Review* 74: 431–61.

Lleó, C. (1990), Homonymy and reduplication: on the extended availability of two strategies in phonological acquisition. *Journal of Child Language* 17: 267–78.

Lleó, C. (1996), To spread or not to spread: different styles in the acquisition of Spanish phonology. In B. Bernhardt, J. Gilbert and D. Ingram (eds), *Proceedings of the UBC International Conference on Phonological Acquisition*. Somerville: Cascadilla Press: 251–28.

Locke, J. (1983), *Phonological acquisition and change*. New York: Academic Press.

Łukaszewicz, B. (2006), Extrasyllabicity, transparency and prosodic constituency in the acquisition of Polish. *Lingua* 116: 1–30.

Łukaszewicz, B. (2007), Reduction in syllable onsets in the acquisition of Polish: deletion, coalescence, metathesis and gemination. *Journal of Child Language* 34.1: 53–82.

McCarthy, J. and A. Prince (1994), The emergence of the unmarked: Optimality in prosodic morphology. In M. González (ed.), *Proceedings of NELS 24*. Amherst: Graduate Student Linguistic Association: 333–79.

McCarthy, J. and A. Prince (1995), Faithfulness and reduplicative identity. In J. Beckman, L. Walsh Dickey and S. Urbanczyk (eds), Papers in optimality theory. *University of Massachusetts Occasional Papers in Linguistics 18*, Amherst: Graduate Student Linguistics Association.

McClelland, J. and D. Rumelhart (1981), An interactive activation model of context effects in letter recognition: Part 1. An account of basic findings. *Psychological Review* 88: 375–407.

McGurk, H. and J. MacDonald (1976), Hearing lips and seeing voices. *Nature* 264: 746–8.

Macken, M. (1980), The child's lexical representation: the 'puzzle-puddle-pickle' evidence. *Journal of Linguistics* 16: 1–17.

Macken, M. (1992), Where's phonology? In C. A. Ferguson, L. Menn and C. Stoel-Gammon (eds), *Phonological Development: Models, Research, Implications*, Timonium, MD: York Press: 249–73.

Macken, M. A. and D. Barton (1980a), The acquisition of the voicing contrast in English: A study of voice onset time in word-initial stop consonants. *Journal of Child Language* 7: 41–74.

Macken, M. A. and D. Barton (1980b), The acquisition of the voicing contrast in Spanish: A phonetic and phonological study of word-initial stop consonants. *Journal of Child Language* 7: 433–58.

Macken, M. and C. Ferguson (1983), Cognitive aspects of phonological development: Model, evidence and issues. In K. Nelson (ed.), *Children's language 4*. Hillsdale NJ: Lawrence Erlbaum: 255–82.

McLeod, S., J. van Doorn and V. A. Reed (2001), Normal acquisition of consonant clusters. *American Journal of Speech-Language Pathology* 10: 2, 99–100.

MacWhinney, B. (1995), *The CHILDES project* (2nd edn). Mahwah: Lawrence Erlbaum.

Maddieson, I. (1984), *Patterns of sounds*. Cambridge: CUP.

Marcus, G., S. Pinker, M. Ullman, M. Hollander, T. Rosen and F. Xu (1992), Overregularization in language acquisition. *Monographs of the Society for Research in Child Development* 57: (Serial No. 228).

Marcus, G., S. Vijayan, S. Bandi Rao and P. Vishton (1999), Rule learning by 7-month-old infants. *Science* 283: 5398, 77–80.

Mattingly, I., A. Liberman, A. Syrdal and T. Halwes (1971), Discrimination in speech and nonspeech modes. *Cognitive Psychology* 2: 131–57.

Mattock, K. and D. Burnham (2006), Chinese and English tone perception: evidence for perceptual re-organisation. *Infancy* 10: 3, 241–65.

Mattys, S., P. Jusczyk, P. Luce and J. Morgan (1999), Phonotactic and prosodic effects on word segmentation in infants. *Cognitive Psychology* 38: 465–94.

Maye, J., J. Werker and L. Gerken (2002), Infant sensitivity to distributional information can affect phonetic discrimination. *Cognition* 82: B101–B111.

Maxwell, E. and G. Weismer (1982), The contribution of phonological, acoustic and perceptive techniques to the characterisation of a misarticulating child's voice contrast in stops. *Applied Psycholinguistics* 3: 29–43.

Mehler, J., P. Jusczyk, G. Lambertz, N. Halsted, J. Bertoncini and C. Amiel-Tison (1988), A precursor of language acquisition in young infants. *Cognition* 29: 143–78.

Menn, L. (1971), Phonotactic rules in beginning speech. *Lingua* 26: 225–51.

Menn, L. (1976), Evidence for an interactionist discovery theory of child phonology. *Papers and Reports on Language Development* 12: 169–77.

Menn, L. (1983), Development of articulatory phonetic, and phonological capabilities. In B. Butterworth (ed.), *Language production* (Vol. II). London: Academic Press.

Menn, L. and E. Matthei (1992), The 'two-lexicon' account of child phonology: looking back, looking ahead. In C. Ferguson, L. Menn and C. Stoel-Gammon (eds), *Phonological development: models, research, implications*. Timonium: York Press: 211–47.

Mithun, M. and H. Basri (1986), The phonology of Selayarese. *Oceanic Linguistics* 25: 210–54.

Miyawaki, K., W. Strange, R. R. Verbrugge, A. M. Liberman, J. J. Jenkins and O. Fujimura (1975), An effect of linguistic experience: the discrimination of /r/ and /l/ by native speakers of Japanese and English. *Perception and Psychophysics* 18: 331–40.

Moffit, A. R. (1971), Consonant cue perception by twenty- to twenty-four-week-old infants. *Child Development* 42: 3, 717–31.

Moon, C., R. Cooper and W. Fifer (1993), Two-day-olds prefer their native language. *Infant Behaviour and Development* 16: 495–500.

Morgan, J. (1996), A rhythmic bias in preverbal speech segmentation. *Journal of Memory and Language* 33: 666–89.

Morse, P. (1972), The discrimination of speech and nonspeech stimuli in early infancy. *Journal of Experimental Child Psychology* 14: 477–92.

Murray, R. and T. Vennemann, (1983), Sound change and syllable structure in Germanic phonology. *Language* 59: 514–28.

Näätänen, R., A. Lehtokoski, M. Lennes, M. Cheour, M. Huotilainen, A. Iivonen, M. Vainio, P. Alku, R. J. Ilmoniemi, A. Luuk, J. Allik, J. Sinkkonen and K. Alho (1997), Language-specific phoneme representations revealed by electric and magnetic brain responses. *Nature* 385: 432–4.

Nazzi, T., J. Bertoncini and J. Mehler (1998), Language discrimination by newborns: towards an understanding of the role of rhythm. *Journal of Experimental Psychology: Human Perception and Performance* 24: 3, 756–66.

Oller, D. K. (2000), *The emergence of the speech capacity*. Mahwah: Lawrence Erlbaum.

O'Neal, C. (1998), A longitudinal study of the phonology acquisition of English consonants. MA dissertation, University of Sussex.

Ota, M. (1998), Phonological constraints and word truncation in early language acquisition. In A. Greenhill, M. Hughes, H. Littlefield and H. Walsh (eds), *Proceedings of the 22nd Annual Conference on Language Development*. Somerville: Cascadilla Press: 598–609.

Ota, M. (2001), Phonological theory and the acquisition of prosodic structure: Evidence from child Japanese. *Annual Review of Language Acquisition* 1: 65–118.

Pačesová, J. (1968), *The development of vocabulary in the child*. Brno, Czechoslovakia: Universita J. E. Purkyne.

Palleroni, A. and M. Hauser (2003), Experience-dependent plasticity for auditory processing in a raptor. *Science* 299: 5610, 1195.

Pallier, C. (2000), Word recognition: do we need phonological representations? In A. Cutler, J. M. McQueen and R. Zondervan (eds), *Proceedings of the Workshop on Spoken Word Access Processes (SWAP)*. Nijmegen, The Netherlands: Max Planck Institute for Psycholinguistics: 159–62.

Paradis, C. and J.-F. Prunet (eds) (1991), *The special status of coronals: internal and external evidence phonetics and phonology* (Vol. 2). San Diego: Academic Press Inc.

Pater, J. (1996), Consequences of constraint ranking. PhD dissertation, McGill University.

Pater, J. (1997), Minimal violation and phonological development. *Language Acquisition* 6: 3, 201–53.

Pater, J. (2004), Bridging the gap between receptive and productive development with minimally violable constraints. In R. Kager, J. Pater and W. Zonneveld (eds), *Constraints in phonological acquisition*. Cambridge: CUP: 219–44.

Pater, J. and J. Barlow (2001), Place-determined onset-selection. Conference handout. Child Phonology Conference, Boston.

Pater, J. and J. Barlow (2002), A typology of cluster reduction: conflicts with sonority. In B Skarabela., S. Fish, and A. Do (eds), *Proceedings of the 26th Annual Conference on Language Development*. Somerville: Cascadilla Press: 533–44.

Pater, J. and J. Barlow (2003), Constraint conflict in cluster reduction. *Journal of Child Language* 30: 487–526.

Pater, J. and J. Paradis (1996), Truncation without templates in child phonology. In A. Stringfellow, D. Cahana-Amitay, E. Hughes and A. Zukowski (eds), *Proceedings of the 20th Annual Boston University Conference on Language Development*. Somerville: Cascadilla Press: 540–51.

Pater, J., L. Stager and J. Werker (1998), Additive effects of phonetic distinctions in word learning. In *Proceedings of the 16th International Congress on Acoustics and 135th Meeting of the Acoustical Society of America*, Norfolk, VA: ASA: 2049–50.

Pater, J. and A. Werle (2001), Typology and variation in child consonant harmony. In C. Féry, A. Dubach Green and R. van de Vijver (eds), *Proceedings of HILPS5*. University of Potsdam: 119–39.

Pater, J. and A. Werle (2003), Direction of assimilation in child consonant harmony. *Canadian Journal of Linguistics* 48: 3/4, 385–408.

Pegg, J. and J. Werker (1997), Adult and infant perception of two English phones. *Journal of the Acoustical Society of America* 102: 6, 3742–53.

Peña, M., A. Maki, D. Kovacic, G. Dehaene-Lambertz, F. Bouquet, H. Koizumi and J. Mehler (2003), Sounds and silence: an optical topography study of language recognition at birth. *Proceedings of the National Academy of Sciences*, USA 10: 11702–5.

Petersen, M. R., M. D. Beecher, S. R. Zoloth, D. Moody and W. L. Stebbins (1978), Neural lateralization of species-specific vocalizations by Japanese macaques (*Macacafuscata*). *Science* 202: 324–7.

Pike, K. (1945), *The intonation of American English*. Ann Arbor: University of Michigan Press.

Pinker, S. (1994), *The language instinct: the new science of language and mind*. London: Penguin Books.

Plante, E. (1991), MRI findings in the parents and siblings of specifically language-impaired boys. *Brain and Language* 41: 67–80.

Polka, L. and O.-S. Bohn (1996), A cross-language comparison of vowel perception in English-learning and German-learning infants. *Journal of the Acoustical Society of America* 100: 577–92.

Polka, L., C. Colantonio and M. Sundara (2001), Cross-language perception of /d – ð/: Evidence for a new developmental pattern. *Journal of the Acoustical Society of America* 109: 5, 2190–200.

Polka, L. and J. Werker (1994), Developmental changes in perception of non-native vowel contrasts. *Journal of Experimental Psychology: Human Perception and Performance* 20: 2, 421–35.

Poole, I. (1934), Genetic development of articulation of consonant sounds in speech. *Elementary English Review* 11: 159–61.

Poremba, A., M. Malloy, R. Saunders, R. Carson, P. Herscovitch, and M. Mishkin (2004), Species-specific calls evoke asymmetric activity in the monkey's temporal poles. *Nature* 427: 448–51.

Prather, E., D. Hedrick, and C. Kern, (1975), Articulation development in children aged 2 to 4 years. *Journal of Speech and Hearing Disorders* 40: 179–91.

Prince, A. (2002), *Arguing optimality*. ROA-652 paper located at Rutgers Optimality Archive, roa.rutgers.edu

Prince, A. and P. Smolensky (2004), *Optimality theory constraint interaction in generative grammar*. Oxford: Blackwell Publishing.

Ramus, F., M. Hauser, C. Miller, D. Morris. and J. Mehler (2000), Language discrimination by human newborns and cotton-top tamarin monkeys. *Science* 288: 349–51.

Ramus, F., M. Nespor and J. Mehler (1999), Correlates of linguistic rhythm in the speech signal. *Cognition* 73: 265–92.

Recasens, D. (1996), An articulatory-perceptual account of vocalisation and elision of dark /l/ in Romance languages. *Language and Speech* 39: 61–89.

Reimers, P. (2006), The role of markedness in the acquisition of phonology. PhD dissertation, University of Essex.

Reimers, P. (2008), The role of UG in the initial state of the phonological grammar. In S. Kern, F. Gayraud and E. Marsico (eds), *Emergence of linguistic abilities: from gestures to grammar*. Newcastle: Cambridge Scholar Publishing Ltd: 133–55.

Remez, R. P. Rubin, D. Pisoni and T. Carell (1981), Speech perception without traditional speech cues. *Science* 212: 947–50.

Rice, K. (1995), Phonological variability in language acquisition. In E. Clarke (ed.) *Proceedings of the 27th Annual Child Language Research Forum*, Stanford: 7–17.

Rice, K. (1996), Aspects of variability in child language acquisition. In B. Bernhardt, J. Gilbert and D. Ingram (eds), *Proceedings of the UBC International Conference on Phonological Acquisition*. Somerville: Cascadilla Press: 1–14.

Rice, K. (2005), Liquid relationships. *Toronto Working Papers in Linguistics* 24: 31–44.

Rice, K (2007), Markedness in phonology. In P. de Lacy (ed.), *The Cambridge handbook of phonology*. Cambridge: CUP: 79–97.

Rice, K. and P. Avery (1995), Variability in child language acquisition: A theory of segmental elaboration. In J. Archibald (ed.), *Phonological acquisition and phonological theory*. Hillsdale: Lawrence Erlbaum Associates.

Rivera-Gaxiola, M., L. Klarman, A. Garcia-Sierra and P. K. Kuhl (2005), Neural patterns to speech and vocabulary growth in American infants. *NeuroReport* 16: 495–8: 23–46.

Roca, I. and Johnson, W. (1999), *A course in phonology*. Oxford: Blackwell Publishing.

Rose Y. (2000), Headedness and prosodic licensing in L1 phonological acquisition. PhD dissertation, McGill University.

Rubino, C. (2005), Reduplication: Form, function and distribution. In B. Hurch (ed.), *Studies on reduplication*. Berlin: Mouton de Gruyter: 11–30.

Saffran, J. (2003), Statistical language learning: Mechanisms and constraints. *Current Directions in Psychological Science* 12: 110–4.

Saffran, J., R. Aslin and E. Newport (1996), Statistical learning by 8-month-old infants. *Science* 274: 1926–8.

Saffran, J., E. Johnson, R. Aslin and E. Newport (1999), Statistical learning of tone sequences by human infants and adults. *Cognition* 70: 27–52.

Saffran, J. and E. Thiessen (2003), Pattern induction by infant language learners. *Developmental Psychology* 39: 484–94.

Sagey, E. (1986), The representation of features and relations in non-linear phonology. PhD dissertation, MIT.

Sakai, K. L., Y. Tatsuno, K. Suzuki, H. Kimura and Y. Ichida (2005), Sign and speech: amodal commonality in left hemisphere dominance for comprehension of sentences. *Brain* 128: 1407–17.

Salidis, J. and J. Johnson (1997), The production of minimal words: a longitudinal case study of phonological development. *Language Acquisition* 6: 11–36.

Sansavini, A., J. Bertoncini and G. Giovanelli (1997), Newborns discriminate the rhythm of multisyllabic stressed words. *Developmental Psychology* 33: 1, 3–11.

Schwartz, R., L. Leonard, M.J. Wilcox and M. K. Folger (1980), Again and again: reduplication in child phonology. *Journal of Child Phonology* 7: 75–87.

Scullen M. (1997), *French prosodic morphology, a unified account*. Bloomington: Indiana University Linguistics Club Publications.

Selkirk, E.O. (1984), On the major class features and syllable theory. In M. Aronoff and R.T. Oehrle (eds), *Language sound structure: studies in phonology*. Dedicated to Morris Halle by his teacher and students. Cambridge, MA: The MIT Press: 107–19.

Sinnott, J. and C. Gilmore (2004), Perception of place-of-articulation information in natural speech by monkeys vs humans. *Perception and Psychophysics* 66: 8, 1341–50.

Sinnott, J. and K. Mosteller (2001), A comparative assessment of the speech sound discrimination in the Mongolian gerbil. *Journal of the Acoustical Society of America* 110: 1729–32.

Skinner, B. F. (1957), *Verbal behavior*. Acton, MA: Copley Publishing Group.

Slobin, D. (1973), Cognitive prerequisites for the development of grammar. In C. Ferguson and D. Slobin (eds), *Studies of child language development*. New York: Holt, Rinehart, and Winston: 175–208.

Smith, N. V. (1973), *The acquisition of phonology: a case study*. Cambridge: CUP.

Smolensky, P. (1996), On the comprehension/production dilemma in child language. *Linguistic Inquiry* 27: 720–31. [ROA-118].

Spencer, A. (1986), A theory of phonological development. *Lingua* 68: 1–38.

Sproat, R. and O, Fujimura (1993), Allophonic variation in English /l/ and its implications for phonetic implementation. *Journal of Phonetics* 291–331.

Stampe, D. (1972/9), How I spent my summer vacation: A dissertation on natural phonology. PhD dissertation, University of Chicago. Published (1979) as *A dissertation on natural phonology*. New York: Garland.

Stemberger, J. (1992), A connectionist view of child phonology: phonological processing without phonological processes. In C. Ferguson, L. Menn and C. Stoel-Gammon (eds), *Phonological development: models, research, implications*. Timonium: York Press: 165–90.

Stemberger, J. and C. Stoel-Gammon (1991), The underspecification of coronals: evidence from language acquisition and performance errors. In C. Paradis and J-F. Prunet (eds), *Phonetics and phonology: The special status of coronals, internal and external evidence*. San Diego: Academic Press: 181–99.

Stites, J., K. Demuth and C. Kirk (2004), Markedness versus frequency effects in coda acquisition. In A. Brugos, L. Micciulla, and C. E. Smith (eds), *Proceedings of the 28th Annual Boston University Conference on Language Development*. Somerville: Cascadilla Press: 565–76.

Stoel-Gammon, C. (1996), On the acquisition of velars in English. In B. Bernhardt, J. Gilbert and D. Ingram (eds), *Proceedings of the UBC International Conference on Phonological Acquisition*. Somerville: Cascadilla Press: 201–14.

Stoel-Gammon, C. and J. Cooper (1984), Patterns in lexical and phonological development. *Journal of Child Language* 11: 247–71.

Stoel-Gammon, C. and J. Dunn (1985), *Normal and disordered phonology in children*. Baltimore: University Park Press.

Strange, W. and P. Broen (1981), The relationship between perception and production of /w/, /r/, and /l/ by three-year-old children. *Journal of Experimental Child Psychology* 31: 81–102.

Streeter, L. (1976), Language perception of 2-month-old infants shows effects of both innate mechanisms and experience. *Nature* 259: 39–41.

Swingley, D. (2008), The roots of the early vocabulary in infants' learning from speech. *Current Directions in Psychological Science* 17: 308–12.

Swoboda, P. J., J. Kass, P. A. Morse and L. A. Leavitt (1976), Memory factors in vowel discrimination of normal and at-risk infants. *Child Development* 49: 2, 332–9.

Templin, M. C. (1957), Certain language skills in children: their development and interrelationships. *Institute of Child Welfare Monographs* (Vol. 26). Minneapolis: University of Minnesota Press.

Toro, J. M., J. Trobalon and N. Sebastián-Galles (2003), The use of prosodic cues in language discrimination tasks by rats. *Animal Cognition* 6: 2, 131–6.

Trehub, S. (1976), The discrimination of foreign speech contrasts by infants and adults. *Child Development* 47: 466–72.

Trubetzkoy, N. (1939), *Grundzüge der Phonologie*, Güttingen: Vandenhoeck and Ruprecht.

Tsao, F.-M., H.-M. Liu and P. Kuhl (2004), Speech perception in infancy predicts language development in the second year of life: A longitudinal study. *Child Development* 75: 1067–84.

Tsao, F.-M., H.-M. Liu and P. K. Kuhl (2006), Perception of native and non-native affricate-fricative contrasts: Cross-language tests on adults and infants. *Journal of the Acoustical Society of America* 120: 2285–94.

Tsushima, T., O. Takizawa, M. Sasaki, S. Shiraki, K. Nishi, M. Kohno, P. Menyuk and C. Best (1994), Discrimination of English /r-l/ and /w-y/ by Japanese infants at 6–12 months: language-specific developmental changes in speech perception abilities. *Third International Conference on Spoken Language Processing (ICSLP)* 1994: 1695–8.

Turk, A., P. Jusczyk and L. Gerken (1995), Do English-learning infants use syllable weight to determine stress? *Language and Speech* 38: 143–58.

Ueda, I. (1996), Segmental acquisition and feature specification in Japanese. In B. Bernhardt, J. Gilbert & D. Ingram (eds), *Proceedings of the UBC International Conference on Phonological Acquisition*, Somerville: Cascadilla Press: 15–27.

Velten, H. (1943), The growth of phonemic and lexical patterns in infant language. *Language* 19: 400–4.

Vihman, M.(1992), Early syllables and the construction of phonology. In C. Ferguson, L. Menn and C. Stoel-Gammon (eds), *Phonological development: models, research, implications*. Timonium: York Press.

Vihman, M. (1993), Variable paths to early word production. *Journal of Phonectics* 21: 61–82.

Vihman, M (1996), *Phonological development: the origins of language in the child*. Cambridge, MA: Blackwell Publishing.

Vihman, M. and B. de Boysson-Bardies (1994), The nature and origins of ambient language influence on infant vocal production and early words. *Phonetica* 51: 159–69.

Vihman, M. (2004), The relationship between production and perception in the transition into language, *ESRC Research Report* (Online at: www.regard.ac.uk).

Vihman, M., S. Nakai and R. DePaolis (2006), Getting the rhythm right: A cross-linguistic study of segmental duration in babbling and first words. In L. Goldstein D. Whalen and C. Best (eds), *Papers in Laboratory Phonology* 8: *Varieties of Phonological Competence*: 341–66.

Vouloumanos, A. and J. Werker (2007), Listening to language at birth: evidence for a bias for speech in neonates. *Developmental Science* 10.2: 159–64.

Vouloumanos, A., M. Hauser, J. Werker and A. Martin (in press). The tuning of human neonates' preference for speech. *Child Development*.

Wada, J. A., R. Clarke and A. Hamm (1975), Cerebral hemispheric asymmetry in humans: Cortical speech zones in 100 adult and 100 infant brains. *Archives of Neurology* 32: 239–46.

Waibel, A. (1986), Suprasegmentals in very large vocabulary word recognition speech perception. In E. Schwab and H. Nusbaum (eds), *Pattern recognition by humans and machines*. New York: Academic Press: 159–86.

Walsh Dickey, L. (1997), The phonology of liquids. PhD dissertation, University of Massachusetts.

Weissenborn, J., B. Höhle, S. Bartels, B. Herold and M. Hoffmann (2002), The development of prosodic competence in German infants. Poster, 13th Biennial International Conference on Infant Studies. Toronto, April 2002. (Online at: www.barbara-hoehle.de/publications.htm).

Werker, J., J. Gilbert, G. Humphrey and R. Tees (1981), Developmental aspects of cross-language speech perception. *Child Development* 52: 349–55.

Werker, J. and C. Lalonde (1988), Cross-language speech perception: initial capabilities and developmental change. *Developmental Psychology* 24: 4, 672–83.

Werker, J. and R. Tees (1984), Cross-language speech perception: evidence for perceptual reorganisation during the first year of life. *Infant Behaviour and Development* 7: 49–63.

Whalen, D.H., A.G. Levitt and Q. Wang (1991), Intonational differences between the reduplicative babbling of French- and English-learning infants. *Journal of Child Language* 18: 501–16.

Woodward, J. and R. Aslin (1990), Segmentation cues in maternal speech to infants. Poster presented at the International Conference on Infant Studies, Montreal, Canada, April.

Yildiz, Y. (2006), The acquisition of English [ɹ] by Turkish learners: explaining the age effects in L2 Phonology. Paper presented at the 15th Postgraduate Conference in Linguistics, University of Manchester.

Yip, M. (1995), Repetition and its avoidance: the case of Javanese. In K. Suzuki and D. Elzinga (eds), *Papers of the South Western Optimality*

Theory Workshop, Arizona Phonology Conference (Vol. 5). University of Arizona Department of Linguistics Coyote Papers, Tucson AZ: 141–66.

Yoneyama, K. H. Koiso and J. Fon (2003), A corpus-based analysis on prosody and discourse structure in Japanese spontaneous monologues. *ISCA and IEEE Workshop on Spontaneous Speech Processing and Recognition*, paper MA03.

Zamuner, T. (2003), *Input-based phonological acquisition.* New York: Routledge.

INDEX

Note: page numbers in italics denote tableaux or figures